D0049528

This 64th edition is dedicated to all those professional and aspiring amateur mixologists throughout the world who seek the most authoritative, accurate, and complete source for perfect drinks.

Mr. BOSTON

OFFICIAL BARTENDER'S AND PARTY GUIDE

WARNER BOOKS

A Time Warner Company

ACKNOWLEDGMENTS

Appreciation is acknowledged to Leo Cotton, who served as originator and editor of the first *Mr. Boston Bartender's Guide,* which was published in 1935. He continued as editor through the guide's 49th printing—a period of over thirty-five years, until his retirement in 1970.

Further appreciation and acknowledgment is extended to:
Susan Suffes, Editor; Patrick Promotion, Creative Direction;
Todd McGowan, Art Direction; Ben Crain, Writing; John Watson,
Photography; Darcy Green, Tom McNichols, Corie Merrill, John Rose,
John Zappa, Marketing and Development.

A very special thanks to Jobson Publishing Corporation, publishers of *Cheers,* for sharing many of the recipes included in this new edition.

Mr. Boston Official Bartender's and Party Guide
Copyright © 1994 by Barton Incorporated
Material from Mr. Boston Bartender's Guide, copyright © 1935, 1936, 1940, 1941, 1946, 1948, 1949, 1951, 1953, 1955, 1957, 1960, 1961, 1962, 1963, 1964, 1965, 1966, 1967, 1968, 1969, 1970, 1974, 1976, 1977, 1978, 1981, 1984 by Mr. Boston Distiller Corporation.

w A Time Warner Company

Printed in the United States of America
First Printing: July 1994
First Reissue: November 1997
10 9 8 7 6 5

64th Edition revised and updated by Renee Cooper and Chris Morris

Photos by Warren Lynch & Associates, Inc., Louisville, Kentucky
Warren Lynch, David English, Jeffery Gardner, Dan Kremer, Photographers

Library of Congress Cataloging-in-Publication Data
Mr. Boston, official bartender's and party guide.—64th ed., rev.
  and updated / [by Renee Cooper and Chris Morris]
       p. cm.
  Rev. and updated ed. of: Mr. Boston official bartender's guide.
  63rd ed. c1988.
  Includes index.
    1. Liquors. 2. Cocktails. 3. Alcoholic beverages. I. Cooper, Renee
II. Morris, Chris. III. Mr. Boston official bartender's guide. IV. Title: Mister
Boston, the official bartender's and party guide.
TX951.M7 1994
641.8'74——dc20   93—41971

Contents

Chocolate-Covered Strawberry, Crocodile Cooler

Introduction

Welcome. You are holding in your hands the 64th Edition of the definitive guide to mixing perfect drinks. The *Mr. Boston Bartender's Guide* has been the official manual of bartenders and spirits professionals since it was first published in 1935. It has been endorsed, consulted, and considered a basic tool for bartenders for decades. In fact, over eleven million copies have been in print since it first appeared shortly after the repeal of Prohibition as an urgently needed source of answers to questions such as: How much is a dash? How do you make a dry Martini? How do you frost glasses?

Even experienced bartenders had trouble making the same drink taste the same way each time they mixed it. So Mr. Boston collected the best-known and best-loved drinks recipes, tested and standardized the measurements, and presented, in alphabetical order, recipes with such clear, easy-to-follow directions that, at last, anyone could be an expert at cocktail time.

Of course, the book was copied. But originators stay original. With this, our 64th Edition, we have completely revised the format, organizing recipes into sections by the primary liquor in the drink. We've also added all-new sections covering today's popular shooters, as well as frozen drinks, hot drinks and punches. More than 300 new recipes have been added, including expanded low-alcohol and no-alcohol drinks sections. As you peruse the book, you'll also find an occasional joke and amusing or surprising trivia. We must also admit to succumbing to a bit of nostalgia and bringing back a few favorite bar tricks that first appeared in our 1959 edition. We hope you'll have some fun trying them!

In addition to more than 1,200 recipes, the 64th Edition now contains a brand-new Party Planning Guide, with a wide range of ideas and tips for entertaining for any occasion during the year, from casual outdoor get-togethers to holiday extravaganzas. We're sure you'll find it helpful in planning all your festive gatherings.

With this book as your guide, you can look at almost any wine and spirits label from any country and know what you are buying, what it will taste like, where it is from, and what foods it complements. You will know how to store and serve wine and beer and a bit about the process and unique conditions that produced them.

None of this is stuffy or complicated. Drinks are meant to go with good times and good friends. So is the *Mr. Boston Bartender's and Party Guide*. Informative but fun to read, complete but concise, it is the only book you need to make memorable drinks for your parties and perfect wine choices for intimate or elegant occasions.

Before you continue reading, however, please take a moment to think about both the responsible use and serving of alcoholic drinks. The consumption of alcohol dates back many centuries, and in many cultures throughout the world, is part of social rituals associated with significant occasions and celebrations. The majority of adults who choose to drink do not abuse alcohol and are aware that responsible drinking is key to their own enjoyment, health, and safety, as well as that of others, particularly when driving. Be a responsible drinker, and if you're under the legal drinking age, our nonalcoholic drinks chapter is the *only* one for you. When entertaining at home, there are steps you can take to encourage responsible drinking. For example, always provide plenty of food and nonalcoholic beverages (try some of the recipes in this book), don't push drinks on your guests, and don't insist on refilling a drink. And if friends have had too much to drink, call them a cab. If you're a professional bartender, take advantage of the responsible server-training programs that are widely available.

So congratulations! You have made an excellent selection to enhance your expertise as a professional bartender or a savvy host. Simply turn the page and you are on your way to making your friends'—and your own—favorite drinks superbly.

S ince the repeal of Prohibition, *Mr. Boston Bartender's Guides* have passed down the secrets of mixing the perfect drink. This newly revised edition now contains over 1,200 recipes, including many new cocktail recipes, made easily accessible by fingertip indexing.

The winning methods are gathered here for you to use with complete confidence. You need only follow this advice to achieve the extra artistry that will mark you as a professional.

There are a few practical rules to follow for stocking your bar and mixing drinks. You'll want to be able to satisfy the tastes of your guests quickly, so that you can enjoy the conviviality of good spirits. Here you'll find the supplies you'll need to keep on hand to take care of anyone's request. And with the mastery of a few simple techniques carefully explained here, you'll find it easy to quickly concoct any drink calling for mixing, mashing, muddling, or simple stirring.

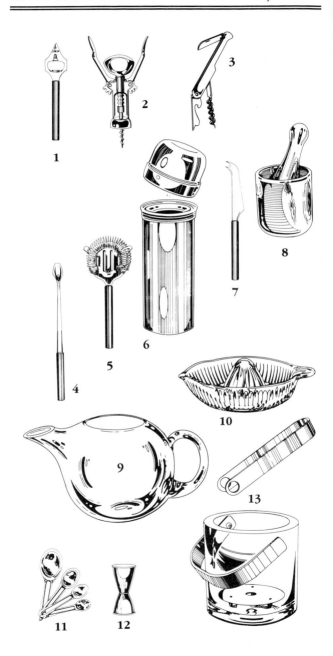

EQUIPMENT

The right tools make the job easier. For a home or professional bar you'll need to have handy:

1. Can and bottle openers
2. Easy-to-use corkscrew
3. Waiter's corkscrew
4. Glass stirring rod or long spoon
5. Coil-rimmed bar strainer
6. A tall, heavy-duty mixing glass or shaker
7. Small, sharp stainless-steel paring knife for cutting fruit or for shearing off rind
8. Wooden muddler or the back of a large wooden spoon for mashing herbs, fruit, etc.
9. Large pitcher
10. Fruit juice extractor
11. Set of measuring spoons
12. A jigger measure with easy-to-read half-and quarter-ounce measures
13. Ice bucket and ice tongs

An electric blender is essential for mixing frozen drinks. Since grinding ice is a heavy-duty job, most manufacturers recommend using cracked or crushed ice rather than cubes in the blender. Consult your owner's manual for guidelines.

Your bar should also have an assortment of straws, swizzle sticks, toothpicks, coasters, and cocktail napkins.

GLASSWARE

The best glasses should be thin-lipped, transparent, and sound off in high registers when "pinged." Clean, sparkling glasses show off good drinks to great advantage. The proper glass enhances a drink. Here are illustrations showing a comprehensive selection. In practice, however, only a few basic types are necessary. Nos. 1, 4, 7, 11, 14, and 17, for example, will answer virtually all your needs. Beside each recipe are line drawings of the classic glass shape used for each drink.

You might also need a coffee cup, coffee mug, or punch cup for some of the recipes.

Glass Name

1. Collins
2. Shot
3. Highball
4. Old-Fashioned
5. Beer Mug
6. Beer Pilsner
7. Irish Coffee Glass
8. Pousse Café
9. Parfait
10. Red Wine
11. White Wine
12. Sherry
13. Champagne Flute
14. Brandy Snifter
15. Cocktail
16. Cordial or Pony
17. Whiskey Sour

STOCKING A BAR

If you keep a 750-milliliter bottle of each of the spirits mentioned here, you'll be able to create just about any combination of drinks and *that* should satisfy just about everybody.

Spirits, Wines, and Beer
- Bourbon
- Brandy and Cognac
- Gin
- Rum (Light and Dark)
- Scotch
- Tequila (White and Gold)
- Vodka
- Whiskey (Blended and Irish)
- Liqueurs
  (see Drink Recipes for kinds)
- Vermouth (Sweet and Dry)
- Red and White Wine (Dry)
- Fruit-flavored Brandies
- Beer (Lager, Ale, and Stout)
- Champagne

Mixers
- Mineral Water
- Cola
- Club Soda
- Ginger Ale
- Lemon-Lime Soda
- Tonic Water
- Water
- Fresh Lemon Juice
- Fresh Lime Juice
- Fresh Orange Juice
- Grapefruit Juice
- Cranberry Juice
- Pineapple Juice
- Tomato Juice
- Coconut Cream

Condiments
- Bitters
- Grenadine
- Powdered Sugar
- Granulated Sugar
- Coarse Salt
- Ground Black Pepper
- Tabasco Sauce
- Worcestershire Sauce
- Orgeat Syrup
  (almond-flavored syrup)
- Horseradish
- Cinnamon Sticks
- Ground Cinnamon
- Ground Nutmeg
- Light Cream
- Whipping Cream
- Passion Fruit Syrup
- Simple Syrup (recipe follows)
- Milk

Garnishes
- Stuffed Olives
- Cocktail Onions
- Lemons
- Limes
- Oranges
- Maraschino Cherries
- Strawberries
- Celery
- Pineapple
- Bananas
- Cucumber
- Fresh Mint

To Make Simple Syrup or Sugar Syrup

In a saucepan, gradually stir one lb. granulated sugar into 13 oz. hot water to make 16 oz. simple syrup. A variety of drinks call for sweetening to offset the tartness of some juices used in their recipes. Granulated sugar does not dissolve easily in cold drinks, but this simple sugar syrup, being liquid, is the perfect alternative.

About Bitters

A little goes a long way. Made from numerous and intricate combinations of growing things (roots, barks, berries, and herbs) that are each uniquely flavored, they add zest to mixed drinks.

Angostura Bitters—Made from a Trinidadian secret recipe.
Abbott's Aged Bitters—Made in Baltimore since 1865.
Peychaud's Bitters—These come from New Orleans.
Orange Bitters—Made from the dried peel of mouth-puckering Seville oranges and sold by several English firms.

Vermouth

Vermouth is a white appetizer wine flavored with as many as thirty to forty different herbs, roots, berries, flowers, and seeds. There are nearly as many vermouth formulas as there are brand labels.

The dry variety (French) is light gold in color and has a delightful nutty flavor. Sweet (Italian) vermouth is red, richer in flavor, and more syrupy. Both are perishable and will lose their freshness if left too long in an opened bottle. Refrigerate after opening. Use with care and discretion in mixed drinks—be sure to follow the recipe since most people now prefer "drier" cocktails.

Ice

Bar ice must be clean and fresh and free of any flavor save water. If necessary, use bottled spring water.

Rule of thumb: For parties, you will always need more ice than you have. Buy or make extra.

Ice goes in the cocktail glass first. That way the spirits get cooled on the way in without any unnecessary splashing. Ice can be crushed, shaved, cracked, or cubed, depending on the drink. If you can store only one kind of ice, buy cubes. Most highballs, old-fashioneds, and on-the-rocks drinks call for ice cubes. Use cracked or cubed ice for stirring and shaking; crushed or shaved ice for special tall drinks, frappes, and other drinks to be sipped through straws. Both manual and electric ice crushers are available, but you can easily make your own crushed version by putting cubes in a tightly closed plastic bag, wrapping the bag in a towel, and smashing the ice with a rolling pin or hammer. Since cubed ice is the most readily available, particularly to home bartenders, it can be used in the recipes throughout this book, unless otherwise specified.

TECHNIQUES

How to Chill a Glass

Always chill before you fill. There are three ways to make a cocktail glass cold:

1. Put the glasses in the refrigerator or freezer a couple of hours before using them.

2. Fill the glasses with crushed ice just before using.

3. Fill the glasses with cracked ice and stir it around before pouring in the drink.

If refrigerator space is not available for pre-chilling, fill each glass with ice before mixing. When the drink is ready, empty the glass, shake out all of the melted ice, and then pour in the drink.

How to Frost a Glass

There are two types of "frosted" glass. For "frosted" drinks, glasses should be stored in a refrigerator or buried in shaved ice long enough to give each glass a white, frosted, ice-cold look and feel.

For a "sugar-frosted" glass, moisten the rim of a pre-chilled glass with a slice of lime or lemon and then dip the rim into powdered sugar.

For margaritas, rub the rim of the glass with a lime, invert glass, and dip into coarse salt.

How to Muddle

Muddling is a simple mashing technique for grinding herbs such as mint smooth in the bottom of a glass. You can buy a wooden muddler in a bar supply store. It crushes the herbs, much as the back of a soup spoon might, without scarring your glassware.

To Stir or Not to Stir

Pitchers of cocktails need at least ten seconds of stirring to mix properly. Carbonated mixers in drinks do much of their own stirring just by naturally bubbling. Two stirs from you will complete the job.

When to Shake
Shake any drink made with juices, sugar, or cream, or use an electric blender. Strain cocktails from shaker or blender to a glass through a coil-rimmed strainer.

Pouring
Pour drinks as soon as you make them or they will wilt. Leftovers should be discarded or they will be too diluted by the time you get to "seconds."

When making a batch of drinks at once, set up the glasses in a row. Pour until each glass is half full, then backtrack until the shaker is empty. That way everyone gets the same amount, thoroughly mixed.

Floating Liqueurs
Creating a rainbow effect in a glass with different colored

cordials requires a special pouring technique. Simply pour each liqueur slowly over an inverted teaspoon (rounded side up) into a glass: Start with the heaviest liqueur first. (Recipes will give proper order.) Pour *slowly*. The rounded surface of the spoon will spread each liqueur over the one beneath without mixing them. You can accomplish the same trick using a glass rod. Pour slowly down the rod.

The Secret of Flaming
The secret of setting brandy (or other high-alcohol spirits) aflame is first to warm it and its glass until almost hot. You can warm a glass by holding it by its stem above the flame or electric coil on your stove until the glass feels warm. (Avoid touching the glass to the flame or coil, which could char or crack it.)

Next, heat some brandy in a saucepan above the flame (or in a cooking pan). When the brandy is hot, ignite it with a match. If it's hot enough, it will flame instantly. Pour the flaming liquid carefully into the other brandy you want flamed. If all the liquid is warm enough, it will ignite.

Warning: Flames can shoot high suddenly. Look up and be sure there's nothing "en route" than can ignite. That includes your hair. Have an open box of baking soda handy in case of accidents. Pour it over flames to extinguish them. Use pot holders to protect your hands from the hot glass, spoon, or pan.

Using Fruit and Fruit Juices
Whenever possible, use only *fresh* fruit. Wash the outside peel before using. Fruit can be cut in wedges or in slices. If slices are used, they should be cut about one-quarter-inch thick and slit toward the center to fix slice on rim of glass. Make sure garnishes are fresh and cold.

When mixing drinks containing fruit juices, always pour the liquor last. Squeeze and strain fruit juices just before using to ensure freshness and good taste. Avoid artificial, concentrated substitutes.

When recipes call for a twist of lemon peel, rub a narrow strip of peel around the rim of the glass to deposit the oil on it. Then twist the peel so that the oil (usually one small drop) will drop into the drink. Then drop in the peel. The lemon oil gives added character to the cocktail, which many prefer.

To Open Champagne or Sparkling Wine

When the bottle is well chilled, wrap it in a clean towel and undo the wire around the cork. Pointing the bottle away from people and priceless objects, hold the cork with one hand, grasp the bottle by the indentation on the bottom, and slowly turn the bottle (not the cork!) until the cork comes free with a pop! Pour slowly into the center of the glass.

To Open Wine
    Cut the seal neatly around the neck with a sharp knife just below the top. Peel off, exposing the cork. Wipe off cork and bottle lip. Insert the corkscrew and turn until the corkscrew is completely inside the cork. With a steady pull, remove cork. If the cork crumbles or breaks, pour the wine through a tea strainer into another container for serving. The host or hostess should taste the wine to check its quality before offering it to guests.

Measurements

Even the most professional bartender measures the ingredients of every drink. So, to make a perfect drink every time, measure all ingredients. Remember, too, that many drinks can be spoiled by being too strong as well as too weak.

SOME STANDARD BAR MEASURES		
	Standard	Metric
1 Dash (or splash)	$\frac{1}{32}$ oz.	0.9 ml.
1 Teaspoon	$\frac{1}{8}$ oz.	3.7 ml.
1 Tablespoon	$\frac{3}{8}$ oz.	11.1 ml.
1 Pony	1 oz.	29.5 ml.
1 Jigger	$1\frac{1}{2}$ oz.	44.5 ml.
1 Wineglass	4 oz.	119 ml.
1 Split	6 oz.	177 ml.
1 Cup	8 oz.	257 ml.

METRIC STANDARDS OF FILL FOR DISTILLED SPIRITS		
Metric Size	Fluid Ounces	Number of Bottles per Case
50 ml.	1.7	120
100 ml.	3.4	48
200 ml.	6.8	48
375 ml.	12.7	24
750 ml.	25.4	12
1 liter	33.8	12
1.75 liters	59.2	6

METRIC SIZES FOR WINE
(ml. = milliliters, 1 liter = 1,000 milliliters)

Name of Package	Metric Equivalent	Equivalent Fluid Ounces	Bottles per Case
Split	187 ml.	6.34	48
Tenth	375 ml.	12.68	24
Fifth	750 ml.	25.36	12
Quart	1 liter	33.81	12
Magnum	1.5 liters	50.72	6
Jeroboam	3 liters	101.44	4

CALORIE COUNTS

To determine the caloric intake of your favorite cocktail, use the following chart as a guide.

Beverage	Calories per 1 oz. Serving
White Wine (24 proof)	23
Red Wine (24 proof)	23
Beer (typical American)	12
Champagne (25 proof)	26
Liqueurs (34–48 proof)	86–105
All Straight Spirits:	
80 proof	65
86 proof	70
90 proof	74

Bourbon

Some like wines — both white and red
And some like brews from grain.
Some like Scotch and Irish
And plenty choose champagne.

Rum by many is preferred
And brandy makes its boast.
The Dutch and English like their gin
And ale goes well with roast.

Requests for rye in eastern states
Quite frequently are heard;
And the hill folk of the southlands
Make corn a favorite word.

But to folks throughout the nation —
Both rural folks and urban,
The king of distillations
Is the whiskey known as Bourbon.
— *Anonymous*

Bourbon was born over 200 years ago in the hollows of Kentucky where the cold, clear limestone spring water flowed—water that made the grass blue, the horses frisky, the corn grow like crazy, and the whiskey sweet and smooth as honey. Bourbon whiskey, America's only native spirit, still makes its home in Kentucky, where today as much as 80 percent of the world's bourbon is produced.

Bourbon is distilled from a mash of grain containing, according to federal law, not less than 51 percent corn, balanced with barley and either wheat or rye. Each distillery has its own unique blend of grain and some of the mash recipes are generations old — family formulas jealously guarded since their creation. *Kentucky Tavern Straight Bourbon Whiskey* has been in existence for over 110 years, while *Ten High Kentucky Straight Sour Mash Bourbon Whiskey* goes back to 1879 and is still matured in select white oak barrels to create a smooth, distinct flavor. *Kentucky Gentleman's* formula produces a unique, classical bourbon offering a well-balanced mix of sweet, aromatic grain and barrel notes.

The rich amber color and characteristic sweetness of bourbon is derived from its signature aging process in new white oak barrels, which are charred to caramelize the natural sugars in the wood and bring them to the surface. While two years is the minimum time for aging established by law, most bourbons are aged between four and twelve years. Federal regulations also stipulate that bourbon cannot be distilled above 160 proof and must be bottled at no less than 80 proof. *Very Old Barton* is a smooth, traditional bourbon backed by generations of distilling experience. This hand-crafted bourbon is slow-aged in the barrel giving it a rich, mellow aroma and "honey barrel" overtone.

Bourbon's distinctive and mellow taste makes it both an excellent complement to food and a versatile ingredient in sauces and dessert recipes, particularly those made with chocolate.

Tennessee whiskey, commonly but incorrectly perceived as a type of bourbon, is made in a similar way, but with one extra step in the process that influences its final character and flavor. Before barreling, the newly distilled whiskey is mellowed — filtered very slowly over a period of ten days through charcoal made from seasoned sugar maple timbers, which gives the whiskey a unique smoky sweetness. This step is so significant that Tennessee whiskey is distinguished by law as a separate category of whiskey.

In 1933, President Franklin D. Roosevelt announced the repeal of Prohibition with the words, "What America needs now is a drink."

Bourbon on the Rocks, Mint Julep

ALLEGHENY

1 oz.   Bourbon
1 oz.   Dry Vermouth
1½ tsps. Blackberry-
          flavored Brandy
1½ tsp. Lemon Juice

Shake with ice and strain
into cocktail glass. Add a
twist of lemon peel on top.

AMERICANA

¼ oz.   Tennessee Whiskey
½ tsp.   Sugar
1–2 dashes Bitters
Chilled Champagne

In collins glass, combine the
Tennessee Whiskey, bitters,
and sugar, stirring until
sugar is dissolved. Fill with
champagne and add a slice
of peach.

BASIN STREET

2 oz.   Bourbon
1 oz.   Triple Sec
1 oz.   Lemon Juice

Shake well with cracked ice
and strain into cocktail glass.

BOURBON A LA CRÈME

2 oz.   Bourbon
1 oz.   Crème de Cacao
          (Brown)
1-2   Vanilla Beans

Combine with ice in mixing
glass and refrigerate for at
least one hour. Shake well
and serve straight up.

BOURBON AND WATER

2 oz.   Bourbon
4 oz.   Water

Pour bourbon and water
into old-fashioned glass.
Add ice and a twist of lemon
peel, if desired, and stir.

BOURBON COBBLER

2½ oz.   Bourbon
1 tbsp.   Lemon Juice
2 tsps.   Grapefruit Juice
1½ tsps. Almond Extract

Combine all ingredients in
mixing glass, pour over ice
into old-fashioned glass.
Decorate with peach slice.

BOURBON HIGHBALL

2 oz.   Bourbon
Ginger Ale or Club Soda

Fill highball glass with
bourbon, ginger ale or club
soda, and ice cubes. Add
twist of lemon peel, if
desired, and stir.

BOURBON ON THE ROCKS

2 oz.   Bourbon

Pour bourbon into old-
fashioned glass half-filled
with ice.

"Here's mud in your eye"
—American toast

BRIGHTON PUNCH

¼ oz.   Bourbon
¼ oz.   Brandy
¾ oz.   Benedictine
Juice of ½ Orange
Juice of ½ Lemon
Club Soda

Shake with ice and pour into collins glass nearly filled with shaved ice. Then fill with club soda and stir gently. Decorate with orange and lemon slices and serve with straw.

BUDDY'S FAVORITE

1½ oz.   Bourbon
6 oz.   Cold Water

Pour ingredients into highball glass. Stir and serve without ice.

BULL AND BEAR

1½ oz.   Bourbon
¾ oz.   Orange Curaçao
1 tbsp.   Grenadine
Juice of ½ Lime

Shake with cracked ice, strain into cocktail glass. Garnish with cherry and orange slice.

CHAPEL HILL

1½ oz.   Bourbon
½ oz.   Triple Sec
1 tbsp.   Lemon Juice

Shake with ice and strain into cocktail glass. Add twist of orange peel.

COFFEE OLD-FASHIONED

1½ tsp.   Instant Coffee
½ cup   Water
2 tsps.   Powdered Sugar
2 dashes Bitters
1 oz.   Bourbon
2 oz.   Club Soda

Dissolve coffee in water; stir in sugar, bitters, and bourbon. Add soda and pour over ice in old-fashioned glass. Garnish with orange slice and cherry.

CREOLE LADY

1½ oz.   Bourbon
1½ oz.   Madeira
1 tsp.   Grenadine

Stir with ice and strain into cocktail glass. Serve with one green and one red cherry.

DAISY DUELLER

1½ oz.   Tennessee Whiskey
1½ tsps. Lemon Juice
1½ tsps. Simple Syrup
Several drops Cointreau
Club Soda

Shake all ingredients except soda with ice. Strain into highball glass; add ice and fill with soda. Decorate with fruit slices.

DIXIE JULEP

1 tsp.   Powdered Sugar
2½ oz.   Bourbon

Put sugar and bourbon into collins glass. Fill with crushed ice and stir gently until glass is frosted. Decorate with sprigs of mint. Serve with straws.

DIXIE WHISKEY COCKTAIL

½ tsp.   Powdered Sugar
1 dash   Bitters
¼ tsp.   Triple Sec
½ tsp.   Crème de Menthe (White)
2 oz.   Bourbon

Shake with ice and strain into cocktail glass.

GENTLEMAN'S COCKTAIL

1½ oz.   Bourbon
½ oz.   Brandy
½ oz.   Crème de Menthe
Club Soda

Pour bourbon, brandy, and crème de menthe over ice into highball glass. Add club soda and garnish with a lemon twist.

> The portion of whiskey that evaporates through the pores of a barrel during the aging process is known as "the angels' share."

JOCOSE JULEP

2½ oz.   Bourbon
½ oz.   Crème de Menthe (Green)
1 oz.   Lime Juice
1 tsp.   Sugar
5 Chopped Mint Leaves
Club Soda

Combine all ingredients in blender without ice. Pour into collins glass over ice cubes. Fill with club soda and decorate with a sprig of mint.

KENTUCKY BLIZZARD

1½ oz.   Bourbon
1½ oz.   Cranberry Juice
½ oz.   Lime Juice
½ oz.   Grenadine
1 tsp.   Sugar

Shake all ingredients with cracked ice. Strain into cocktail glass or over fresh cracked ice in old-fashioned glass. Garnish with a half-slice of orange.

KENTUCKY COCKTAIL

¾ oz.   Pineapple Juice
1½ oz.   Bourbon

Shake with ice and strain into cocktail glass.

KENTUCKY COLONEL COCKTAIL

½ oz.   Benedictine
1½ oz.   Bourbon

Stir with ice and strain into cocktail glass. Add a twist of lemon peel.

KISS ON THE LIPS

2 oz.   Bourbon
6 oz.   Apricot Nectar

Pour over ice into collins glass and stir. Serve with a straw.

LIMESTONE

1½ oz.   Bourbon
Collins Mix
Lime Juice

Into ice-filled highball glass, pour bourbon, fill glass with collins mix, and add lime juice to taste.

LOUISVILLE COOLER

1½ oz.   Bourbon
1 oz.   Orange Juice
1 tbsp.   Lime Juice
1 tsp.   Powdered Sugar

Shake all ingredients with cracked ice. Strain into old-fashioned glass over fresh cracked ice. Garnish with a half-slice of orange.

LOUISVILLE LADY

1 oz.   Bourbon
¼ oz.   Crème de Cacao
           (White)
¼ oz.   Cream

Shake with ice and strain into cocktail glass.

MAGNOLIA MAIDEN

1¼ oz.   Bourbon
1¼ oz.   Mandarine Napoléon
1 splash Simple Syrup
1 splash Club Soda

Shake bourbon, Mandarine Napoléon, and simple syrup with crushed ice. Strain into old-fashioned glass with ice. Top with club soda.

MINT JULEP

4 sprigs Mint
1 tsp.   Powdered Sugar
2 tsps.   Water
2½ oz.   Bourbon

In silver julep cup, silver mug, or collins glass, muddle mint leaves, powdered sugar, and water. Fill glass or mug with shaved or crushed ice and add bourbon. Top with more ice and garnish with a mint sprig and straws.

Recipe For a Mint Julep

Pluck the mint gently from its bed, just as the dew of the evening is about to form on it. Select the choice sprigs only, but do not rinse them. Prepare the simple syrup and measure out a half-tumbler of whiskey. Pour the whiskey into a well-frosted silver cup, throw the other ingredients away, and drink the whiskey!

—*attributed to a Louisville, Kentucky newspaper editor*

MINT JULEP (SOUTHERN STYLE)

5–6 sprigs Mint
1 tsp.   Powdered Sugar
2 tsps.   Water
2½ oz.   Bourbon

In silver mug or collins glass, dissolve powdered sugar with water. Fill with finely shaved ice and add bourbon. Stir until glass is heavily frosted, adding more ice if necessary. (Do not hold glass with hand while stirring.) Decorate with sprigs of fresh mint so that the tops are about two inches above the rim of glass. Use short straws so that it will be necessary to bury nose in mint, which is intended for scent rather than taste.

NARRAGANSETT

1½ oz.   Bourbon
1 oz.   Sweet Vermouth
1 dash Anisette

Stir in old-fashioned glass with ice cubes. Add a twist of lemon peel.

NEVINS

1½ oz.   Bourbon
1½ tsps. Apricot-flavored
         Brandy
1 tbsp. Grapefruit Juice
1½ tsps. Lemon Juice
1 dash Bitters

Shake with ice and strain into cocktail glass.

PENDENNIS TODDY

1 cube Sugar
1 tsp.   Water
2 oz.   Bourbon

Muddle cube of sugar with water in sour glass. Fill with ice, add bourbon, and stir. Decorate with two slices of lemon.

RED-HOT PASSION

½ oz.   Bourbon
½ oz.   Amaretto
½ oz.   Southern Comfort
¼ oz.   Sloe Gin
1 splash Triple Sec
1 splash Orange Juice
1 splash Pineapple Juice

Pour all ingredients over ice into parfait or hurricane glass and stir gently. Garnish with an orange slice.

RED RAIDER

1 oz.   Bourbon
½ oz.   Triple Sec
1 oz.   Lemon Juice
1 dash Grenadine

Shake with ice and strain into cocktail glass.

SOUTHERN BELLE

1¼ oz. Tennessee Whiskey
8 oz.   Pineapple Juice
¾ oz.   Triple Sec
2 oz.   Orange Juice
1 splash Grenadine

Combine Tennessee Whiskey, triple sec, and juices in tall glass with ice. Top with grenadine and stir once.

SOUTHERN LADY

2 oz.	Bourbon
1 oz.	Southern Comfort
1 oz.	Crème de Noyaux
3 oz.	Pineapple Juice
1 oz.	Lime Juice
2 oz.	Lemon-lime Soda

Shake first four ingredients with ice and strain into parfait or hurricane glass half-filled with ice. Fill with soda to within one inch of top of glass and top with lime juice. Garnish with pineapple wheel and cherry.

SOUTHERN PEACH

1½ oz.	Bourbon
⅛ oz.	Grenadine
2 oz.	Orange Juice
2 oz.	Sour Mix
1 oz.	Peach Schnapps

Fill parfait or hurricane glass with ice. Pour grenadine over ice; add bourbon. Into a blender jar, pour orange juice, sour mix, and schnapps and blend well. Slowly pour mixture into hurricane glass. Garnish with a peach slice.

STILETTO

Juice of ½ Lemon	
1½ tsps.	Amaretto
1½ oz.	Bourbon or Blended Whiskey

Pour into old-fashioned glass over ice cubes and stir.

THOROUGHBRED COOLER

1 oz.	Bourbon
1 oz.	Sour Mix
1 oz.	Orange Juice
1 dash	Grenadine
Lemon-lime Soda	

Pour all ingredients over ice in highball glass. Fill with lemon-lime soda and stir. Add dash of grenadine, garnish with an orange wedge.

TRILBY COCKTAIL

1½ oz.	Bourbon
¼ oz.	Sweet Vermouth
2 dashes	Orange Bitters

Stir with ice and strain into cocktail glass.

TOUCH COIN TRICK PROBLEM

Taking five pennies, propose that they be placed in such a way that each coin touches all remaining coins. Few people can solve this one, but it is relatively easy. Lay one penny on the table and two other pennies side by side upon it. With the remaining two pennies arrange them to form an inverted V on the first coin. Then two coins ride over the other two and thus each coin will touch all the others.

Brandy is distilled from fermented fruit, sometimes aged in oak casks, and usually bottled at 80 proof. Long enjoyed as an after-dinner drink, brandy is also widely used in mixed drinks and cooking. It is produced in a number of countries. The term *brandy,* used alone, means that the spirit has been distilled from grape wine. *Jacques Bonet Three Star Brandy* is made in the great French tradition. It features a smooth, full-bodied richness and bouquet which will delight the most exacting taste.

Cognac is fine brandy known for its smoothness and heady scent. It is produced only in the Cognac region of France. (Hence all cognac is brandy, but not all brandy is cognac.) The age of cognac is guaranteed by authorities only up to six years. Beyond that there is no official standard, so you might find quite a range of designations.

To help consumers differentiate among the various cognacs, a special descriptor system was created. Sometimes known as Three Star, VS (Very Special) cognac is a blend from brandies that have aged a minimum of two years, although many have aged longer. VSOP (Very Special Old Pale) refers to blends that are not less than four years old. The descriptor XO (Extra Old) denotes a blend of considerable age. Other descriptors such as Napoleon, Extra, Vieille, Reserve, and Vieux mean the same thing.

Armagnac is much like cognac but has a richer taste. This brandy is produced only in the Armagnac region of France.

American brandy, virtually all of which is distilled in California, has its own taste characteristics. Unlike European brandies, California brandies are usually produced by individual firms that grow the grapes, distill, age, blend, bottle, and market the brandies under their own brand names. They are typically light and smooth. *Mr. Boston Five Star California Brandy* offers a smooth, mellow taste perfect in a brandy snifter, on the rocks, or mixed as a cocktail.

Apple Brandy, Applejack, and Calvados are apple brandies distilled from apple cider. Calvados is produced only in Normandy, France. Germany also has a long tradition of making fine brandy, even though the country is at the northernmost limit of wine production. One pioneer of fine brandy was Hugo Asbach, who described his brandy as "Weinbrand," the German word for grape brandy, which subsequently became the generic term for high-quality wine spirits. In an attempt to emulate the qualities of cognac, some German brandies are blended solely from grape spirits produced in pot-stills. However, the best German brandy is blended from spirits derived from both pot and continuous stills, giving it its own style, with an emphasis on flavor and smoothness. *Asbach Uralt Brandy* is a blend of both types of wine spirit, aged for over two years in small oak casks. The result epitomizes German brandy at its best and is richer and rounder than many cognac brandies.

Fruit brandies—eaux de vie—are water-white, 80- to 90-proof spirits distilled directly from fruits. Fruit brandies made from cherries are called Kirsch or Kirschwasser; from pears, Poire; and from raspberries, Framboise. They are best served chilled or over ice. Fruit-flavored brandies are brandy-based liqueurs flavored with blackberries, peaches, apricots, cherries, and so on. Made with all-natural fruit flavors, *Mr. Boston Flavored Brandies* are among the largest-selling and most complete line of fruit-flavored brandies in the country. Often used in mixed drinks, they are also excellent ingredients in a variety of dessert recipes.

Brandies fine enough to be drunk undiluted out of a snifter do not need to be heated over a candle. The warmth of a hand is sufficient to enhance the bouquet.

Singapore Sling

AFTER DINNER COCKTAIL

1 oz.	Apricot-flavored Brandy
1 oz.	Triple Sec
Juice of	1 Lime

Shake with ice and strain into cocktail glass. Leave lime in glass.

ALEXANDER COCKTAIL NO. 2

1 oz.	Crème de Cacao (White)
1 oz.	Brandy
1 oz.	Light Cream

Shake with ice and strain into cocktail glass. Sprinkle nutmeg on top.

AMERICAN BEAUTY COCKTAIL

1 tbsp.	Orange Juice
1 tbsp.	Grenadine
½ oz.	Dry Vermouth
½ oz.	Brandy
¼ tsp.	Crème de Menthe (White)
1 dash	Port

Shake with ice and strain into cocktail glass and top with a dash of port.

APPLE BRANDY COCKTAIL

1½ oz.	Apple Brandy
1 tsp.	Grenadine
1 tsp.	Lemon Juice

Shake with ice and strain into cocktail glass.

APPLE BRANDY HIGHBALL

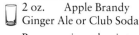

2 oz.	Apple Brandy

Ginger Ale or Club Soda

Pour over ice cubes into highball glass. Fill with ginger ale or club soda. Add a twist of lemon peel, if desired, and stir.

APPLE BRANDY RICKEY

Juice of	½ Lime
1½ oz.	Apple Brandy

Club Soda

Fill highball glass with club soda and ice cubes. Leave lime in glass. Stir.

APPLE BRANDY SOUR

Juice of	½ Lemon
½ tsp.	Powdered Sugar
2 oz.	Apple Brandy

Shake with ice and strain into sour glass. Decorate with a half-slice of lemon and a cherry.

APRICOT BRANDY RICKEY

Juice of	½ Lime
2 oz.	Apricot-flavored Brandy

Club Soda

Pour into highball glass over ice cubes and fill with club soda. Drop a rind of lime into glass. Stir.

APRICOT COCKTAIL

Juice of ¼ Lemon
Juice of ¼ Orange
1½ oz.   Apricot-flavored
         Brandy
1 tsp.   Gin

Shake with ice and strain
into cocktail glass.

APRICOT COOLER

½ tsp.   Powdered Sugar
2 oz.   Club Soda or
        Ginger Ale
2 oz.   Apricot-flavored
        Brandy

In collins glass, dissolve
powdered sugar and club
soda. Stir and fill glass with
cracked ice and add brandy.
Add club soda or ginger ale
and stir again. Insert a spiral
of orange or lemon peel (or
both) and dangle end over
rim of glass.

APRICOT FIZZ

Juice of ½ Lemon
Juice of ½ Lime
1tsp.   Powdered Sugar
2 oz.   Apricot-flavored
        Brandy
Club Soda

Shake with cracked ice and
strain into highball glass
with two ice cubes. Fill with
club soda.

B & B

½ oz.   Benedictine
½ oz.   Brandy

Use cordial glass and
carefully float the brandy on
top of the Benedictine.

BABBIE'S SPECIAL COCKTAIL

1 tbsp.   Light Cream
1½ oz.   Apricot- flavored
        Brandy
¼ tsp.   Gin

Shake with ice and strain
into cocktail glass.

BEE STINGER

½ oz.   Crème de Menthe
        (White)
1½ oz.   Blackberry Brandy

Shake with ice and strain
into cocktail glass.

BETSY ROSS

1½ oz.   Brandy
1½ oz.   Port
1 dash   Triple Sec

Stir with cracked ice and
strain into cocktail glass.

BOMBAY COCKTAIL

½ oz.   Dry Vermouth
½ oz.   Sweet Vermouth
1 oz.   Brandy
¼ tsp.   Anisette
½ tsp.   Triple Sec

Stir with ice and strain into
cocktail glass.

BOSOM CARESSER

1 oz.   Brandy
1 oz.   Madeira
½ oz.   Triple Sec

Stir with cracked ice and strain into cocktail glass.

BRANDIED MADEIRA

1 oz.   Brandy
1 oz.   Madeira
½ oz.   Dry Vermouth

Stir with cracked ice and strain into old-fashioned glass over ice cubes. Add a twist of lemon peel.

BRANDIED PORT

1 oz.   Brandy
1 oz.   Tawny Port
1 tbsp.   Lemon Juice
1 tsp.   Maraschino

Shake all ingredients and strain into old-fashioned glass with ice cubes. Add a slice of orange.

BRANDY ALEXANDER

½ oz.   Crème de Cacao
            (Brown)
½ oz.   Brandy
½ oz.   Heavy Cream

Shake well with cracked ice and strain into cocktail glass.

BRANDY CASSIS

1½ oz.   Brandy
1 oz.   Lemon Juice
1 dash   Crème de Cassis

Shake with cracked ice and strain into cocktail glass. Add a twist of lemon peel.

BRANDY COBBLER

1 tsp.   Powdered Sugar
2 oz.   Club Soda
2 oz.   Brandy

Dissolve powdered sugar in club soda. Fill 10-oz. goblet with shaved ice. Add brandy. Stir well and decorate with fruits in season. Serve with straws.

BRANDY COCKTAIL

2 oz.   Brandy
¼ tsp.   Simple Syrup
2 dashes Bitters

Stir ingredients with ice and strain into cocktail glass. Add a twist of lemon peel.

BRANDY COLLINS

Juice of ½ Lemon
1 tsp.   Powdered Sugar
2 oz.   Brandy
Club Soda

Shake with cracked ice and strain into collins glass. Add cubes of ice, fill with club soda, and stir. Decorate with a slice of orange or lemon and a cherry. Serve with straws.

In nineteenth century Italy, the Jesuits became known as "Brandy Fathers" because they dispensed brandy to the poor as medicine.

Brandy-making in the United States began in California in the mid-1800's when prospectors who had failed to make it rich during the Gold Rush turned their attention to wine production and distillation.

BRANDY CRUSTA COCKTAIL

1 tsp.	Maraschino
1 dash	Bitters
1 tsp.	Lemon Juice
½ oz.	Triple Sec
2 oz.	Brandy

Moisten the edge of a cocktail glass with lemon and dip into sugar. Cut the rind of half a lemon into a spiral and place in glass. Stir above ingredients with ice and strain into sugar-rimmed glass. Add a slice of orange.

BRANDY DAISY

Juice of	½ Lemon
½ tsp.	Powdered Sugar
1 tsp.	Raspberry Syrup or Grenadine
2 oz.	Brandy

Shake with ice and strain into stein or 8-oz. metal cup. Add cubes of ice and decorate with fruit.

BRANDY FIX

Juice of	½ Lemon
1 tsp.	Powdered Sugar
1 tsp.	Water
2½ oz.	Brandy

Mix lemon juice, powdered sugar, and water in highball glass. Stir. Then fill glass with shaved ice and brandy. Stir, add a slice of lemon. Serve with straws.

BRANDY FIZZ

Juice of	½ Lemon
1 tsp.	Powdered Sugar
2 oz.	Brandy
Club Soda	

Shake with cracked ice and strain into highball glass over two ice cubes. Fill with club soda.

BRANDY GUMP COCKTAIL

1½ oz.	Brandy
Juice of	½ Lemon
½ tsp.	Grenadine

Shake with ice and strain into cocktail glass.

BRANDY HIGHBALL

| 2 oz. | Brandy |
| Ginger Ale or Club Soda | |

Pour brandy over ice into highball glass. Fill with ginger ale or club soda. Add a twist of lemon peel and stir gently.

BRANDY JULEP

5–6	Mint Leaves
1 tsp.	Powdered Sugar
2½ oz.	Brandy

Into collins glass put sugar, mint leaves, and brandy. Fill glass with finely shaved ice and stir until mint rises to top, being careful not to bruise leaves. (Do not hold glass with hand while stirring.) Decorate with a slice of pineapple, orange or lemon, and a cherry. Serve with straws.

BRANDY MILK PUNCH

1 tsp. Powdered Sugar
2 oz. Brandy
1 cup Milk

Shake with ice, strain into collins glass, and sprinkle nutmeg on top.

BRANDY SANGAREE

½ tsp. Powdered Sugar
1 tsp. Water
2 oz. Brandy
Club Soda
1 tbsp. Port

Dissolve sugar in water and add brandy. Pour over ice into highball glass. Fill with club soda and stir. Float port on top and sprinkle lightly with nutmeg.

BRANDY SLING

1 tsp. Powdered Sugar
1 tsp. Water
Juice of ½ Lemon
2 oz. Brandy

Dissolve sugar in water and lemon juice. Add brandy. Serve in old-fashioned glass with cubed ice and a twist of lemon peel.

Prosit
    —a German toast

BRANDY SMASH

1 cube Sugar
1 oz. Club Soda
4 sprigs Mint
2 oz. Brandy

Muddle cube of sugar with club soda and mint in old-fashioned glass. Add brandy and ice cubes. Stir and decorate with a slice of orange and a cherry. Add a twist of lemon peel on top.

BRANDY AND SODA

2 oz. Brandy
Club Soda

Pour brandy into collins glass with ice cubes. Fill with club soda.

BRANDY SOUR

Juice of ½ Lemon
½ tsp. Powdered Sugar
2 oz. Brandy

Shake with ice and strain into sour glass. Decorate with a half-slice of lemon and a cherry.

BRANDY SQUIRT

1½ oz. Brandy
1 tbsp. Powdered Sugar
1 tsp. Grenadine
Club Soda

Shake with ice and strain into highball glass and fill with club soda. Decorate with stick of pineapple and strawberries.

BRANDY SWIZZLE

Juice of 1 Lime
1 tsp.   Powdered Sugar
2 oz.   Club Soda
2 dashes Bitters
2 oz.   Brandy

Put lime juice, sugar, and
club soda into collins glass.
Fill glass with ice and stir.
Add bitters and brandy. Add
club soda and serve with a
swizzle stick.

BRANDY TODDY

½ tsp.   Powdered Sugar
1 tsp.   Water
2 oz.   Brandy
1   Ice Cube

Dissolve the sugar and water
in old-fashioned glass. Add
the brandy and the ice cube.
Stir and add a twist of lemon
peel on top.

BRANDY VERMOUTH COCKTAIL

½ oz.   Sweet Vermouth
2 oz.   Brandy
1 dash   Bitters

Stir with ice and strain into
cocktail glass.

BRANTINI

1½ oz.   Brandy
1 oz.   Gin
1 dash   Dry Vermouth

Stir with cracked ice and
strain into old-fashioned
glass with cubed ice. Add a
twist of lemon peel.

BULLDOG COCKTAIL

1½ oz.   Cherry-flavored
           Brandy
¾ oz.   Gin
Juice of ½ Lime

Shake with ice and strain
into cocktail glass.

BULL'S EYE

1 oz.   Brandy
2 oz.   Hard Cider
Ginger Ale

Pour into highball glass over
ice cubes and fill with ginger
ale. Stir.

BULL'S MILK

1 tsp.   Powdered Sugar
1 oz.   Light Rum
1½ oz.   Brandy
1 cup   Milk

Shake with ice and strain
into collins glass. Sprinkle
nutmeg and pinch of
cinnamon on top.

BUTTON HOOK COCKTAIL

½ oz.   Crème de Menthe
           (White)
½ oz.   Apricot-flavored
           Brandy
½ oz.   Anisette
½ oz.   Brandy

Shake with ice and strain
into cocktail glass.

CADIZ

¾ oz.	Dry Sherry
¾ oz.	Blackberry-flavored Brandy
½ oz.	Triple Sec
1 tbsp.	Light Cream

Shake with ice and strain into old-fashioned glass over ice cubes.

CARA SPOSA

1 oz.	Coffee-flavored Brandy
1 oz.	Triple Sec
½ oz.	Light Cream

Shake with ice and strain into cocktail glass.

CARROL COCKTAIL

1½ oz.	Brandy
¾ oz.	Sweet Vermouth

Stir with ice and strain into cocktail glass. Serve with a cherry.

CHAMPS ÉLYSÉES COCKTAIL

1 oz.	Brandy
½ oz.	Chartreuse (Yellow)
Juice of ¼ Lemon	
½ tsp.	Powdered Sugar
1 dash	Bitters

Shake with ice and strain into cocktail glass.

CHARLES COCKTAIL

1½ oz.	Sweet Vermouth
1½ oz.	Brandy
1 dash	Bitters

Stir with ice and strain into cocktail glass.

CHERRY BLOSSOM

1½ oz.	Brandy
½ oz.	Cherry-flavored Brandy
1½ tsps.	Triple Sec
1½ tsps.	Grenadine
2 tsps.	Lemon Juice

Shake with ice and strain into cocktail glass that has had its rim moistened with cherry brandy and dipped into powdered sugar. Add a maraschino cherry.

CHERRY FIZZ

Juice of ½ Lemon	
2 oz.	Cherry-flavored Brandy
Club Soda	

Shake with ice and strain into highball glass with two ice cubes. Fill with club soda and decorate with a cherry.

CHERRY SLING

2 oz.	Cherry-flavored Brandy
Juice of ½ Lemon	

Serve in old-fashioned glass filled with ice cubes and stir. Add a twist of lemon peel.

CHICAGO COCKTAIL

2 oz.	Brandy
1 dash	Bitters
¼ tsp.	Triple Sec

Prepare old-fashioned glass by rubbing slice of lemon around rim and then dip into powdered sugar. Stir ingredients with ice and strain into prepared glass.

CLASSIC COCKTAIL
Juice of ¼ Lemon
1½ tsps. Curaçao
1½ tsps. Maraschino
1 oz.   Brandy

Prepare rim of old-fashioned glass by rubbing with lemon and dipping into powdered sugar. Shake ingredients with ice and strain into prepared glass.

COFFEE GRASSHOPPER
¼ oz.   Coffee-flavored
          Brandy
¼ oz.   Crème de
          Menthe (White)
¾ oz.   Light Cream

Shake with ice and strain into old-fashioned glass over ice cubes.

COGNAC HIGHBALL
2 oz.   Cognac
Ginger Ale or Club Soda

Pour cognac into highball glass over ice cubes and fill with ginger ale or club soda. Add a twist of lemon peel, if desired, and stir.

COLD DECK COCKTAIL
½ tsp.   Crème de Menthe
          (White)
½ oz.   Sweet Vermouth
1 oz.   Brandy

Stir with ice and strain into cocktail glass.

CRÈME DE CAFÉ

1 oz.   Coffee-flavored
          Brandy
½ oz.   Rum
½ oz.   Anisette
1 oz.   Light Cream

Shake with ice and strain into old-fashioned glass.

CUBAN COCKTAIL NO. 2
Juice of ½ Lime or ¼ Lemon
½ oz.   Apricot-flavored
          Brandy
1½ oz.   Brandy
1 tsp.   Light Rum

Shake with ice and strain into cocktail glass.

DEAUVILLE COCKTAIL
Juice of ¼ Lemon
½ oz.   Brandy
½ oz.   Apple Brandy
½ oz.   Triple Sec

Shake with ice and strain into cocktail glass.

DEPTH BOMB

1 oz.   Apple Brandy
1 oz.   Brandy
1 dash   Lemon Juice
1 dash   Grenadine

Shake with ice and strain into old-fashioned glass over ice cubes.

DREAM COCKTAIL

¾ oz.   Triple Sec
1½ oz.   Brandy
¼ tsp.   Anisette

Shake with ice and strain into cocktail glass.

EAST INDIA COCKTAIL NO. 1

1½ oz.   Brandy
½ tsp.   Pineapple Juice
½ tsp.   Triple Sec
1 tsp.   Jamaica Rum
1 dash   Bitters

Shake with ice and strain into cocktail glass. Add a twist of lemon peel and a cherry.

ETHEL DUFFY COCKTAIL

¾ oz.   Apricot-flavored Brandy
¾ oz.   Crème de Menthe (White)
¾ oz.   Triple Sec

Shake with ice and strain into cocktail glass.

FANCY BRANDY

2 oz.   Brandy
1 dash   Bitters
¼ tsp.   Triple Sec
¼ tsp.   Powdered Sugar

Shake with ice and strain into cocktail glass. Add a twist of lemon peel.

FANTASIO COCKTAIL

1 tsp.   Crème de Menthe (White)
1 tsp.   Maraschino
1 oz.   Brandy
¾ oz.   Dry Vermouth

Stir with ice and strain into cocktail glass.

FONTAINEBLEAU SPECIAL

1 oz.   Brandy
1 oz.   Anisette
½ oz.   Dry Vermouth

Shake with ice and strain into cocktail glass.

FROUPE COCKTAIL

1½ oz.   Sweet Vermouth
1½ oz.   Brandy
1 tsp.   Benedictine

Stir with ice and strain into cocktail glass.

GEORGIA MINT JULEP

2 sprigs   Mint
1 tsp.   Powdered Sugar
1 splash   Water
1½ oz.   Brandy
1 oz.   Peach-flavored Brandy

Put mint into collins glass with ice. Add sugar and splash of water. Muddle, then add brandy and peach liqueur. Decorate with mint leaves.

GILROY COCKTAIL

Juice of ¼ Lemon
1 tbsp.   Dry Vermouth
¾ oz.   Cherry-flavored Brandy
¾ oz.   Gin
1 dash   Orange Bitters

Shake with ice and strain into cocktail glass.

GOLDEN DAWN

1 oz.	Apple Brandy
½ oz.	Apricot-flavored Brandy
½ oz.	Gin
1 oz.	Orange Juice
1 tsp.	Grenadine

Shake all ingredients except grenadine with ice and strain into old-fashioned glass filled with ice cubes. Add grenadine.

HARVARD COCKTAIL

1½ oz.	Brandy
¾ oz.	Sweet Vermouth
1 dash	Bitters
1 tsp.	Grenadine
2 tsps.	Lemon Juice

Shake with ice and strain into cocktail glass.

HARVARD COOLER

½ tsp.	Powdered Sugar
2 oz.	Club Soda or Ginger Ale
2 oz.	Apple Brandy

Into collins glass put sugar and club soda. Stir. Then add ice cubes and apple brandy. Fill with club soda or ginger ale and stir again. Insert a spiral of orange or lemon peel (or both) and dangle end over rim of glass.

HENNESSY MARTINI

| 2 oz. | Hennessy V.S Cognac |
| ½ tsp. | Lemon Juice |

Fill shaker or mixing glass with ice. Add Hennessy and lemon juice. Stir gently, don't shake. Let settle. Strain into chilled martini glass. Garnish with twist of lemon peel.

HONEYMOON COCKTAIL

¼ oz.	Benedictine
¼ oz.	Apple Brandy
Juice of ½ Lemon	
1 tsp.	Triple Sec

Shake with ice and strain into cocktail glass.

JACK-IN-THE-BOX

1 oz.	Apple Brandy
1 oz.	Pineapple Juice
1 dash	Bitters

Shake with ice and strain into cocktail glass.

JACK ROSE COCKTAIL

1½ oz.	Apple Brandy
Juice of ½ Lime	
1 tsp.	Grenadine

Shake with ice and strain into cocktail glass.

JAMAICA GRANITO

1 small scoop Lemon or
    Orange Sherbet
1½ oz.   Brandy
1 oz.   Triple Sec
Club Soda

Combine in collins glass and
stir. Sprinkle nutmeg on top.

JAMAICA HOP

1 oz.   Coffee-flavored
        Brandy
1 oz.   Crème de Cacao
        (White)
1 oz.   Light Cream

Shake well with ice and
strain into cocktail glass.

JERSEY LIGHTNING

1½ oz.   Apple Brandy
½ oz.   Sweet Vermouth
Juice of 1 Lime

Shake with ice and strain
into cocktail glass.

LADY BE GOOD

1½ oz.   Brandy
½ oz.   Crème de Menthe
        (White)
½ oz.   Sweet Vermouth

Shake with ice and strain
into cocktail glass.

LA JOLLA

1½ oz.   Brandy
½ oz.   Crème de Banana
1 tsp.   Orange Juice
2 tsps.   Lemon Juice

Shake with ice and strain
into cocktail glass.

LIBERTY COCKTAIL

¾ oz.   Light Rum
1½ oz.   Apple Brandy
¼ tsp.   Simple Syrup

Stir with ice and strain into
cocktail glass.

LUGGER

1 oz.   Brandy
1 oz.   Apple Brandy
1 dash   Apricot-flavored
        Brandy

Shake with ice and strain
into cocktail glass.

LUXURY COCKTAIL

3 oz.   Brandy
2 dashes Orange Bitters
3 oz.   Well-chilled
        Champagne

Stir and pour into
champagne flute.

MERRY WIDOW
COCKTAIL NO. 2

1¼ oz.   Maraschino
1¼ oz.   Cherry-flavored
        Brandy

Stir with ice and strain into
cocktail glass. Serve with a
cherry.

METROPOLITAN
COCKTAIL

1¼ oz.   Brandy
1¼ oz.   Sweet Vermouth
½ tsp.   Sugar Syrup
1 dash   Bitters

Stir with ice and strain into
cocktail glass.

MIDNIGHT COCKTAIL

1 oz.   Apricot-flavored
            Brandy
½ oz.   Triple Sec
1 tbsp.   Lemon Juice

Shake with ice and strain
into cocktail glass.

MIKADO COCKTAIL

1 oz.   Brandy
1 dash   Triple Sec
1 dash   Grenadine
1 dash   Crème de Noyaux
1 dash   Bitters

Stir in old-fashioned glass
over ice cubes.

MONTANA

1½ oz.   Brandy
1 oz.   Port
½ oz.   Dry Vermouth

Stir in old-fashioned glass
filled with ice cubes.

MOONLIGHT

2 oz.   Apple Brandy
Juice of 1 Lemon
1 tsp.   Powdered Sugar

Shake with ice and strain
into old-fashioned glass over
ice cubes.

MORNING COCKTAIL

1 oz.   Brandy
1 oz.   Dry Vermouth
¼ tsp.   Triple Sec
¼ tsp.   Maraschino
¼ tsp.   Anisette
2 dashes Orange Bitters

Stir with ice and strain into
cocktail glass. Serve with a
cherry.

NETHERLAND

1 oz.   Brandy
1 oz.   Triple Sec
1 dash   Orange Bitters

Stir in old-fashioned glass
with ice cubes.

OLYMPIC COCKTAIL

¾ oz.   Orange Juice
¾ oz.   Triple Sec
¾ oz.   Brandy

Shake with ice and strain
into cocktail glass.

PARADISE COCKTAIL

1 oz.   Apricot-flavored
            Brandy
¾ oz.   Gin
Juice of ¼ Orange

Shake with ice and strain
into cocktail glass.

PEACH SANGAREE

1 oz.   Peach-flavored
            Brandy
Club Soda
1 tsp.   Port

Put brandy into highball
glass with ice cubes. Fill
glass with club soda. Stir and
float port on top. Sprinkle
lightly with nutmeg.

POLONAISE

1½ oz.   Brandy
1 tbsp.   Blackberry-flavored
          Brandy
½ oz.   Dry Sherry
1 dash   Lemon Juice

Shake with ice and strain
into old-fashioned glass over
ice cubes.

POOP DECK COCKTAIL

1 oz.   Brandy
1 oz.   Port
1 tbsp. Blackberry-flavored
         Brandy

Shake with ice and strain
into cocktail glass.

PRESTO COCKTAIL

1 tbsp.   Orange Juice
½ oz.   Sweet Vermouth
1½ oz.   Brandy
¼ tsp.   Anisette

Shake with ice and strain
into cocktail glass.

PRINCESS POUSSE CAFÉ

¾ oz.   Apricot-flavored
          Brandy
1½ tsps. Light Cream

Pour cream carefully on top
of brandy, so that it does not
mix with the other
ingredients. Use pousse-café
glass.

ROYAL SMILE COCKTAIL

Juice of ¼ Lemon
1 tsp.   Grenadine
½ oz.   Gin
1 oz.   Apple Brandy

Stir with ice and strain into
cocktail glass.

ST. CHARLES PUNCH

1 oz.   Brandy
½ oz.   Triple Sec
3 oz.   Port
Juice of 1 Lemon
1 tsp.   Sugar

Shake all ingredients except
port with ice. Strain into
collins glass with ice. Top
with port. Add a slice of
lemon and a cherry.

SARATOGA COCKTAIL

2 oz.   Brandy
2 dashes Bitters
1 tsp.   Lemon Juice
1 tsp.   Pineapple Juice
½ tsp.   Maraschino

Shake with ice and strain
into cocktail glass.

SAUCY SUE COCKTAIL

½ tsp.   Apricot-flavored
          Brandy
½ tsp.   Pernod
2 oz.   Apple Brandy

Stir with ice and strain into
cocktail glass.

SHRINER COCKTAIL

1½ oz. Brandy
1½ oz. Sloe Gin
2 dashes Bitters
½ tsp. Simple Syrup

Stir with ice and strain into cocktail glass. Add a twist of lemon peel.

SIDECAR COCKTAIL

Juice of ¼ Lemon
1 oz. Triple Sec
1 oz. Brandy

Shake with ice and strain into cocktail glass.

SINGAPORE SLING

Juice of ½ Lemon
1 tsp. Powdered Sugar
2 oz. Gin
Club Soda
½ oz. Cherry-flavored Brandy

Shake lemon, sugar, and gin with ice and strain into collins glass. Add ice cubes and fill with club soda. Float cherry-flavored brandy on top. Decorate with fruits in season and serve with straws.

SLOPPY JOE'S COCKTAIL NO. 2

¾ oz. Pineapple Juice
¾ oz. Brandy
¾ oz. Port
¼ tsp. Triple Sec
¼ tsp. Grenadine

Shake with ice and strain into cocktail glass.

SOMBRERO

1½ oz. Coffee-flavored Brandy
1 oz. Light Cream

Pour brandy into old-fashioned glass over ice cubes. Float cream on top.

SOOTHER COCKTAIL

½ oz. Brandy
½ oz. Apple Brandy
½ oz. Triple Sec
Juice of ½ Lemon
1 tsp. Powdered Sugar

Shake with ice and strain into cocktail glass.

SPECIAL ROUGH COCKTAIL

1½ oz. Apple Brandy
1½ oz. Brandy
½ tsp. Anisette

Stir with ice and strain into cocktail glass.

STAR COCKTAIL

1 oz. Apple Brandy
1 oz. Sweet Vermouth
1 dash Bitters

Stir with ice and strain into cocktail glass. Add a twist of lemon peel.

STINGER

½ oz. Crème de Menthe (White)
1½ oz. Brandy

Shake with ice and strain into cocktail glass.

STIRRUP CUP

1 oz. Cherry-flavored Brandy
1 oz. Brandy
Juice of ½ Lemon
1 tsp. Sugar

Shake with ice and strain into old-fashioned glass over ice cubes.

TEMPTER COCKTAIL

1 oz. Port
1 oz. Apricot-flavored Brandy

Stir with ice and strain into cocktail glass.

THANKSGIVING SPECIAL

¾ oz. Apricot-flavored Brandy
¾ oz. Gin
¾ oz. Dry Vermouth
¼ tsp. Lemon Juice

Shake with ice and strain into cocktail glass. Serve with a cherry.

TULIP COCKTAIL

1½ tsps. Lemon Juice
1½ tsps. Apricot-flavored Brandy
¾ oz. Sweet Vermouth
¾ oz. Apple Brandy

Shake with ice and strain into cocktail glass.

VALENCIA COCKTAIL

1 tbsp. Orange Juice
1½ oz. Apricot-flavored Brandy
2 dashes Orange Bitters

Shake with ice and strain into cocktail glass.

VANDERBILT COCKTAIL

¾ oz. Cherry-flavored Brandy
1½ oz. Brandy
1 tsp. Simple Syrup
2 dashes Bitters

Stir with ice and strain into cocktail glass.

WHIP COCKTAIL

½ oz. Dry Vermouth
½ oz. Sweet Vermouth
1½ oz. Brandy
¼ tsp. Anisette
1 tsp. Triple Sec

Stir with ice and strain into cocktail glass.

WIDOW'S KISS

1 oz. Brandy
½ oz. Chartreuse (Yellow)
½ oz. Benedictine
1 dash Bitters

Shake with ice and strain into cocktail glass.

WINDY CORNER COCKTAIL

2 oz.   Blackberry-flavored
         Brandy

Stir brandy with ice and strain
into cocktail glass. Sprinkle
a little nutmeg on top.

TWO BOTTLES AND A BILL

Place a dollar bill across the open end of a
soda bottle. Then balance another soda bottle upside down on the first one so that the
two rims coincide, as shown. Then claim
that you will remove the bill from between
the two bottles without upsetting the bottles.
METHOD: Hold the bill firmly in your left
hand, and smartly strike the bill with the
forefinger of your right hand about halfway
between left hand and the bottles. If you hold
the bill taut—a new bill is best—it will slip
out without upsetting the bottles.

Gin

"**S**haken, not stirred." A classic line, for a classic cocktail—the preferred martini of James Bond, the debonair British secret agent immortalized in Ian Fleming's novels.

Purists claim that shaking a martini can "bruise" the gin, a dubious, though amusing, contention. There's no question, however, that gin itself has had a controversial past.

Used today in more crisply refreshing drinks than any other distilled spirit, gin was first created as a medicine by a Dutch chemist some 300 years ago. Its supposed curative powers became irrelevant—people *felt* better, so in the seventeenth century, the English took the Dutch potion back to their country and drank it liberally, with or without toasting anyone's health. In fact, they became so enamored of the spirit that they soon were making it themselves. Once called "Mother's Ruin," and scorned by the upper classes because it was the drink of the oft-sodden poor, gin perhaps owes its modern sophisticated cachet to the Martini.

Gins are more than neutral spirits distilled from grain. They are reprocessed and redistilled with a flavorist's collection of assorted herbs and spices, primarily juniper berries. Gin, like other clear spirits, is basically clean and bracing in flavor, but has fruity and herby overtones as well.

The most common style of gin is London Dry. In eighteenth-century London, most gins were sweetened to disguise their rawness. Pioneering distillers experimented with making unsweetened gin, which was smooth in character, with elegant aromatic flavors, giving rise to the style of gin known as London Dry, now produced around the world. *Barton London Extra Dry Gin* offers the crisp, dry taste most gin drinkers prefer.

Martini, Salty Dog

Fleischmann's Gin was introduced in 1870 as the first American-made gin. Today it still features a lighter gin taste—perfect in a Salty Dog, Martini, or Gin and Tonic.

Carbonated water was originally developed in the eighteenth century to emulate naturally sparkling mineral water. Later it was found that this water was the most effective and palatable medium in which to give quinine medicine to British servicemen in India, who were at risk for contracting malaria. Thus Indian Tonic Water was born. It wasn't long before British army officers, who found gin an indispensable antidote to the tropical heat, began mixing tonic water with gin—creating one of the most famous mixed drinks in the world.

Gin and Tonic

ABBEY COCKTAIL

1½ oz.   Gin
Juice of ¼ Orange
1 dash   Orange Bitters

Shake with ice and strain
into cocktail glass. Add a
maraschino cherry.

ADAM AND EVE

1 oz.   Forbidden Fruit
               Liqueur
1 oz.   Gin
1 oz.   Brandy
1 dash   Lemon Juice

Shake well with cracked ice
and strain into cocktail glass.

ALABAMA FIZZ

Juice of ½ Lemon
1 tsp.   Powdered Sugar
2 oz.   Gin
Club Soda

Shake well with cracked ice
and strain into highball glass
over two ice cubes. Fill with
club soda. Garnish with two
sprigs of fresh mint.

ALASKA COCKTAIL

2 dashes Orange Bitters
1½ oz.   Gin
¼ oz.   Chartreuse (Yellow)

Stir with ice and strain into
cocktail glass.

ALBEMARLE FIZZ

Juice of ½ Lemon
1 tsp.   Powdered Sugar
2 oz.   Gin
1 tsp.   Raspberry Syrup
Club Soda

Shake with ice and strain
into highball glass over two
ice cubes. Fill with club soda.

ALEXANDER COCKTAIL NO. 1

1 oz.   Gin
1 oz.   Crème de Cacao
               (White)
1 oz.   Light Cream

Shake with ice and strain
into cocktail glass. Sprinkle
nutmeg on top.

ALEXANDER'S SISTER COCKTAIL

1 oz.   Dry Gin
1 oz.   Crème de Menthe
               (Green)
1 oz.   Light Cream

Shake with ice and strain
into cocktail glass. Sprinkle
nutmeg on top.

ALLEN COCKTAIL

1½ tsps. Lemon Juice
¼ oz.   Maraschino
1½ oz.   Gin

Shake with ice and strain
into cocktail glass.

Cheers
   —an English toast

ANGLER'S COCKTAIL

2 dashes Bitters
3 dashes Orange Bitters
1½ oz.   Gin
1 dash   Grenadine

Shake with cracked ice and pour into old-fashioned glass over ice cubes.

APRICOT ANISETTE COLLINS

1½ oz.   Gin
½ oz.   Apricot-flavored Brandy
1½ tsps. Anisette
1 tbsp. Lemon Juice
Club Soda

Shake with ice and strain into collins glass over ice. Fill with club soda and stir lightly. Garnish with a slice of lemon.

ARTILLERY

1½ oz.   Gin
1½ tsps. Sweet Vermouth
2 dashes Bitters

Stir with ice and strain into cocktail glass.

BARBARY COAST

½ oz.   Gin
½ oz.   Rum
½ oz.   White Crème de Cacao
½ oz.   Scotch
½ oz.   Light Cream

Shake with ice and strain into cocktail glass.

BARON COCKTAIL

½ oz.   Dry Vermouth
1½ oz.   Gin
1½ tsps. Triple Sec
½ tsp.   Sweet Vermouth

Stir with ice and strain into cocktail glass. Add a twist of lemon peel.

BEAUTY SPOT COCKTAIL

1 tsp.   Orange Juice
½ oz.   Sweet Vermouth
½ oz.   Dry Vermouth
1 oz.   Gin
1 dash   Grenadine

Shake first four ingredients with ice and strain into cocktail glass, with a dash of grenadine in bottom of glass.

BELMONT COCKTAIL

2 oz.   Gin
1 tsp.   Raspberry Syrup
¾ oz.   Light Cream

Shake with ice and strain into cocktail glass.

BENNETT COCKTAIL

Juice of ½ Lime
1½ oz.   Gin
½ tsp.   Powdered Sugar
2 dashes Orange Bitters

Shake with ice and strain into cocktail glass.

Proost
—a Dutch toast

BERMUDA BOUQUET

Juice of ¼ Orange
Juice of ½ Lemon
1 tsp.   Powdered Sugar
1½ oz.   Gin
1 oz.   Apricot-flavored
         Brandy
1 tsp.   Grenadine
½ tsp.   Triple Sec

Shake with ice and strain
into highball glass with ice
cubes.

BERMUDA HIGHBALL

¾ oz.   Gin
¾ oz.   Brandy
¾ oz.   Dry Vermouth
Ginger Ale or Club Soda

Pour into highball glass over
ice cubes. Fill with ginger ale
or club soda. Add a twist of
lemon peel and stir.

BERMUDA ROSE

1¼ oz.   Gin
1½ tsps. Apricot-flavored
         Brandy
1½ tsps. Grenadine

Shake with ice and strain
into cocktail glass.

BIJOU COCKTAIL

¾ oz.   Gin
¾ oz.   Chartreuse (Green)
¾ oz.   Sweet Vermouth
1 dash   Orange Bitters

Stir with ice and strain into
cocktail glass. Add a cherry
on top.

BILLY TAYLOR

Juice of ½ Lime
2 oz.   Gin
Club Soda

Fill collins glass with club
soda and ice cubes. Stir in
lime juice and gin.

BLOODHOUND COCKTAIL

½ oz.   Dry Vermouth
½ oz.   Sweet Vermouth
1 oz.   Gin

Shake with ice and strain
into cocktail glass. Decorate
with two or three crushed
strawberries.

BLUE BIRD

1½ oz.   Gin
½ oz.   Triple Sec
1 dash   Bitters

Stir with ice cubes and strain
into cocktail glass. Add a
twist of lemon peel and a
cherry.

BLUE CANARY

¾ oz.   Gin
3 tbsps. Grapefruit Juice
1 tbsp. Blue Curaçao

Combine ingredients with
ice in mixing glass and stir
gently. Strain into chilled
cocktail glass filled with
crushed ice. Garnish with a
mint sprig.

BLUE DEVIL COCKTAIL

1 oz. Gin
Juice of ½ Lemon or
1 Lime
1 tbsp. Maraschino
½ tsp. Blue Curaçao

Shake with ice and strain
into cocktail glass.

BLUE MOON COCKTAIL

1½ oz. Gin
¾ oz. Blue Curaçao

Stir with ice and strain into
cocktail glass. Add a twist of
lemon peel.

BOOMERANG

1 oz. Dry Vermouth
1½ oz. Gin
1 dash Bitters
1 dash Maraschino

Stir with ice cubes and strain
into cocktail glass. Add a
twist of lemon peel.

BOSTON COCKTAIL

¾ oz. Gin
¾ oz. Apricot-flavored
Brandy
Juice of ¼ Lemon
1½ tsps. Grenadine

Shake with ice and strain
into cocktail glass.

BRONX COCKTAIL

1 oz. Gin
½ oz. Dry Vermouth
½ oz. Sweet Vermouth
Juice of ¼ Orange

Shake with ice and strain
into cocktail glass. Serve
with slice of orange.

BRONX COCKTAIL (DRY)

1 oz. Gin
1 oz. Dry Vermouth
Juice of ¼ Orange

Shake with ice and strain
into cocktail glass. Serve
with a slice of orange.

BRONX TERRACE COCKTAIL

1½ oz. Gin
1½ oz. Dry Vermouth
Juice of ½ Lime

Shake with ice and strain
into cocktail glass. Add a
cherry.

BROWN COCKTAIL

¾ oz. Gin
¾ oz. Light Rum
¾ oz. Dry Vermouth

Stir with ice and strain into
cocktail glass.

BULLDOG HIGHBALL

Juice of ½ Orange
2 oz. Gin
Ginger Ale

Pour into highball glass over
ice cubes and fill with ginger
ale. Stir.

CABARET

1½ oz. Gin
2 dashes Bitters
½ tsp. Dry Vermouth
¼ tsp. Benedictine

Stir with ice and strain into
cocktail glass. Serve with a
cherry.

CARUSO

1½ oz.   Gin
1 oz.   Dry Vermouth
½ oz.   Crème de Menthe
          (Green)

Stir with ice and strain into cocktail glass.

CASINO COCKTAIL

2 dashes Orange Bitters
¼ tsp.   Maraschino
¼ tsp.   Lemon Juice
2 oz.   Gin

Shake with ice and strain into cocktail glass. Serve with a cherry.

CHELSEA SIDECAR

Juice of ¼ Lemon
¾ oz.   Triple Sec
¾ oz.   Gin

Shake with ice and strain into cocktail glass.

CLARIDGE COCKTAIL

¾ oz.   Gin
¾ oz.   Dry Vermouth
1 tbsp.   Apricot-flavored
          Brandy
1 tbsp.   Triple Sec

Stir with ice and strain into cocktail glass.

CLUB COCKTAIL

1½ oz.   Gin
¾ oz.   Sweet Vermouth

Stir with ice and strain into cocktail glass. Add a cherry or olive.

COLONIAL COCKTAIL

½ oz.   Grapefruit Juice
1 tsp.   Maraschino
1½ oz.   Gin

Shake with ice and strain into cocktail glass. Serve with an olive.

COOPERSTOWN COCKTAIL

½ oz.   Dry Vermouth
½ oz.   Sweet Vermouth
1 oz.   Gin

Shake with ice and strain into cocktail glass. Add a sprig of mint.

COUNT CURREY

1½ oz.   Gin
1 tsp.   Powdered Sugar
Chilled Champagne

Shake gin and sugar with ice and strain into champagne flute over ice cubes. Fill with champagne.

CREAM FIZZ

Juice of ½ Lemon
1 tsp.   Powdered Sugar
2 oz.   Gin
1 tsp.   Light Cream
Club Soda

Shake with ice and strain into highball glass over two ice cubes. Fill with club soda and stir.

CRIMSON COCKTAIL

1½ oz. Gin
2 tsps. Lemon Juice
1 tsp. Grenadine
¾ oz. Port

Shake with ice and strain into cocktail glass, leaving enough room on top to float port.

CRYSTAL SLIPPER COCKTAIL

½ oz. Blue Curaçao
2 dashes Orange Bitters
1½ oz. Gin

Stir with ice and strain into cocktail glass.

DAMN-THE-WEATHER COCKTAIL

1 tsp. Triple Sec
1 tbsp. Orange Juice
1 tbsp. Sweet Vermouth
1 oz. Gin

Shake with ice and strain into cocktail glass.

DARB COCKTAIL

1 tsp. Lemon Juice
¾ oz. Dry Vermouth
¾ oz. Gin
¾ oz. Apricot-flavored Brandy

Shake with ice and strain into cocktail glass.

DEEP SEA COCKTAIL

1 oz. Dry Vermouth
¼ tsp. Anisette
1 dash Orange Bitters
1 oz. Gin

Stir with ice and strain into cocktail glass.

DELMONICO NO. 1

¾ oz. Gin
½ oz. Dry Vermouth
½ oz. Sweet Vermouth
½ oz. Brandy

Stir with ice and strain into cocktail glass. Add a twist of lemon peel.

DELMONICO NO. 2

1 dash Orange Bitters
1 oz. Dry Vermouth
1½ oz. Gin

Stir with ice and strain into cocktail glass. Add a twist of lemon peel.

DEMPSEY COCKTAIL

1 oz. Gin
1 oz. Apple Brandy
½ tsp. Anisette
½ tsp. Grenadine

Stir with ice and strain into cocktail glass.

DIAMOND FIZZ

Juice of ½ Lemon
1 tsp. Powdered Sugar
2 oz. Gin
Chilled Champagne

Shake with ice and strain into highball glass over two cubes of ice. Fill with champagne and stir.

DIXIE COCKTAIL

Juice of ¼ Orange
1 tbsp.   Anisette
½ oz.   Dry Vermouth
1 oz.   Gin

Shake with ice and strain into cocktail glass.

DRY MARTINI
(5-to-1)

1⅔ oz.   Gin
⅓ oz.   Dry Vermouth

Stir vermouth and gin over ice cubes in mixing glass. Strain into cocktail glass. Serve with a twist of lemon peel or olive, if desired.

DU BARRY COCKTAIL

1 dash   Bitters
¾ oz.   Dry Vermouth
½ tsp.   Anisette
1½ oz.   Gin

Stir with ice and strain into cocktail glass. Add a slice of orange.

EMERALD ISLE COCKTAIL

2 oz.   Gin
1 tsp.   Crème de Menthe
         (Green)
3 dashes Bitters

Stir with ice and strain into cocktail glass.

EMERSON

1½ oz.   Gin
1 oz.   Sweet Vermouth
Juice of ½ Lime
1 tsp.   Maraschino

Shake with ice and strain into cocktail glass.

ENGLISH HIGHBALL

¾ oz.   Gin
¾ oz.   Brandy
¾ oz.   Sweet Vermouth
Ginger Ale or Club Soda

Pour into highball glass over ice cubes and fill with ginger ale or club soda. Add a twist of lemon peel, if desired, and stir.

ENGLISH ROSE COCKTAIL

1½ oz.   Gin
¾ oz.   Apricot-flavored
         Brandy
¾ oz.   Dry Vermouth
1 tsp.   Grenadine
¼ tsp.   Lemon Juice

Prepare rim of glass by rubbing with lemon and dipping in sugar. Shake all ingredients with ice and strain into cocktail glass. Serve with a cherry.

FALLEN ANGEL

Juice of 1 Lime or ½ Lemon
1½ oz.   Gin
1 dash   Bitters
½ tsp.   Crème de Menthe
         (White)

Shake with ice and strain into cocktail glass. Serve with a cherry.

FANCY GIN

2 oz.   Gin
1 dash   Bitters
¼ tsp.   Triple Sec
¼ tsp.   Powdered Sugar

Shake with ice and strain into cocktail glass. Add a twist of lemon peel.

FARE THEE WELL

1½ oz.   Gin
½ oz.   Dry Vermouth
1 dash   Sweet Vermouth
1 dash   Triple Sec

Shake with ice and strain
into cocktail glass.

FARMER'S COCKTAIL

1 oz.   Gin
½ oz.   Dry Vermouth
½ oz.   Sweet Vermouth
2 dashes Bitters

Stir with ice and strain into
cocktail glass.

FAVORITE COCKTAIL

¾ oz.   Apricot-flavored
          Brandy
¾ oz.   Dry Vermouth
¾ oz.   Gin
¼ tsp.   Lemon Juice

Shake with ice and strain
into cocktail glass.

FIFTY-FIFTY COCKTAIL

1½ oz.   Gin
1½ oz.   Dry Vermouth

Stir with ice and strain into
cocktail glass.

FINE-AND-DANDY COCKTAIL

Juice of ¼ Lemon
½ oz.   Triple Sec
1½ oz.   Gin
1 dash   Bitters

Shake with ice and strain
into cocktail glass. Serve
with a cherry.

FINO MARTINI

2 oz.   Gin
2 tsps.   Fino Sherry

Stir gin and sherry over ice
cubes in mixing glass. Strain
into cocktail glass. Serve
with a twist of lemon peel.

FLAMINGO COCKTAIL

Juice of ½ Lime
½ oz.   Apricot-flavored
          Brandy
1½ oz.   Gin
1 tsp.   Grenadine

Shake with ice and strain
into cocktail glass.

FLORADORA COOLER

Juice of 1 Lime
½ tsp.   Powdered Sugar
1 tbsp.   Grenadine
2 oz.   Club Soda or
          Ginger Ale
2 oz.   Gin

Stir first four ingredients in
collins glass. Fill glass with
ice and add gin. Fill with
club soda or ginger ale and
stir again.

FLORIDA

½ oz.   Gin
1½ tsps. Kirschwasser
1½ tsps. Triple Sec
1 oz.   Orange Juice
1 tsp.   Lemon Juice

Shake with ice and strain
into cocktail glass.

FLYING DUTCHMAN

2 oz.   Gin
1 dash Triple Sec

Shake with ice and strain into old-fashioned glass over ice cubes.

FOG HORN

Juice of ½ Lime
1½ oz. Gin
Ginger Ale

Pour into highball glass over ice cubes. Fill with ginger ale. Stir. Add a slice of lime.

FRANKENJACK COCKTAIL

1 oz.   Gin
¼ oz.   Dry Vermouth
½ oz.   Apricot-flavored Brandy
1 tsp.   Triple Sec

Stir with ice and strain into cocktail glass. Serve with a cherry.

FREE SILVER

Juice of ¼ Lemon
½ tsp. Powdered Sugar
1½ oz. Gin
½ oz.   Dark Rum
1 tbsp. Milk
Club Soda

Shake with ice and strain into collins glass over ice cubes. Fill with club soda.

FRENCH "75"

Juice of 1 Lemon
2 tsps. Powdered Sugar
2 oz.   Gin
Chilled Champagne

Stir in collins glass. Then add ice cubes, fill with champagne and stir. Decorate with a slice of lemon or orange and a cherry. Serve with straws.

GIMLET

1 oz.   Lime Juice
1 tsp.   Powdered Sugar
1½ oz. Gin

Shake with ice and strain into cocktail glass.

GIN ALOHA

1½ oz. Gin
1½ oz. Triple Sec
1 tbsp. Unsweetened Pineapple Juice
1 dash Orange Bitters

Shake with ice and strain into cocktail glass.

GIN AND BITTERS

½ tsp. Bitters
Gin

Put bitters into cocktail glass and revolve the glass until it is entirely coated with the bitters. Then fill with gin. (No ice is used in this drink.)

GIN BUCK

Juice of ½ Lemon
1½ oz.   Gin
Ginger Ale

Pour lemon juice and gin into old-fashioned glass over ice cubes. Fill with ginger ale and stir.

GIN COBBLER

1 tsp.   Powdered Sugar
2 oz.   Club Soda
2 oz.   Gin

Dissolve sugar and club soda in goblet, then fill with ice and add gin. Stir and decorate with fruits in season. Serve with straws.

GIN COCKTAIL

2 oz.   Gin
2 dashes Bitters

Stir with ice and strain into cocktail glass. Serve with a twist of lemon peel.

GIN COOLER

½ tsp.   Powdered Sugar
2 oz.   Club Soda
2 oz.   Gin
Club Soda or Ginger Ale

Into collins glass stir sugar with 2 oz. club soda. Fill glass with ice and add gin. Fill with club soda or ginger ale and stir again. Insert a spiral of orange or lemon peel (or both) and dangle end over rim of glass.

GIN DAISY

Juice of ½ Lemon
½ tsp.   Powdered Sugar
1 tsp.   Grenadine
2 oz.   Gin

Shake with ice and strain into stein or metal cup. Add ice cubes and decorate with fruit.

GIN FIX

Juice of ½ Lemon
1 tsp.   Powdered Sugar
1 tsp.   Water
2 ½ oz. Gin

Mix lemon juice, sugar, and water in highball glass. Stir and fill glass with ice. Add gin. Stir, add a slice of lemon. Serve with straws.

GIN FIZZ

Juice of ½ Lemon
1 tsp.   Powdered Sugar
2 oz.   Gin
Club Soda

Shake with ice and strain into highball glass with two ice cubes. Fill with club soda and stir.

GIN HIGHBALL

2 oz.   Gin
Ginger Ale or Club Soda

Pour into highball glass over ice cubes and fill with ginger ale or club soda. Add a twist of lemon peel, if desired, and stir.

GIN AND IT

2 oz.   Gin
1 oz.   Sweet Vermouth

Stir ingredients in cocktail glass. (No ice is used in this drink.)

GIN MILK PUNCH

1 tsp.   Powdered Sugar
2 oz.   Gin
1 cup   Milk

Shake with ice, strain into collins glass, and sprinkle nutmeg on top.

GIN RICKEY

Juice of ½ Lime
1½ oz.   Gin
Club Soda

Pour ingredients into highball glass over ice cubes and fill with club soda. Stir. Add a wedge of lime.

GIN SANGAREE

½ tsp.   Powdered Sugar
1 tsp.   Water
2 oz.   Gin
Club Soda
1 tbsp.   Port

Dissolve sugar in water and add gin. Pour into highball glass over ice cubes. Fill with club soda and stir. Float port on top and sprinkle lightly with nutmeg.

GIN AND SIN

1 oz.   Gin
1 oz.   Lemon Juice
1 tbsp.   Orange Juice
1 dash   Grenadine

Shake with ice and strain into cocktail glass.

GIN SLING

1 tsp.   Powdered Sugar
1 tsp.   Water
Juice of ½ Lemon
2 oz.   Gin

Dissolve sugar in water and lemon juice. Add gin. Pour into old-fashioned glass over ice cubes and stir. Add a twist of orange peel.

GIN SMASH

1 cube   Sugar
1 oz.   Club Soda
4 sprigs   Mint
2 oz.   Gin

Muddle sugar with club soda and mint in old-fashioned glass. Add gin and one ice cube. Stir and decorate with a slice of orange and a cherry. Add a twist of lemon peel.

GIN SOUR

Juice of ½ Lemon
½ tsp.   Powdered Sugar
2 oz.   Gin

Shake with ice and strain into sour glass. Decorate with half-slice of lemon and a cherry.

GIN SQUIRT

1½ oz.   Gin
1 tbsp.   Powdered Sugar
1 tsp.   Grenadine
Club Soda

Stir with ice and strain into highball glass over ice cubes. Fill with club soda and stir. Decorate with cubes of pineapple and strawberries.

GIN SWIZZLE

Juice of 1 Lime
1 tsp.   Powdered Sugar
2 oz.   Club Soda
2 dashes Bitters
2 oz.   Gin

Combine first three ingredients in collins glass. Fill glass with ice and stir. Add bitters and gin. Fill with club soda and serve with swizzle stick.

GIN THING

1½ oz.   Gin
Juice of ½ Lime
Ginger Ale

Pour gin and lime juice into highball glass over ice cubes and fill with ginger ale.

GIN TODDY

½ tsp.   Powdered Sugar
2 tsps.   Water
2 oz.   Gin

In old-fashioned glass, mix sugar and water. Add gin and one ice cube. Stir and add a twist of lemon peel.

GIN AND TONIC

 2 oz.   Gin
Tonic Water

Pour gin into highball glass over ice cubes and fill with tonic water. Stir.

GOLDEN DAZE

 1½ oz.   Gin
½ oz.   Peach-flavored Brandy
1 oz.   Orange Juice

Shake with ice and strain into cocktail glass.

GOLF COCKTAIL

 1½ oz.   Gin
¾ oz.   Dry Vermouth
2 dashes Bitters

Stir with ice and strain into cocktail glass.

GRAND ROYAL FIZZ

Juice of ½ Orange
Juice of ½ Lemon
1 tsp.   Powdered Sugar
2 oz.   Gin
½ tsp.   Maraschino
2 tsps.   Light Cream
Club Soda

Shake with ice and strain into highball glass over two ice cubes. Fill with club soda and stir.

GRAPEFRUIT COCKTAIL

1 oz.   Grapefruit Juice
1 oz.   Gin
1 tsp.   Maraschino

Shake with ice and strain into cocktail glass. Serve with a cherry.

GREENBACK

1½ oz.   Gin
1 oz.   Crème de Menthe
(Green)
1 oz.   Lemon Juice

Shake with ice and strain
into old-fashioned glass over
ice cubes.

GREEN DEVIL

1½ oz.   Gin
1½ oz.   Crème de Menthe
(Green)
1 tbsp.   Lime Juice

Shake with ice and strain
into old-fashioned glass over
ice cubes. Decorate with
mint leaves.

GREEN DRAGON

Juice of ½ Lemon
½ oz.   Kümmel
½ oz.   Crème de Menthe
(Green)
1½ oz.   Gin
4 dashes Orange Bitters

Shake with ice and strain
into cocktail glass.

GREYHOUND

1½ oz.   Gin
5 oz.   Grapefruit Juice

Pour into highball glass over
ice cubes. Stir well.

GYPSY COCKTAIL

1½ oz.   Sweet Vermouth
1½ oz.   Gin

Stir with ice and strain into
cocktail glass. Serve with a
cherry.

HARLEM COCKTAIL

¾ oz.   Pineapple Juice
1½ oz.   Gin
½ tsp.   Maraschino

Shake with ice and strain
into cocktail glass. Decorate
with two pineapple chunks.

HASTY COCKTAIL

¾ oz.   Dry Vermouth
1½ oz.   Gin
¼ tsp.   Anisette
1 tsp.   Grenadine

Stir with ice and strain into
cocktail glass.

HAWAIIAN COCKTAIL

2 oz.   Gin
1 tbsp.   Pineapple Juice
½ oz.   Triple Sec

Shake with ice and strain
into cocktail glass.

HOFFMAN HOUSE COCKTAIL

¾ oz.   Dry Vermouth
1½ oz.   Gin

Stir with ice and strain into
cocktail glass. Serve with an
olive.

HOKKAIDO COCKTAIL

1½ oz.   Gin
1 oz.   Sake
½ oz.   Triple Sec

Shake with ice and strain
into cocktail glass.

HOMESTEAD COCKTAIL

1½ oz.	Gin
¾ oz.	Sweet Vermouth

Stir with ice and strain into cocktail glass. Serve with a slice of orange.

HONOLULU COCKTAIL NO. 1

1 dash	Bitters
¼ tsp.	Orange Juice
¼ tsp.	Pineapple Juice
¼ tsp.	Lemon Juice
½ tsp.	Powdered Sugar
1½ oz.	Gin

Shake with ice and strain into cocktail glass.

HONOLULU COCKTAIL NO. 2

¾ oz.	Gin
¾ oz.	Maraschino
¾ oz.	Benedictine

Stir with ice and strain into cocktail glass.

HOTEL PLAZA COCKTAIL

¾ oz.	Sweet Vermouth
¾ oz.	Dry Vermouth
¾ oz.	Gin

Stir with ice and strain into cocktail glass. Decorate with a slice of pineapple.

H.P.W. COCKTAIL

1½ tsps.	Dry Vermouth
1½ tsps.	Sweet Vermouth
1½ oz.	Gin

Stir with ice and strain into cocktail glass. Add a twist of orange peel.

HUDSON BAY

1 oz.	Gin
½ oz.	Cherry-flavored Brandy
1½ tsps.	151-Proof Rum
1 tbsp.	Orange Juice
1½ tsps.	Lime Juice

Shake with ice and strain into cocktail glass.

HULA-HULA COCKTAIL

¾ oz.	Orange Juice
1½ oz.	Gin
¼ tsp.	Powdered Sugar

Shake with ice and strain into cocktail glass.

IDEAL COCKTAIL

1 oz.	Dry Vermouth
1 oz.	Gin
¼ tsp.	Maraschino
½ tsp.	Grapefruit or Lemon Juice

Shake with ice and strain into cocktail glass. Serve with a cherry.

IMPERIAL COCKTAIL

1½ oz.	Dry Vermouth
1½ oz.	Gin
½ tsp.	Maraschino
1 dash	Bitters

Stir with ice and strain into cocktail glass. Serve with a cherry.

INCOME TAX COCKTAIL

1½ tsps. Dry Vermouth
1½ tsps. Sweet Vermouth
1 oz.   Gin
1 dash   Bitters
Juice of ¼ Orange

Shake with ice and strain
into cocktail glass.

JAMAICA GLOW

1 oz.   Gin
1 tbsp. Claret
1 tbsp. Orange Juice
1 tsp.   Jamaica Rum

Shake with ice and strain
into cocktail glass.

JEWEL COCKTAIL

¾ oz.   Chartreuse (Green)
¾ oz.   Sweet Vermouth
¾ oz.   Gin
1 dash   Orange Bitters

Stir with ice and strain into
cocktail glass. Serve with a
cherry.

JEYPLAK COCKTAIL

1½ oz.   Gin
¾ oz.   Sweet Vermouth
¼ tsp.   Anisette

Shake with ice and strain
into cocktail glass. Serve
with a cherry.

JOCKEY CLUB COCKTAIL

1 dash   Bitters
¼ tsp.   Crème de Cacao
         (White)
Juice of ¼ Lemon
1½ oz.   Gin

Shake with ice and strain
into cocktail glass.

JOULOUVILLE

1 oz.   Gin
½ oz.   Apple Brandy
1½ tsps. Sweet Vermouth
1 tbsp. Lemon Juice
2 dashes Grenadine

Shake with ice and strain
into cocktail glass.

JOURNALIST COCKTAIL

1½ tsps. Dry Vermouth
1½ tsps. Sweet Vermouth
1½ oz.   Gin
½ tsp.   Lemon Juice
½ tsp.   Triple Sec
1 dash   Bitters

Shake with ice and strain
into cocktail glass.

JUDGE JR. COCKTAIL

¾ oz.   Gin
¾ oz.   Light Rum
Juice of ¼ Lemon
½ tsp.   Powdered Sugar
¼ tsp.   Grenadine

Shake with ice and strain
into cocktail glass.

JUDGETTE COCKTAIL

¾ oz. Peach-flavored
      Brandy
¾ oz. Gin
¾ oz. Dry Vermouth
Juice of ¼ Lime

Shake with ice and strain
into cocktail glass. Serve
with a cherry.

K.G.B. COCKTAIL

½ oz. Kümmel
1½ oz. Gin
¼ tsp. Apricot-flavored
       Brandy
¼ tsp. Lemon Juice

Shake with ice and strain
into cocktail glass. Add a
twist of lemon peel.

KISS-IN-THE-DARK

¾ oz. Gin
¾ oz. Cherry-flavored
      Brandy
¾ oz. Dry Vermouth

Stir with ice and strain into
cocktail glass.

KNICKERBOCKER COCKTAIL

¼ tsp. Sweet Vermouth
¾ oz. Dry Vermouth
1½ oz. Gin

Stir with ice and strain into
cocktail glass. Add a twist of
lemon peel.

KNOCK-OUT COCKTAIL

½ oz. Anisette
¾ oz. Gin
¾ oz. Dry Vermouth
1 tsp. Crème de Menthe
       (White)

Stir with ice and strain into
cocktail glass. Serve with a
cherry.

KUP'S INDISPENSABLE COCKTAIL

½ oz. Light Vermouth
½ oz. Dry Vermouth
1½ oz. Gin
1 dash Bitters

Stir with ice and strain into
cocktail glass.

LADY FINGER

1 oz. Gin
½ oz. Kirschwasser
1 oz. Cherry-flavored
      Brandy

Shake with ice and strain
into cocktail glass.

LEAP FROG HIGHBALL

Juice of ½ Lemon
2 oz. Gin
Ginger Ale

Pour into highball glass over
ice cubes and fill with ginger
ale. Stir.

LEAVE-IT-TO-ME COCKTAIL NO. 1

½ oz. Apricot-flavored Brandy
½ oz. Dry Vermouth
1 oz. Gin
¼ tsp. Lemon Juice
¼ tsp. Grenadine

Shake with ice and strain into cocktail glass.

LEAVE-IT-TO-ME COCKTAIL NO. 2

1 tsp. Raspberry Syrup
1 tsp. Lemon Juice
¼ tsp. Maraschino
1½ oz. Gin

Stir with ice and strain into cocktail glass.

LONDON BUCK

2 oz. Gin
Juice of ½ Lemon
Ginger Ale

Pour gin and lemon juice over ice cubes in highball glass. Fill with ginger ale and stir.

LONDON COCKTAIL

2 oz. Gin
2 dashes Orange Bitters
½ tsp. Simple Syrup
½ tsp. Maraschino

Stir with ice and strain into cocktail glass. Add a twist of lemon peel.

LONE TREE COCKTAIL

¾ oz. Sweet Vermouth
1½ oz. Gin

Stir with ice and strain into cocktail glass.

LONE TREE COOLER

½ tsp. Powdered Sugar
2 oz. Club Soda
2 oz. Gin
1 tbsp. Dry Vermouth
Club Soda or Ginger Ale

Put sugar and 2 oz. club soda into collins glass. Stir, fill glass with ice, and add gin and vermouth. Fill with club soda or ginger ale and stir again. Insert a spiral of orange or lemon peel (or both) and dangle end over rim of glass.

MAIDEN'S BLUSH COCKTAIL

¼ tsp. Lemon Juice
1 tsp. Triple Sec
1 tsp. Grenadine
1½ oz. Gin

Shake with ice and strain into cocktail glass.

MAIDEN'S PRAYER

1½ oz. Gin
½ oz. Triple Sec
1 oz. Lemon Juice

Shake with ice and strain into cocktail glass.

MAJOR BAILEY

1½ tsps. Lime Juice
1½ tsps. Lemon Juice
½ tsp. Powdered Sugar
12 Mint Leaves
2 oz. Gin

Muddle first four ingredients well, pour into collins glass filled with ice and add gin. Stir until glass is frosted. Decorate with sprig of mint and serve with straws.

MAMIE'S SISTER
Juice of 1 Lime
2 oz.   Gin
Ginger Ale

Put the juice of one lime and a lime twist into collins glass, and add gin. Fill glass with ginger ale and ice. Stir.

MARTINEZ COCKTAIL
1 dash   Orange Bitters
1 oz.   Dry Vermouth
¼ tsp.   Triple Sec
1 oz.   Gin

Stir with ice and strain into cocktail glass. Serve with a cherry.

MARTINI
(**Traditional 2-to-1**)
1½ oz.   Gin
¾ oz.   Dry Vermouth

Stir vermouth and gin over ice cubes in mixing glass. Strain into cocktail glass. Serve with a twist of lemon peel or olive, if desired.

MARTINI (DRY)
(**5-to-1**)
1⅔ oz.   Gin
⅓ oz.   Dry Vermouth

Follow directions for Martini preparation.

MARTINI (EXTRA DRY)
(**8-to-1**)
2 oz.   Gin
¼ oz.   Dry Vermouth

Follow directions for Martini preparation.

MARTINI (MEDIUM)
1½ oz.   Gin
½ oz.   Dry Vermouth
½ oz.   Sweet Vermouth

Follow directions for Martini preparation.

MARTINI (SWEET)
1 oz.   Gin
1 oz.   Sweet Vermouth

Follow directions for Martini preparation.

MAURICE COCKTAIL
Juice of ¼ Orange
½ oz.   Sweet Vermouth
½ oz.   Dry Vermouth
1 oz.   Gin
1 dash   Bitters

Shake with ice and strain into cocktail glass.

MAXIM

1½ oz.   Gin
1 oz.   Dry Vermouth
1 dash   Crème de Cacao
          (White)

Shake with ice and strain into cocktail glass. Serve with a cherry.

MELON COCKTAIL
2 oz.   Gin
¼ tsp.   Lemon Juice
¼ tsp.   Maraschino

Shake with ice and strain into cocktail glass. Serve with a cherry.

MERRY WIDOW COCKTAIL NO. 1

1¼ oz. Gin
1¼ oz. Dry Vermouth
½ tsp. Benedictine
½ tsp. Anisette
1 dash Orange Bitters

Stir with ice and strain into cocktail glass. Add a twist of lemon peel.

MR. MANHATTAN COCKTAIL

1 cube Sugar
4 sprigs Mint
¼ tsp. Lemon Juice
1 tsp. Orange Juice
1½ oz. Gin

Muddle ingredients. Shake with ice and strain into cocktail glass.

MONTE CARLO IMPERIAL HIGHBALL

2 oz. Gin
½ oz. Crème de Menthe (White)
Juice of ¼ Lemon
Chilled Champagne

Shake with ice and strain into highball glass over ice cubes. Fill glass with champagne and stir.

MONTMARTRE COCKTAIL

1¼ oz. Dry Gin
½ oz. Sweet Vermouth
½ oz. Triple Sec

Stir with ice and strain into cocktail glass. Serve with a cherry.

MONTREAL CLUB BOUNCER

1½ oz. Gin
½ oz. Anisette

Pour into old-fashioned glass over ice cubes. Stir.

MORRO

1 oz. Gin
½ oz. Dark Rum
1 tbsp. Pineapple Juice
1 tbsp. Lime Juice
½ tsp. Powdered Sugar

Shake with ice and strain into sugar-rimmed old-fashioned glass over ice cubes.

NEGRONI

¾ oz. Gin
¾ oz. Campari
¾ oz. Sweet or Dry Vermouth
1 splash Club Soda (optional)

Stir with ice and strain into cocktail glass, or into old-fashioned glass over ice cubes, with or without a splash of club soda. Add a twist of lemon peel.

NIGHTMARE

1½ oz. Gin
½ oz. Madeira
½ oz. Cherry-flavored Brandy
1 tsp. Orange Juice

Shake with ice and strain into cocktail glass.

NINETEENTH HOLE

1½ oz.   Gin
1 oz.   Dry Vermouth
1 tsp.   Sweet Vermouth
1 dash   Bitters

Stir with ice in mixing glass
and strain into cocktail
glass. Garnish with an olive.

OPAL COCKTAIL

1 oz.   Gin
½ oz.   Triple Sec
1 tbsp.   Orange Juice
¼ tbsp. Powdered Sugar

Shake with ice and strain
into cocktail glass.

ORANGE BLOSSOM

1 oz.   Gin
1 oz.   Orange Juice
¼ tsp.   Powdered Sugar

Shake with ice and strain
into cocktail glass.

ORANGE BUCK

1½ oz.   Gin
1 oz.   Orange Juice
1 tbsp.   Lime Juice
Ginger Ale

Shake with ice and strain
into highball glass over ice
cubes. Fill with ginger ale
and stir.

Martini di Arma di Taggia, head
bartender at the Knickerbocker
Hotel in New York, is said to
have invented the Dry Martini
for John D. Rockefeller, the famous oil magnate.

ORANGE OASIS

1½ oz.   Gin
½ oz.   Cherry-flavored
           Brandy
4 oz.   Orange Juice
Ginger Ale

Shake with ice and strain
into highball glass over ice
cubes. Fill with ginger ale
and stir.

PAISLEY MARTINI

2 oz.   Gin
½ oz.   Dry Vermouth
1 tsp.   Scotch

Stir in old-fashioned glass
over ice cubes. Add a twist
of lemon peel.

PALL MALL

1½ oz.   Gin
½ oz.   Sweet Vermouth
½ oz.   Dry Vermouth
½ oz.   Crème de Menthe
           (White)

Stir in old-fashioned glass
over ice cubes.

PALM BEACH
COCKTAIL

1½ oz.   Gin
1½ tsps. Sweet Vermouth
1½ tsps. Grapefruit Juice

Shake with ice and strain
into cocktail glass.

PAPAYA SLING

1½ oz.   Gin
1 dash   Bitters
Juice of 1 Lime
1 tbsp.   Papaya Syrup
Club Soda

Shake with ice and strain into collins glass over ice cubes. Fill with club soda and stir. Add a pineapple stick.

PARISIAN

1 oz.   Gin
1 oz.   Dry Vermouth
¼ oz.   Crème de Cassis

Shake with ice and strain into cocktail glass.

PARK AVENUE

1½ oz.   Gin
¼ oz.   Sweet Vermouth
1 tbsp. Pineapple Juice

Stir with ice and strain into cocktail glass.

PERFECT COCKTAIL

1½ tsps. Dry Vermouth
1½ tsps. Sweet Vermouth
1½ oz.   Gin
1 dash   Bitters

Stir with ice and strain into cocktail glass.

PETER PAN COCKTAIL

2 dashes Bitters
¼ oz.   Orange Juice
¼ oz.   Dry Vermouth
¼ oz.   Gin

Shake with ice and strain into cocktail glass.

PICCADILLY COCKTAIL

¾ oz.   Dry Vermouth
1½ oz.   Gin
¼ tsp.   Anisette
¼ tsp.   Grenadine

Stir with ice and strain into cocktail glass.

PLAZA COCKTAIL

¾ oz.   Sweet Vermouth
¾ oz.   Dry Vermouth
¾ oz.   Gin

Shake with ice and strain into cocktail glass. Add a strip of pineapple.

POLLYANNA

3 slices Orange
3 slices Pineapple
2 oz.   Gin
½ oz.   Sweet Vermouth
½ tsp.   Grenadine

Muddle ingredients. Shake with ice and strain into cocktail glass.

POLO COCKTAIL

1 tbsp. Lemon Juice
1 tbsp. Orange Juice
1 oz.   Gin

Shake with ice and strain into cocktail glass.

POMPANO

1 oz.   Gin
½ oz.   Dry Vermouth
1 oz.   Grapefruit Juice

Shake with ice and strain into cocktail glass.

POPPY COCKTAIL

¾ oz.   Crème de Cacao (White)
1½ oz.   Gin

Shake with ice and strain into cocktail glass.

PRINCE'S SMILE

½ oz.   Apricot-flavored Brandy
½ oz.   Apple Brandy
1 oz.   Gin
¼ tsp.   Lemon Juice

Shake with ice and strain into cocktail glass.

PRINCETON COCKTAIL

1 oz.   Gin
1 oz.   Dry Vermouth
Juice of ½ Lime

Stir with ice and strain into cocktail glass.

QUEEN ELIZABETH

1½ oz.   Gin
½ oz.   Dry Vermouth
1½ tsps. Benedictine

Stir with ice and strain into cocktail glass.

RACQUET CLUB COCKTAIL

1½ oz.   Gin
¾ oz.   Dry Vermouth
1 dash   Orange Bitters

Stir with ice and strain into cocktail glass.

RED CLOUD

1½ oz.   Gin
½ oz.   Apricot-flavored Brandy
1 tbsp.   Lemon Juice
1 tsp.   Grenadine

Shake with ice and strain into cocktail glass.

REMSEN COOLER

½ tsp.   Powdered Sugar
2 oz.   Club Soda or Ginger Ale
2 oz.   Gin

Into collins glass, put sugar and 2 oz. club soda. Stir. Add ice cubes and gin. Fill with club soda or ginger ale and stir again. Insert a spiral of orange or lemon peel (or both) and dangle end over rim of glass.

RENAISSANCE COCKTAIL

1½ oz.   Gin
½ oz.   Dry Sherry
1 tbsp.   Light Cream

Shake with ice and strain into cocktail glass. Sprinkle with nutmeg.

RESOLUTE COCKTAIL

Juice of ¼ Lemon
½ oz.   Apricot-flavored Brandy
1 oz.   Gin

Shake with ice and strain into cocktail glass.

ROBERT E. LEE COOLER

Juice of ½ Lime
½ tsp. Powdered Sugar
2 oz. Club Soda
¼ tsp. Anisette
2 oz. Gin
Ginger Ale

Put first three ingredients into collins glass. Stir. Add ice cubes, anisette, and gin. Fill with ginger ale and stir again. Add a spiral of orange or lemon peel (or both) and dangle end over rim of glass.

ROLLS-ROYCE

½ oz. Dry Vermouth
½ oz. Sweet Vermouth
1½ oz. Gin
¼ tsp. Benedictine

Stir with ice and strain into cocktail glass.

ROSE COCKTAIL (ENGLISH)

½ oz. Apricot-flavored Brandy
½ oz. Dry Vermouth
1 oz. Gin
½ tsp. Lemon Juice
1 tsp. Grenadine

Moisten rim of cocktail glass with lemon juice and dip into powdered sugar. Shake all ingredients above with ice and strain into prepared glass.

Alcohol is a liquid good for preserving almost everything except secrets.

ROSE COCKTAIL (FRENCH)

½ oz. Cherry-flavored Brandy
½ oz. Dry Vermouth
1½ oz. Gin

Stir with ice and strain into cocktail glass.

ROSELYN COCKTAIL

¾ oz. Dry Vermouth
1½ oz. Gin
½ tsp. Grenadine

Stir with ice and strain into cocktail glass. Add a twist of lemon peel.

RUM RUNNER

1½ oz. Gin
Juice of 1 Lime
1 oz. Pineapple Juice
1 tsp. Sugar
1 dash Bitters

Shake with ice and strain over ice cubes into old-fashioned glass rimmed with salt.

SALTY DOG

1½ oz. Gin
5 oz. Grapefruit Juice
¼ tsp. Salt

Pour into highball glass over ice cubes. Stir well. Vodka may be substituted for the gin.

SAND-MARTIN COCKTAIL

1 tsp. Chartreuse (Green)
1½ oz. Sweet Vermouth
1½ oz. Gin

Stir with ice and strain into cocktail glass.

SAN SEBASTIAN

1 oz. Gin
1½ tsps. Light Rum
1 tbsp. Grapefruit Juice
1½ tsps. Triple Sec
1 tbsp. Lemon Juice

Shake with ice and strain
into cocktail glass.

SENSATION COCKTAIL

Juice of ¼ Lemon
1½ oz. Gin
1 tsp. Maraschino

Shake with ice and strain
into cocktail glass. Add two
sprigs of fresh mint.

SEVENTH HEAVEN COCKTAIL

2 tsps. Grapefruit Juice
1 tbsp. Maraschino
1½ oz. Gin

Shake with ice and strain
into cocktail glass. Decorate
with a sprig of fresh mint.

SHADY GROVE

1½ oz. Gin
Juice of ½ Lemon
1 tsp. Powdered Sugar
Ginger Beer

Shake with ice and strain
into highball glass with ice
cubes. Fill with ginger beer.

SILVER BULLET

1 oz. Gin
1 oz. Kümmel
1 tbsp. Lemon Juice

Shake with ice and strain
into cocktail glass.

SILVER COCKTAIL

1 oz. Dry Vermouth
1 oz. Gin
2 dashes Orange Bitters
¼ tsp. Simple Syrup
½ tsp. Maraschino

Stir with ice and strain into
cocktail glass. Add a twist of
lemon peel.

SILVER STREAK

1½ oz. Gin
1 oz. Kümmel

Shake with ice and strain
into cocktail glass.

SMILE COCKTAIL

1 oz. Grenadine
1 oz. Gin
½ tsp. Lemon Juice

Shake with ice and strain
into cocktail glass.

SMILER COCKTAIL

½ oz. Sweet Vermouth
½ oz. Dry Vermouth
1 oz. Gin
1 dash Bitters
¼ tsp. Orange Juice

Shake with ice and strain
into cocktail glass.

SNOWBALL

1½ oz. Gin
½ oz. Anisette
1 tbsp. Light Cream

Shake with ice and strain
into cocktail glass.

SNYDER

1½ oz. Gin
½ oz. Dry Vermouth
½ oz. Triple Sec

Shake with ice and strain into cocktail glass. Add a twist of lemon peel.

SOCIETY COCKTAIL

1½ oz. Gin
¾ oz. Dry Vermouth
¼ tsp. Grenadine

Stir with ice and strain into cocktail glass.

SOUTHERN BRIDE

1½ oz. Gin
1 oz. Grapefruit Juice
1 dash Maraschino

Shake with ice and strain into cocktail glass.

SOUTHERN GIN COCKTAIL

2 oz. Gin
2 dashes Orange Bitters
½ tsp. Triple Sec

Stir with ice and strain into cocktail glass. Add a twist of lemon peel.

SOUTH-SIDE COCKTAIL

Juice of ½ Lemon
1 tsp. Powdered Sugar
1½ oz. Gin

Shake with ice and strain into cocktail glass. Add two sprigs of fresh mint.

SOUTH-SIDE FIZZ

Juice of ½ Lemon
1 tsp. Powdered Sugar
2 oz. Gin
Club Soda

Shake with ice and strain into highball glass with ice cubes. Fill with club soda and stir. Garnish fresh mint leaves.

SPENCER COCKTAIL

¾ oz. Apricot-flavored Brandy
1½ oz. Gin
1 dash Bitters
¼ tsp. Orange Juice

Shake with ice and strain into cocktail glass. Add a cherry and a twist of orange peel.

SPHINX COCKTAIL

1½ oz. Gin
1½ tsps. Sweet Vermouth
1½ tsps. Dry Vermouth

Stir with ice and strain into cocktail glass. Serve with a slice of lemon.

SPRING FEELING COCKTAIL

1 tbsp. Lemon Juice
½ oz. Chartreuse (Green)
1 oz. Gin

Shake with ice and strain into cocktail glass.

STANLEY COCKTAIL

Juice of ¼ Lemon
1 tsp.   Grenadine
¾ oz.   Gin
¼ oz.   Light Rum

Shake with ice and strain into cocktail glass.

STAR DAISY

Juice of ½ Lemon
½ tsp.   Powdered Sugar
1 tsp.   Grenadine
1 oz.   Gin
1 oz.   Apple Brandy

Shake with ice and strain into stein or metal cup. Add an ice cube and decorate with fruit.

STRAIGHT LAW COCKTAIL

¾ oz.   Gin
1½ oz.   Dry Sherry

Stir with ice and strain into cocktail glass.

SUNSHINE COCKTAIL

¾ oz.   Sweet Vermouth
1½ oz.   Gin
1 dash   Bitters

Stir with ice and strain into cocktail glass. Add a twist of orange peel.

SWEET PATOOTIE COCKTAIL

1 oz.   Gin
½ oz.   Triple Sec
1 tbsp.   Orange Juice

Shake with ice and strain into cocktail glass.

T & T

2 oz.   Tanqueray Gin
Tonic Water

Pour gin over ice cubes into highball glass and fill with tonic water. Stir. Garnish with a lime wedge.

TAILSPIN COCKTAIL

¾ oz.   Gin
¾ oz.   Sweet Vermouth
¾ oz.   Chartreuse (Green)
1 dash   Orange Bitters

Stir with ice and strain into cocktail glass. Add a twist of lemon peel and a cherry or olive.

TANGO COCKTAIL

1 tbsp.   Orange Juice
½ oz.   Dry Vermouth
½ oz.   Sweet Vermouth
1 oz.   Gin
½ tsp.   Triple Sec

Shake with ice and strain into cocktail glass.

TANQ-A-RITA

1½ oz.   Tanqueray Gin
3 oz.   Margarita Mix
1 splash   Triple Sec

Shake with ice and strain into cocktail glass.

THIRD-DEGREE COCKTAIL

1½ oz.   Gin
¾ oz.   Dry Vermouth
1 tsp.   Anisette

Stir with ice and strain into cocktail glass.

THREE STRIPES COCKTAIL

1 oz.	Gin
½ oz.	Dry Vermouth
1 tbsp.	Orange Juice

Shake with ice and strain into cocktail glass.

THUNDERCLAP

¾ oz.	Gin
¾ oz.	Blended Whiskey
¾ oz.	Brandy

Shake with ice and strain into cocktail glass.

TOM COLLINS

Juice of ½ Lemon	
1 tsp.	Powdered Sugar
2 oz.	Gin
Club Soda	

Shake with ice and strain into collins glass. Add several ice cubes, fill with club soda, and stir. Decorate with slices of lemon and orange and a cherry. Serve with a straw.

TRINITY COCKTAIL

¾ oz.	Sweet Vermouth
¾ oz.	Dry Vermouth
¾ oz.	Gin

Stir with ice and strain into cocktail glass.

TROPICAL SPECIAL

1½ oz.	Gin
1 oz.	Orange Juice
1 oz.	Lime Juice
2 oz.	Grapefruit Juice
½ oz.	Triple Sec

Shake with ice, then strain into highball glass over ice. Decorate with fruit slices and a cherry.

TURF COCKTAIL

¼ tsp.	Anisette
2 dashes	Bitters
1 oz.	Dry Vermouth
1 oz.	Gin

Stir with ice and strain into cocktail glass. Add a twist of orange peel.

TUXEDO COCKTAIL

1½ oz.	Gin
1½ oz.	Dry Vermouth
¼ tsp.	Maraschino
¼ tsp.	Anisette
2 dashes	Orange Bitters

Stir with ice and strain into cocktail glass. Serve with a cherry.

TYPHOON

1 oz.	Gin
½ oz.	Anisette
1 oz.	Lime Juice
Chilled Champagne	

Shake all ingredients, except champagne, with ice. Strain into collins glass with ice cubes. Fill glass with champagne.

UNION JACK COCKTAIL
¾ oz. Sloe Gin
1½ oz. Gin
½ tsp. Grenadine

Shake with ice and strain
into cocktail glass.

VICTOR
1½ oz. Gin
½ oz. Brandy
½ oz. Sweet Vermouth

Shake with ice and strain
into cocktail glass.

WAIKIKI BEACHCOMBER
¾ oz. Gin
¾ oz. Triple Sec
1 tbsp. Fresh Pineapple
          Juice

Shake with ice and strain
into cocktail glass.

WALLICK COCKTAIL
1½ oz. Dry Vermouth
1½ oz. Gin
1 tsp. Triple Sec

Stir with ice and strain into
cocktail glass.

WALLIS BLUE COCKTAIL
1 oz. Triple Sec
1 oz. Gin
Juice of 1 Lime

Moisten rim of old-
fashioned glass with lime
juice and dip into powdered
sugar. Shake ingredients
with ice and strain into
prepared glass over ice
cubes.

WEBSTER COCKTAIL
Juice of ½ Lime
1½ tsps. Apricot-flavored
          Brandy
½ oz. Dry Vermouth
1 oz. Gin

Shake with ice and strain
into cocktail glass.

WEMBLY COCKTAIL
¾ oz. Dry Vermouth
1½ oz. Gin
¼ tsp. Apricot-flavored
          Brandy
½ tsp. Apple Brandy

Stir with ice and strain into
cocktail glass.

WESTERN ROSE
½ oz. Apricot-flavored
          Brandy
1 oz. Gin
½ oz. Dry Vermouth
¼ tsp. Lemon Juice

Shake with ice and strain
into cocktail glass.

WHAT THE HELL
1 oz. Gin
1 oz. Dry Vermouth
1 oz. Apricot-flavored
          Brandy
1 dash Lemon Juice

Stir in old-fashioned glass
over ice cubes.

WHITE WAY COCKTAIL
¾ oz. Crème de Menthe
          (White)
1½ oz. Gin

Shake with ice and strain
into cocktail glass.

WHY NOT?

1 oz.	Gin
1 oz.	Apricot-flavored Brandy
½ oz.	Dry Vermouth
1 dash	Lemon Juice

Shake with ice and strain into cocktail glass.

WILL ROGERS

1½ oz.	Gin
1 tbsp.	Orange Juice
½ oz.	Dry Vermouth
1 dash	Triple Sec

Shake with ice and strain into cocktail glass.

WOODSTOCK

1½ oz.	Gin
1 oz.	Lemon Juice
1½ tsps.	Maple Syrup
1 dash	Orange Bitters

Shake with ice and strain into cocktail glass.

The poor fellow had fallen forty feet to the concrete outside a seaside hotel. He lay bruised, battered, and semi-conscious. The hotel-keeper rushed out and, raising the victim's reeling head, held a glass of sherry to his lips.

"I say!" he gasped, "how far do I have to fall to get a gin?"

XANTHIA COCKTAIL

¾ oz.	Cherry-flavored Brandy
¾ oz.	Chartreuse (Yellow)
¾ oz.	Gin

Stir with ice and strain into cocktail glass.

YALE COCKTAIL

1½ oz.	Gin
½ oz.	Dry Vermouth
1 dash	Bitters
1 tsp.	Blue Curaçao

Stir with ice and strain into cocktail glass.

YELLOW RATTLER

1 oz.	Gin
1 tbsp.	Orange Juice
½ oz.	Dry Vermouth
½ oz.	Sweet Vermouth

Shake with ice and strain into cocktail glass. Add a cocktail onion.

YOLANDA

½ oz.	Brandy
½ oz.	Gin
½ oz.	Anisette
1 oz.	Sweet Vermouth
1 dash	Grenadine

Shake with ice and strain into cocktail glass. Add a twist of orange peel.

BOTTOMS UP MONEY TRICK

Bet that you can remove a dollar bill from under a bottle without touching or upsetting the bottle. METHOD: Roll up the bill and carefully shove the bottle off the bill with the rolled portion without letting your hands touch the bottle.

Rum

Rum is a spirit for all seasons—a favorite in tall, chilled summer drinks and a traditional ingredient of winter holiday cheer. It is the drink of romantics and adventurers. It was the pirates' drink: "Yo, ho, ho and a bottle of rum."

While the simple Rum and Cola has long been among America's top ten favorite drinks, rums are also the base for many tropical cocktails, including the Daiquiri, Zombie, Mai Tai, and Piña Colada. Often mixed with a potpourri of fruit, juices, these drinks are usually distinguished by exotic garnishes such as orchids. Paper parasols and plastic monkeys also often decorate these drinks, which adventurous bartenders sometimes serve in unusual containers, such as hollowed-out coconut shells.

Rum is made from sugar cane boiled down to a rich residue called molasses, which is then fermented and distilled. Light rums are clear to pale gold in color; dark rums are amber to a rich mahogany in color. Both light and dark versions are normally 80 proof.

Light rums are traditionally produced in southern Caribbean islands like Puerto Rico, Trinidad, and Barbados. They do not require extensive aging, with six months in oak casks often being long enough, although a year's aging is more common. *Barton Rum* is produced in the Virgin Islands as both a white and gold rum. The white has a lightly sweet aroma and clean rum flavor, while the gold is light, smooth, and sweet.

Dark rums results from aging the spirit for a period of three to twelve years and, in some cases, from the addition of caramel. It is very aromatic and has a heavier, richer flavor than light rum. Dark rum is produced in the tropics: Jamaica,

Haiti, or Martinique. While supplying the punch in Planter's Punch and the rich flavor in a variety of tropical and hot drinks, the best dark rums can also be savored like a fine brandy.

There are also 151-proof rums, which are excellent in drinks and desserts that call for flaming.

In recent years, a number of specialty rums have been introduced, flavored with coconut, spices, or fruit. These flavored rums can give mainstream rum drinks a different twist.

There are two stories about the origin of the Daiquiri. One says that it was invented by a barman in Havana, Cuba, in the early 1900s. The other maintains that the cocktail was named after the town of Daiquiri, Cuba, where it supposedly originated in 1898, when the town's doctors used local rum as malaria medicine. To make the dose taste better, American engineers who were working for a local mining company added lime juice and sugar to the rum.

A DAY AT THE BEACH

1 oz.	Coconut Rum
½ oz.	Amaretto
4 oz.	Orange Juice
½ oz.	Grenadine

Shake rum, amaretto, and orange juice with ice and pour into highball glass over ice. Top with grenadine and garnish with a pineapple wedge and a strawberry.

APPLE PIE NO. 1

¾ oz.	Light Rum
¾ oz.	Sweet Vermouth
1 tsp.	Apple Brandy
½ tsp.	Grenadine
1 tsp.	Lemon Juice

Shake with ice and strain into cocktail glass.

BACARDI COCKTAIL

1½ oz.	Bacardi Rum
Juice of ½ Lime	
½ tsp.	Grenadine

Shake with ice and strain into cocktail glass.

BAHAMA MAMA

½ oz.	Dark Rum
½ oz.	Coconut Liqueur
¼ oz.	151-proof Rum
¼ oz.	Coffee Liqueur
Juice of ½ Lemon	
4 oz.	Pineapple Juice

Combine ingredients and pour over cracked ice into highball glass. Garnish with a strawberry or cherry.

BANANA COW

1 oz.	Light Rum
1 oz.	Crème de Banana
1½ oz.	Cream
1 dash	Grenadine

Shake ingredients with crushed ice and strain into cocktail glass. Garnish with a banana slice and sprinkle with nutmeg.

BEACHCOMBER

1½ oz.	Light Rum
½ oz.	Triple Sec
½ oz.	Grenadine
1 oz.	Sour Mix

Shake with ice and strain into cocktail glass with sugared rim. Garnish with a lime wheel.

BERMUDA TRIANGLE

1 oz.	Peach Schnapps
½ oz.	Spiced Rum
3 oz.	Orange Juice

Pour ingredients into ice-filled old-fashioned glass.

BLACK DEVIL

2 oz.	Light Rum
½ oz.	Dry Vermouth

Stir with cracked ice and strain into cocktail glass. Add a black olive.

BLACK MARIA

2 oz.	Coffee-flavored Brandy
2 oz.	Light Rum
4 oz.	Strong Black Coffee
2 tsps.	Powdered Sugar

Stir in brandy snifter and add cracked ice.

BLUE HAWAIIAN

1 oz.	Light Rum
1 oz.	Blue Curaçao
2 oz.	Pineapple Juice
1 oz.	Cream of Coconut

Combine ingredients with one cup crushed ice in blender at high speed. Pour into highball glass. Garnish with a slice of pineapple and a cherry.

BOLERO

1½ oz.	Light Rum
¾ oz.	Apple Brandy
¼ tsp.	Sweet Vermouth

Stir well with cracked ice and strain into cocktail glass.

BORINQUEN

1½ oz.	Light Rum
1 tbsp.	Passion Fruit Syrup
1 oz.	Lime Juice
1 oz.	Orange Juice
1 tsp.	151-proof Rum

Put half a cup of crushed ice into blender. Add all ingredients and blend at low speed. Pour into old-fashioned glass.

Rum drinking became a tradition in the British Royal Navy in the mid-1600s, when every sailor was issued a daily ration of a half-pint of rum. It wasn't until 1970 that this rum allowance was phased out.

BOSTON COOLER

Juice of ½ Lemon	
1 tsp.	Powdered Sugar
2 oz.	Club Soda
2 oz.	Light Rum
Club Soda or Ginger Ale	

Into collins glass, pour lemon juice, sugar, and 2 oz. club soda, stir. Fill glass with cracked ice and add rum. Fill with club soda or ginger ale and stir again. Add spiral of orange or lemon peel and dangle end over rim of glass.

BOSTON SIDECAR

¾ oz.	Brandy
¾ oz.	Light Rum
¾ oz.	Triple Sec
Juice of ½ Lime	

Shake with ice and strain into cocktail glass.

BUCK JONES

1½ oz.	Light Rum
1 oz.	Sweet Sherry
Juice of ½ Lime	
Ginger Ale	

Pour ingredients into highball glass over ice cubes and stir. Fill with ginger ale.

BURGUNDY BISHOP

Juice of ¼ Lemon	
1 tsp.	Powdered Sugar
1 oz.	Light Rum
Red Wine	

Shake with ice and strain into highball glass over ice cubes. Fill with red wine and stir. Decorate with fruits.

CANADO SALUDO

1½ oz.   Light Rum
1 oz.   Orange Juice
1 oz.   Pineapple Juice
5 dashes Lemon Juice
5 dashes Grenadine
5 dashes Bitters

Serve over ice cubes in 6-oz. glass, with pineapple slices, an orange slice, and a cherry.

CARIBBEAN CHAMPAGNE

½ tsp.   Light Rum
½ tsp.   Crème de Banana
Chilled Champagne

Pour rum and banana liqueur into champagne flute. Fill with champagne and stir lightly. Add a slice of banana.

CARIBBEAN ROMANCE

1½ oz.   Light Rum
1 oz.   Amaretto
1½ oz.   Orange Juice
1½ oz.   Pineapple Juice
1 splash Grenadine

Shake well with ice, pour into highball glass. Float grenadine on top and garnish with an orange, lemon, or lime slice.

CASA BLANCA

2 oz.   Light Rum
1½ tsps. Lime Juice
1½ tsps. Triple Sec
1½ tsps. Maraschino

Shake with ice and strain into cocktail glass.

CHERIE

Juice of 1 Lime
½ oz.   Triple Sec
1 oz.   Light Rum
½ oz.   Cherry-flavored Brandy

Shake with ice and strain into cocktail glass. Add a cherry.

CHERRY RUM

1¼ oz.   Light Rum
1½ tsps. Cherry-flavored Brandy
1 tbsp.   Light Cream

Shake with ice and strain into cocktail glass.

CHINESE COCKTAIL

1 tbsp.   Grenadine
1½ oz.   Jamaica Rum
1 dash   Bitters
1 tsp.   Maraschino
1 tsp.   Triple Sec

Shake with ice and strain into cocktail glass.

CHOCOLATE RUM

1 oz.   Light Rum
½ oz.   Crème de Cacao (Brown)
½ oz.   Crème de Menthe (White)
1 tbsp.   Light Cream
1 tsp.   151-proof Rum

Shake with ice and strain into old-fashioned glass over ice cubes.

COCOMACOQUE

Juice of ½ Lemon
2 oz.   Pineapple Juice
2 oz.   Orange Juice
1½ oz. Light Rum
2 oz.   Red Wine

Shake all ingredients except
wine. Pour into collins glass
over ice cubes and top with
wine. Add pineapple stick.

CONTINENTAL

1¼ oz. Light Rum
1 tbsp. Lime Juice
1½ tsps. Crème de Menthe
          (Green)
½ tsp.   Powdered Sugar

Shake with ice and strain
into cocktail glass. Add a
twist of lemon peel.

COOL CARLOS

1½ oz. Dark Rum
2 oz.   Cranberry Juice
2 oz.   Pineapple Juice
1 oz.   Orange Curaçao
1 splash Sour Mix

Mix all ingredients except
curaçao with ice, shake well.
Pour into collins glass and
float curaçao on top.
Garnish with pineapple and
orange slices, and a cherry.

CORKSCREW

1½ oz. Light Rum
½ oz.   Dry Vermouth
½ oz.   Peach-flavored
         Brandy

Shake with ice and strain
into cocktail glass. Garnish
with a lime slice.

CREAM PUFF

2 oz.   Light Rum
1 oz.   Light Cream
½ tsp.   Powdered Sugar
Club Soda

Shake with ice and strain
into highball glass over two
ice cubes. Fill with club soda
and stir.

CREOLE

1½ oz. Light Rum
1 dash Tabasco Sauce
1 tsp.   Lemon Juice
1½ oz. Beef Bouillon
Salt and Pepper to taste

Shake with ice and strain
into old-fashioned glass over
ice cubes.

CUBA LIBRE

Juice of ½ Lime
2 oz.   Light Rum
Cola

Put lime juice and twist of
lime into highball glass, and
add rum. Fill with cola and
ice cubes.

CUBAN COCKTAIL
NO. 1

Juice of ½ Lime
½ tsp.   Powdered Sugar
2 oz.   Light Rum

Shake with ice and strain
into cocktail glass.

Okole Maluna Hauoli Maoli Oe
          —a Hawaiian toast

CUBAN SPECIAL

1 tbsp.　Pineapple Juice
Juice of　½ Lime
1 oz.　　Light Rum
½ tsp.　Triple Sec

Shake with ice and strain into cocktail glass. Decorate with a slice of pineapple and a cherry.

DAIQUIRI

Juice of　1 Lime
1 tsp.　　Powdered Sugar
1½ oz.　Light Rum

Shake with ice and strain into cocktail glass.

DERBY DAIQUIRI

1½ oz.　Light Rum
1 oz.　　Orange Juice
1 tbsp.　Lime Juice
1 tsp.　　Sugar

Combine all ingredients with a half-cup of shaved ice in blender. Blend at low speed. Pour into champagne flute.

DINGO

½ oz.　　Light Rum
½ oz.　　Amaretto
½ oz.　　Southern Comfort
2 oz.　　Sour Mix
2 oz.　　Orange Juice
1 splash Grenadine

Combine all ingredients and shake with ice. Pour into highball glass and garnish with an orange slice.

EL PRESIDENTE COCKTAIL NO. 1

Juice of　1 Lime
1 tsp.　　Pineapple Juice
1 tsp.　　Grenadine
1½ oz.　Light Rum

Shake with ice and strain into cocktail glass.

EL PRESIDENTE COCKTAIL NO. 2

¾ oz.　　Dry Vermouth
1½ oz.　Light Rum
1 dash　Bitters

Stir with ice and strain into cocktail glass.

FAIR-AND-WARMER COCKTAIL

¾ oz.　　Sweet Vermouth
1½ oz.　Light Rum
½ tsp.　Triple Sec

Stir with ice and strain into cocktail glass.

FIREMAN'S SOUR

Juice of　2 Limes
½ tsp.　Powdered Sugar
1 tbsp.　Grenadine
2 oz.　　Light Rum
Club Soda

Shake with ice and strain into sour glass. Fill with club soda, if desired. Decorate with a half-slice of lemon and a cherry.

FOG CUTTER

1½ oz.   Light Rum
½ oz.   Brandy
½ oz.   Gin
1 oz.   Orange Juice
3 tbsps. Lemon Juice
1½ tsps. Orgeat Syrup
1 tsp.   Sweet Sherry

Shake all ingredients except
sherry and strain into collins
glass over ice cubes. Top
with sherry.

FORT LAUDERDALE

1½ oz.   Light Rum
½ oz.   Sweet Vermouth
Juice of ¼ Orange
Juice of ¼ Lime

Shake with ice and strain
into old-fashioned glass over
ice cubes. Add a slice of
orange.

GAUGUIN

2 oz.   Light Rum
1 tbsp. Passion Fruit Syrup
1 tbsp. Lemon Juice
1 tbsp. Lime Juice

Combine ingredients with a
cup of crushed ice in blender
and blend at low speed.
Serve in old-fashioned glass.
Top with a cherry.

GOLDEN FRIENDSHIP

Equal parts:
Amaretto
Sweet Vermouth
Light Rum
Ginger Ale

Mix first three ingredients in
collins glass with ice, then fill
with ginger ale. Garnish with
an orange spiral and a cherry.

GORILLA MILK

1 oz.   Light Rum
½ oz.   Coffee Liqueur
½ oz.   Irish Cream
          Liqueur
½ oz.   Crème de Banana
1 oz.   Light Cream

Shake with ice and pour over
ice into hurricane or parfait
glass. Garnish with a banana
slice.

HAVANA COCKTAIL

1½ oz.   Pineapple Juice
½ tsp.   Lemon Juice
¾ oz.   Light Rum

Shake with ice and strain
into cocktail glass.

HOP TOAD

Juice of ½ Lime
¾ oz.   Apricot-flavored
          Brandy
¾ oz.   Light Rum

Stir with ice and strain into
cocktail glass.

HURRICANE

1 oz.   Dark Rum
1 oz.   Light Rum
1 tbsp.   Passion Fruit Syrup
2 tsps.   Lime Juice

Shake with ice and strain
into cocktail glass.

HURRICANE LEAH

¼ oz.   Light Rum
¼ oz.   Gin
¼ oz.   Vodka
¼ oz.   Tequila
¼ oz.   Blue Curaçao
1 dash   Cherry Brandy
3 oz.   Sour Mix
3 oz.   Orange Juice

Pour over ice into hurricane
or parfait glass, stir. Garnish
with an orange wheel.

JACQUELINE

1 oz.   Triple Sec
2 oz.   Dark Rum
1 oz.   Lime Juice
1 pinch   Powdered Sugar

Shake well with cracked ice
and strain into cocktail glass.

JADE

1½ oz.   Light Rum
½ tsp.   Crème de Menthe
            (Green)
½ tsp.   Triple Sec
1 tbsp.   Lime Juice
1 tsp.   Powdered Sugar

Shake with ice and strain
into cocktail glass. Add a
lime slice.

JAMAICAN CRAWLER

1 oz.   Light Rum
1 oz.   Melon Liqueur
3 oz.   Pineapple Juice
1 splash   Grenadine

Combine rum, melon
liqueur, and pineapple juice
with ice, stir well. Pour into
collins glass, then float
grenadine on top.

KNICKERBOCKER
SPECIAL COCKTAIL

1 tsp.   Raspberry Syrup
1 tsp.   Lemon Juice
1 tsp.   Orange Juice
2 oz.   Light Rum
½ tsp.   Triple Sec

Shake with ice and strain
into cocktail glass. Decorate
with a small slice of
pineapple.

LITTLE DEVIL
COCKTAIL

Juice of ¼ Lemon
1½ tsps. Triple Sec
¾ oz.   Light Rum
¾ oz.   Gin

Shake with ice and strain
into cocktail glass.

LITTLE PRINCESS
COCKTAIL

1½ oz.   Sweet Vermouth
1½ oz.   Light Rum

Shake with ice and strain
into cocktail glass.

LOOK OUT BELOW

1½ oz.   151-proof Rum
Juice of ¼ Lime
1 tsp.   Grenadine

Shake with ice and strain
into old-fashioned glass over
ice cubes.

LOUNGE LIZARD

1 oz.   Dark Rum
½ oz.   Amaretto
Cola

Pour rum and amaretto into
ice-filled collins glass. Fill
with cola. Garnish with a
slice of lime.

MAI-TAI

½ tsp.   Powdered Sugar
2 oz.   Light Rum
1 oz.   Triple Sec
1 tbsp.   Orgeat or Almond-
          flavored Syrup
1 tbsp.   Grenadine
1 tbsp.   Lime Juice

Shake with ice and strain
into large old-fashioned
glass about 1/3 full with
crushed ice. Decorate with a
maraschino cherry speared
to a wedge of fresh
pineapple. For a hair-raiser,
top with a dash of 151-proof
rum; for a true Polynesian
effect, float an orchid on
each drink. Serve with
straws.

MALMAISON

Juice of ½ Lemon
1 oz.   Light Rum
½ oz.   Cream Sherry

Shake with ice and strain
into cocktail glass rimmed
with Anisette.

MANDEVILLE

1½ oz.   Light Rum
1 oz.   Dark Rum
1 tsp.   Anisette
1 tbsp.   Lemon Juice
1 tbsp.   Cola
¼ tsp.   Grenadine

Shake with ice and strain
into old-fashioned glass over
ice cubes.

MARIPOSA

1 oz.   Light Rum
½ oz.   Brandy
1 tbsp.   Lemon Juice
1 tbsp.   Orange Juice
1 dash   Grenadine

Shake with ice and strain
into cocktail glass.

MARY PICKFORD
COCKTAIL

1 oz.   Light Rum
1 oz.   Pineapple Juice
¼ tsp.   Grenadine
¼ tsp.   Maraschino

Shake with ice and strain
into cocktail glass.

MIAMI

1½ oz.   Light Rum
½ oz.   Crème de Menthe
         (White)
1 dash Lemon Juice

Shake with ice and strain into cocktail glass.

MIDNIGHT EXPRESS

1½ oz.   Dark Rum
½ oz.   Cointreau
¾ oz.   Lime Juice
1 splash Sour Mix

Shake with ice and pour over ice into old-fashioned glass.

MISSISSIPPI PLANTERS PUNCH

1 tbsp. Powdered Sugar
Juice of 1 Lemon
½ oz.   Light Rum
½ oz.   Bourbon
1 oz.   Brandy
Club Soda

Shake all ingredients with ice and strain into collins glass filled with cubed ice. Fill with club soda and stir.

MONKEY WRENCH

1½ oz.   Light Rum
Grapefruit Juice

Pour rum into ice-filled collins glass. Fill with grapefruit juice and stir.

MOON QUAKE SHAKE

1½ oz.   Dark Rum
1 oz.   Coffee-flavored
         Brandy
1 tbsp. Lemon Juice

Shake with ice and strain into cocktail glass.

NEVADA COCKTAIL

1½ oz.   Light Rum
1 oz.   Grapefruit Juice
Juice of 1 Lime
1 dash Bitters
3 tsps. Powdered Sugar

Shake with ice and strain into cocktail glass.

NEW ORLEANS BUCK

1½ oz.   Light Rum
1 oz.   Orange Juice
½ oz.   Lemon Juice
Ginger Ale

Shake all ingredients with ice and strain into collins glass over ice cubes. Fill with ginger ale and stir.

NIGHT CAP

2 oz.   Light Rum
1 tsp. Powdered Sugar
Warm Milk

Put rum and sugar in Irish coffee glass, fill with warm milk, and stir. Sprinkle a little nutmeg on top.

PALMETTO COCKTAIL

1½ oz.   Light Rum
1½ oz.   Dry Vermouth
2 dashes Bitters

Stir with ice and strain into cocktail glass.

PASSION DAIQUIRI

1½ oz.   Light Rum
Juice of 1 Lime
1 tsp. Powdered Sugar
1 tbsp. Passion Fruit Juice

Shake with ice and strain into cocktail glass.

PIÑA COLADA

3 oz.   Light Rum
3 tbsps.   Coconut Milk
3 tbsps.   Crushed Pineapple

Place in blender with two cups of crushed ice and blend at high speed for a short time. Strain into collins glass and serve with a straw.

PINEAPPLE COCKTAIL

¾ oz.   Pineapple Juice
1½ oz.   Light Rum
½ tsp.   Lemon Juice

Shake with ice and strain into cocktail glass.

PINEAPPLE FIZZ

1 oz.   Pineapple Juice
½ tsp.   Powdered Sugar
2 oz.   Light Rum
Club Soda

Shake with ice and strain into highball glass over two ice cubes. Fill with club soda and stir.

PINK CREOLE

1½ oz.   Light Rum
1 tbsp.   Lime Juice
1 tsp.   Grenadine
1 tsp.   Light Cream

Shake with ice and strain into cocktail glass. Add a black cherry soaked in rum.

PINK PARADISE

1½ oz.   Coconut Rum
1 oz.   Amaretto
3 oz.   Cranberry Juice
1½ oz.   Pineapple Juice

Combine ingredients over ice in hurricane or parfait glass. Garnish with a pineapple wedge and a cherry.

PLANTER'S COCKTAIL

Juice of ¼ Lemon
½ tsp.   Powdered Sugar
1½ oz.   Jamaica Rum

Shake with ice and strain into cocktail glass.

PLANTER'S PUNCH NO. 1

Juice of 2 Limes
2 tsps.   Powdered Sugar
2 oz.   Club Soda
2 dashes Bitters
2½ oz.   Light Rum
1 dash   Grenadine

Mix first three ingredients in collins glass, add ice cubes, and stir until glass is frosted. Add bitters and rum. Stir and top with grenadine. Decorate with slices of lemon, orange, and pineapple, and a cherry. Serve with a straw.

British Admiral Vernon issued an order to his captains in 1740 that the sailors' daily rum ration was henceforth to be diluted with water, which outraged the crews. Vernon's nickname was "Old Grog," because he always wore a coat made of grogram, a coarse material made of silk and mohair. British sailors soon began to call their watered rum "grog" as an irreverent tribute to their commander.

PLANTER'S PUNCH NO. 2

Juice of 1 Lime
Juice of ½ Lemon
Juice of ½ Orange
1 tsp.   Pineapple Juice
2 oz.   Light Rum
1 oz.   Jamaica Rum
2 dashes Triple Sec
1 dash Grenadine

Pour first five ingredients into collins glass filled with ice. Stir until glass is frosted. Add Jamaica Rum, stir, and top with triple sec and grenadine. Decorate with slices of orange, lemon, and pineapple, a cherry, and a sprig of mint dipped in powdered sugar. Serve with a straw.

POKER COCKTAIL

1½ oz.   Sweet Vermouth
1½ oz.   Light Rum

Stir with ice and strain into cocktail glass.

QUAKER'S COCKTAIL

¾ oz.   Light Rum
¾ oz.   Brandy
Juice of 1/4 Lemon
2 tsps.   Raspberry Syrup

Shake with ice and strain into cocktail glass.

QUARTER DECK COCKTAIL

⅓ oz.   Cream Sherry
1½ oz.   Light Rum
Juice of ½ Lime

Stir with ice and strain into cocktail glass.

RAIN MAN

1¼ oz.   151-proof Rum
¾ oz.   Melon Liqueur
4 oz.   Orange Juice

Shake and pour into hurricane or parfait glass filled with ice.

ROBSON COCKTAIL

2 tsps.   Lemon Juice
1 tbsp.   Orange Juice
1½ tsps.   Grenadine
1 oz.   Jamaica Rum

Shake with ice and strain into cocktail glass.

RUM COBBLER

1 tsp.   Powdered Sugar
2 oz.   Club Soda
2 oz.   Light Rum

In goblet, dissolve sugar in club soda. Fill goblet with shaved ice and add rum. Stir and decorate with fruits in season. Serve with a straw.

RUM COLLINS

Juice of 1 Lime
1 tsp.   Powdered Sugar
2 oz.   Light Rum
Club Soda

Shake with ice and strain into collins glass. Add several ice cubes, fill with club soda, and stir. Decorate with a slice of lemon and a cherry. Serve with a straw.

RUM COOLER

½ tsp.	Powdered Sugar
2 oz.	Club Soda
2 oz.	Light Rum
Club Soda or Ginger Ale	

In collins glass, dissolve sugar in 2 oz. club soda. Stir. Fill glass with ice and add rum. Fill with club soda or ginger ale and stir again. Insert a spiral of orange or lemon peel (or both) and dangle end over rim of glass.

RUM DAISY

Juice of ½ Lemon	
½ tsp.	Powdered Sugar
1 tsp.	Grenadine
2 oz.	Light Rum

Shake with ice and strain into stein or metal cup. Add one ice cube and decorate with fruit.

RUM FIX

Juice of ½ Lemon or 1 Lime	
1 tsp.	Powdered Sugar
1 tsp.	Water
2½ oz.	Light Rum

Stir together in highball glass and fill glass with ice. Add rum. Stir and add a slice of lemon. Serve with a straw.

RUM HIGHBALL

| 2 oz. | Light or Dark Rum |
| Ginger Ale or Club Soda | |

Pour rum into highball glass over ice cubes and fill with ginger ale or club soda. Add a twist of lemon peel and stir.

RUM MARTINI

| 4–5 parts | Light Rum |
| 1 dash | Dry Vermouth |

Serve over ice in cocktail glass with a twist of lemon.

RUM MILK PUNCH

1 tsp.	Powdered Sugar
2 oz.	Light Rum
1 cup	Milk

Shake with ice, strain into collins glass, and sprinkle nutmeg on top.

RUM OLD-FASHIONED

½ tsp.	Powdered Sugar
1 dash	Bitters
1 tsp.	Water
1½ oz.	Light Rum
1 tsp.	151-proof Rum

Stir sugar, bitters, and water in old-fashioned glass. When sugar is dissolved, add ice cubes and light rum. Add a twist of lime peel and float the 151-proof rum on top.

RUM RELAXER

1½ oz.	Light Rum
1 oz.	Pineapple Juice
½ oz.	Grenadine
Lemon-lime Soda	

Pour first three ingredients over ice, shake well. Pour into hurricane or parfait glass, fill with lemon-lime soda. Garnish with an orange slice and a cherry.

RUM RICKEY

Juice of ½ Lime
1½ oz. Light Rum
Club Soda

Pour into highball glass over ice cubes and fill with club soda and ice cubes. Stir. Add a wedge of lime.

RUM SCREWDRIVER

1½ oz. Light Rum
5 oz. Orange Juice

Combine ingredients in highball glass with ice cubes.

RUM SOUR

Juice of ½ Lemon
½ tsp. Powdered Sugar
2 oz. Light Rum

Shake with ice and strain into sour glass. Decorate with a half-slice of lemon and a cherry.

RUM SWIZZLE

Juice of 1 Lime
1 tsp. Powdered Sugar
2 oz. Club Soda
2 dashes Bitters
2 oz. Light or Dark Rum

Put lime juice, sugar, and 2 oz. club soda into collins glass. Fill glass with ice and stir. Add bitters and rum. Fill with club soda and serve with a swizzle stick.

RUM TODDY

½ tsp. Powdered Sugar
2 tsps. Water
2 oz. Light or Dark Rum

In old-fashioned glass, dissolve sugar in water. Stir and add rum and a cube of ice. Stir again and add a twist of lemon peel.

SANTIAGO COCKTAIL

½ tsp. Powdered Sugar
¼ tsp. Grenadine
Juice of 1 Lime
1½ oz. Light Rum

Shake with ice and strain into cocktail glass.

SAXON COCKTAIL

Juice of ½ Lime
½ tsp. Grenadine
1¼ oz. Light Rum

Shake with ice and strain into cocktail glass. Serve with a twist of orange peel.

SEWER WATER

1 oz. 151-proof Rum
½ oz. Gin
¾ oz. Melon Liqueur
Pineapple Juice
Lime Juice
Grenadine

In hurricane or parfait glass, splash some grenadine. Add ice, then rum, gin, and melon liqueur. Fill with pineapple juice and float lime juice on top.

SHANGHAI COCKTAIL

Juice of ¼ Lemon
1 tsp.   Anisette
1 oz.   Jamaica Light Rum
½ tsp.   Grenadine

Shake with ice and strain
into cocktail glass.

SIR WALTER COCKTAIL

¾ oz.   Light Rum
¾ oz.   Brandy
1 tsp.   Grenadine
1 tsp.   Triple Sec
1 tsp.   Lemon Juice

Shake with ice and strain
into cocktail glass.

SLOPPY JOE'S
COCKTAIL NO. 1

Juice of 1 Lime
¼ tsp.   Triple Sec
¼ tsp.   Grenadine
¾ oz.   Light Rum
¾ oz.   Dry Vermouth

Shake with ice and strain
into cocktail glass.

SPANISH TOWN
COCKTAIL

2 oz.   Light Rum
1 tsp.   Triple Sec

Stir with ice and strain into
cocktail glass.

STONE COCKTAIL

½ oz.   Light Rum
½ oz.   Sweet Vermouth
1 oz.   Dry Sherry

Stir with ice and strain into
cocktail glass.

STRAWBERRY
DAIQUIRI

1 oz.   Light Rum
½ oz.   Strawberry
              Schnapps
1 oz.   Lime Juice
1 tsp.   Powdered Sugar
1 oz.   Fresh or Frozen
              Strawberries

Shake with ice and strain
into cocktail glass.

SUSIE TAYLOR

Juice of ½ Lime
2 oz.   Light Rum
Ginger Ale

Pour into collins glass over
ice cubes and fill with ginger
ale. Stir.

TAHITI CLUB

2 oz.   Light Rum
1 tbsp.   Lemon Juice
1 tbsp.   Lime Juice
1 tbsp.   Pineapple Juice
½ tsp.   Maraschino

Shake with ice and strain
into old-fashioned glass over
ice cubes. Add a slice of
lemon.

THIRD-RAIL COCKTAIL

¼ oz.   Light Rum
¼ oz.   Apple Brandy
¼ oz.   Brandy
¼ tsp.   Anisette

Shake with ice and strain
into cocktail glass.

THREE MILLER COCKTAIL

1½ oz.	Light Rum
¾ oz.	Brandy
1 tsp.	Grenadine
¼ tsp.	Lemon Juice

Shake with ice and strain into cocktail glass.

TORRIDORA COCKTAIL

1½ oz.	Light Rum
½ oz.	Coffee-flavored Brandy
1½ tsps.	Light Cream
1 tsp.	151-proof Rum

Shake with ice and strain into cocktail glass. Float rum on top.

TROPICA COCKTAIL

1¼ oz.	Light Rum
5 oz.	Pineapple Juice
2 oz.	Grapefruit Juice
1 dash	Grenadine

Mix ingredients in collins glass filled with ice cubes. Garnish with a pineapple wedge.

"One of sour, two of sweet, three of strong and four of weak." It's the classic formula for a rum punch in Martinique. If you order one there, you'll be given a slice of lime, a small bottle of syrup, a bottle of rum, a jug of water and left to mix it yourself. The lime is the sour, the syrup the sweet, the rum the strong, and the water the weak.

VAN VLEET

3 oz.	Light Rum
1 oz.	Maple Syrup
1 oz.	Lemon Juice

Shake with ice and strain into old-fashioned glass over ice cubes.

WHITE LILY COCKTAIL

¾ oz.	Triple Sec
¾ oz.	Light Rum
¾ oz.	Gin
¼ tsp.	Anisette

Shake with ice and strain into cocktail glass.

WHITE LION COCKTAIL

Juice of ½ Lemon	
1 tsp.	Powdered Sugar
2 dashes Bitters	
½ tsp.	Grenadine
1½ oz.	Light Rum

Shake with ice and strain into cocktail glass.

WIKI WAKI WOO

½ oz.	Vodka
½ oz.	Rum
½ oz.	151-proof Rum
½ oz.	Tequila
½ oz.	Triple Sec
1 oz.	Amaretto
1 oz.	Orange Juice
1 oz.	Pineapple Juice
1 oz.	Cranberry Juice

Combine all ingredients with ice, pour into hurricane or parfait glass. Garnish with an orange slice and a cherry.

X.Y.Z. COCKTAIL

1 tbsp.	Lemon Juice
½ oz.	Triple Sec
1 oz.	Light Rum

Shake with ice and strain into cocktail glass.

ZOMBIE

1 oz.	Unsweetened Pineapple Juice
Juice of	1 Lime
Juice of	1 Small Orange
1 tsp.	Powdered Sugar
½ oz.	Apricot-flavored Brandy
2½ oz.	Light Rum
1 oz.	Jamaica Rum
1 oz.	Passion Fruit Syrup (if desired)
½ oz.	151-proof Rum

Put all ingredients with a half-cup of crushed ice into blender. Blend at low speed for one minute and strain into frosted highball glass. Decorate with a stick of pineapple and one green and one red cherry. Carefully float rum and then top with sprig of fresh mint dipped in powdered sugar. Serve with a straw.

THE UPSIDE DOWN BILL

Place a dollar bill on the table with portrait facing you (fig.1). Then claim that you will fold the bill in such a way that when it is reopened, the portrait will be upside down. METHOD: Fold in half by lifting right side over left, as in fig. 2. Next, fold again, taking top of bill and folding down as in fig. 3. Turn the dollar from left to right—fig. 4. Open it as in fig. 5, and behold, the dollar is upside down. Once the trick has been mastered it is most effective if these movements are done very rapidly without pause.

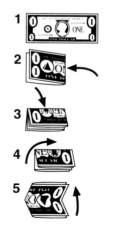

Ah, bonnie Scotland—where men in skirts spend hours whacking little dimpled balls with metal sticks. Where ponies no bigger than a dog roam the moors and the celebrated Loch Ness monster has mystified many the world round. But ask any Scotsman what his native land is most renowned for and you'll hear a story about a spirit as old as its originating braes and burns—Scotch whisky.

Produced only in Scotland, Scotch whiskies fall into two primary categories: single malt and blended. While blended Scotches are the most familiar and have long been popular in the United States, single malts have been gaining aficionados rapidly in recent years.

Single malt Scotches are the product of more than 100 distilleries, each of which produces its own distinctive spirit. Though each distillery uses malted barley as the base for its Scotch, variants in the water, peat, atmospheric characteristics, shape of the pot-still, and the aging casks are factors in determining the uniqueness of the resulting spirit. Most single malts are aged at least eight years, some considerably longer. Generally, characteristics of single malts are best described by those of the region in which they are produced.

Highland malts are smoky and smooth, the dryness from the peat balanced by the sweetness of the barley malt. Island malts are influenced by their proximity to the salt-laden atmosphere of the Atlantic, producing a whisky with a powerful peatiness in both the bouquet and taste. Islay malts are distinguished by peat, which, affected by the sea atmosphere, lends its quality to both the local water, which runs off the peat moors, and the malted barley, which is dried by burning peat. Lowland malts, the mildest of all, lack the smoky, pungent taste of peat but have many subtle flavors of barley malt. Speyside malts are produced by distilleries on the banks of the River Spey, where pure, soft water from the granite mountains runs over massive peat bogs, imparting a firm-bodied taste, with a hint of malt sweetness and a smoky character. Western Highlands malts, produced where the Highlands come down to the sea, are a balance between pungent Island malts and smooth Highland malts. *Speyburn 10 Year Old Single Highland Malt Scotch Whisky,* first produced in 1897, gets its unique flavor and bouquet by using the crystal-clear, fresh spring water from the Granty Burn, one of the major tributaries of the River Spey. And it's still the only Highland distillery to use this particular soft Speyside water in the production of its whisky. *Speyburn Single Highland Malt* is now distributed throughout the world, allowing connoisseurs to savor its character and excellence.

Blended Scotch whiskies derive their individual personalities from the single malts comprising them. All Scotch blends contain malt whisky and grain whisky, similar to American grain neutral spirits. Anywhere from twenty to as many as forty different malt whiskies may be part of a blend. The age of the spirit refers to the youngest whisky included. All blended Scotch imported to the United States is at least four years old and is usually the standard 80 proof.

Blended Scotch traces its roots to the merchants who perfected the art of blending. After creating their own brands, they set out to market their product to the world. Steeped in taste and history, *Lauder's Scotch* was the Gold Medal Winner at the 1893 Chicago World's Fair. *Lauder's* features a distinct smooth taste which has made it one of the finest imported blended Scotch whiskies. *House of Stuart* is a high-quality, robust blended Scotch whisky with good balance of smoke and grain. Aging has also given this Scotch mellow aromatic notes. Blended in Glasgow, Scotland, from the highest quality stocks, *Highland Mist Blended Scotch Whisky* offers up a light, smooth, sophisticated taste. *Highland Mist's* unique bottle and label reinforce the image and heritage of its name. *Inver House Very Rare Scotch Whisky* features a distinct blend of superbly light, 100% rare Scotch whiskies, distilled and blended in Scotland. Its light taste profile has made it the 10th largest Scotch in America.

Speyburn on the Rocks

The word *whisky* is derived from the Gaelic term *usquebaugh* — meaning "water of life."

Whisky was drunk primarily by the lower class until the 19th century, when it rose rapidly in social status.

When scotch whisky first begins aging in the cask its alcohol volume is usually around 70%. As the whisky matures, evaporation occurs which can drop the alcohol volume as low as 57%. This lost alcohol is referred to as "the angels' share."

In the early 20th century, single malts virtually disappeared from public view until the late 1960's. Since then it has undergone a remarkable renaissance and become one of the fastest growing liquor categories.

AFFINITY COCKTAIL

1 oz.   Dry Vermouth
1 oz.   Sweet Vermouth
1 oz.   Scotch
3 dashes Orange Bitters

Stir with ice and strain into cocktail glass.

BEADLESTONE COCKTAIL

1½ oz.   Dry Vermouth
1½ oz.   Scotch

Stir with ice and strain into cocktail glass.

BEALS COCKTAIL

1½ oz.   Scotch
½ oz.   Dry Vermouth
½ oz.   Sweet Vermouth

Stir with ice and strain into cocktail glass.

BLOOD-AND-SAND COCKTAIL

1 tbsp. Orange Juice
½ oz.   Scotch
½ oz.   Cherry-flavored
           Brandy
½ oz.   Sweet Vermouth

Shake with ice and strain into cocktail glass.

BOBBY BURNS COCKTAIL

1½ oz.   Sweet Vermouth
1½ oz.   Scotch
1¼ tsps. Benedictine

Stir with ice and strain into cocktail glass. Add a twist of lemon peel.

CAMERON'S KICK COCKTAIL

¾ oz.   Scotch
¾ oz.   Irish Whiskey
Juice of ¼ Lemon
2 dashes Orange Bitters

Shake with ice and strain into cocktail glass.

FLYING SCOTCHMAN

1 oz.   Sweet Vermouth
1 oz.   Scotch
1 dash   Bitters
¼ tsp.   Simple Syrup

Stir with ice and strain into cocktail glass.

GODFATHER

1½ oz.   Scotch
¾ oz.   Amaretto

Serve in old-fashioned glass over ice. (Bourbon may be used instead of Scotch.)

HEATHER BLUSH

1 oz.   Scotch
1 oz.   Strawberry Liqueur
3 oz.   Chilled Sparkling
           Wine

Pour scotch and liqueur into champagne flute. Top with sparkling wine. Garnish with a strawberry.

HIGHLAND COOLER

½ tsp.   Powdered Sugar
2 oz.   Club Soda
2 oz.   Scotch
Club Soda or Ginger Ale

Into collins glass, put powdered sugar and 2 oz. club soda. Stir. Then add ice cubes and scotch. Fill with club soda or ginger ale and stir again. Insert a spiral of orange or lemon peel (or both) and dangle end over rim of glass.

HIGHLAND FLING COCKTAIL

¾ oz.   Sweet Vermouth
1½ oz.   Scotch
2 dashes Orange Bitters

Stir with ice and strain into cocktail glass. Serve with an olive.

HOLE-IN-ONE

1¾ oz.   Scotch
¾ oz.   Vermouth
¼ tsp.   Lemon Juice
1 dash   Orange Bitters

Shake with ice and strain into cocktail glass.

HOOT MON COCKTAIL

¾ oz.   Sweet Vermouth
1½ oz.   Scotch
1 tsp.   Benedictine

Stir with ice and strain into cocktail glass. Twist a lemon peel and drop into glass.

LOCH LOMOND

1 oz.   Scotch
½ oz.   Peach Schnapps
1 oz.   Blue Curaçao
3 oz.   Grapefruit Juice
½ oz.   Lemon Juice

Shake all ingredients with ice. Strain into parfait or hurricane glass filled with crushed ice. Garnish with slice of star fruit.

MAMIE GILROY

Juice of ½ Lime
2 oz.   Scotch
Ginger Ale

Combine in collins glass filled with ice. Stir.

MIAMI BEACH COCKTAIL

¾ oz.   Scotch
¾ oz.   Dry Vermouth
¾ oz.   Grapefruit Juice

Shake with ice and strain into cocktail glass.

MODERN COCKTAIL

1½ oz.   Scotch
½ tsp.   Lemon Juice
¼ tsp.   Anisette
½ tsp.   Jamaica Rum
1 dash   Orange Bitters

Shake with ice and strain into cocktail glass. Serve with a cherry.

ROB ROY

¾ oz.   Sweet Vermouth
1½ oz.   Scotch

Stir with ice and strain into cocktail glass.

RUSTY NAIL

¾ oz.   Scotch
¼ oz.   Drambuie

Serve in old-fashioned glass
with ice cubes. Float
Drambuie on top.

SCOTCH BISHOP COCKTAIL

1 oz.   Scotch
1 tbsp.   Orange Juice
½ oz.   Dry Vermouth
½ tsp.   Triple Sec
¼ tsp.   Powdered Sugar

Shake with ice and strain
into cocktail glass. Add a
twist of lemon peel.

SCOTCH BOUNTY

1 oz.   Scotch
1 oz.   Coconut Rum
1 oz.   Crème de Cacao
          (White)
½ oz.   Grenadine
4 oz.   Orange Juice

Shake with ice and pour into
hurricane or parfait glass.
Garnish with a pineapple
wedge and a cherry. Serve
with a straw.

SCOTCH COBBLER

2 oz.   Scotch
4 dashes Curaçao
4 dashes Brandy

Pour ingredients over ice in
old-fashioned glass. Garnish
with slice of orange and a
mint sprig.

SCOTCH COOLER

2 oz.   Scotch
3 dashes Crème de Menthe
          (White)
Chilled Club Soda

Pour into highball glass over
ice cubes. Fill with club soda
and stir.

SCOTCH HIGHBALL

2 oz.   Scotch
Ginger Ale or Club Soda

Put scotch into highball glass
with ice cubes and fill with
ginger ale or club soda. Add
a twist of lemon peel and
stir.

SCOTCH HOLIDAY SOUR

1½ oz.   Scotch
1 oz.   Cherry-flavored
           Brandy
½ oz.   Sweet Vermouth
1 oz.   Lemon Juice

Shake with ice and strain
into old-fashioned glass over
ice cubes. Add a slice of
lemon.

SCOTCH MILK PUNCH

2 oz.   Scotch
6 oz.   Milk
1 tsp.   Powdered Sugar

Shake with ice and strain
into collins glass. Sprinkle
with nutmeg.

SCOTCH MIST

2 oz.   Scotch

Pack old-fashioned glass
with crushed ice. Pour in
scotch, add a twist of lemon
peel. Serve with a short
straw.

SCOTCH OLD-FASHIONED

1 cube   Sugar
1 dash   Bitters
1 tsp.   Water
2 oz.   Scotch

In old-fashioned glass,
muddle sugar cube, water,
and bitters. Add scotch and
stir. Add a twist of lemon
peel and ice cubes. Decorate
with slices of orange and
lemon, and a cherry.

SCOTCH RICKEY

Juice of ½ Lime
1½ oz.   Scotch
Club Soda

Pour into highball glass over
ice and fill with club soda.
Add a twist of lime. Stir.

SCOTCH ON THE ROCKS

2 oz.   Scotch

Pour scotch into old-
fashioned glass half-filled
with ice.

SCOTCH ROYALE

1 cube   Sugar
1½ oz.   Scotch
1 dash   Bitters
Chilled Champagne

Place sugar cube in
champagne flute. Add scotch
and bitters, fill with
champagne.

SCOTCH SOUR

1½ oz.   Scotch
Juice of ½ Lime
1/2 tsp.   Powdered Sugar

Shake with ice and strain
into sour glass. Decorate
with a half-slice of lemon
and a cherry.

SCOTCH STINGER

½ oz.   Crème de Menthe
             (White)
1½ oz.   Scotch

Shake with ice and strain
into cocktail glass.

THE SHOOT

1 oz.   Scotch
1 oz.   Dry Sherry
1 tsp.   Orange Juice
1 tsp.   Lemon Juice
½ tsp.   Powdered Sugar

Shake with ice and strain
into cocktail glass.

Schlante
    —a Scottish toast

SILENT THIRD

1 oz. Cointreau
2 oz. Scotch
1 oz. Lemon Juice

Shake well with cracked ice and strain into cocktail glass.

> "Now, McTavish," said the doctor, "it's like this. You've either to stop the whisky or lose your eyesight, and you must choose."
> "Ay, weel, doctor," said McTavish, "I'm an old man, an' I was thinkin' I ha'e seen about everythin' worth seein'."

STONE FENCE

2 dashes Bitters
2 oz. Scotch
Club Soda or Cider

Fill highball glass with ice cubes. Add scotch and bitters and fill with club soda or cider. Stir.

THISTLE COCKTAIL

1½ oz. Sweet Vermouth
1½ oz. Scotch
2 dashes Bitters

Stir with ice and strain into cocktail glass.

WALTERS

1½ oz. Scotch
1 tbsp. Orange Juice
1 tbsp. Lemon Juice

Shake with ice and strain into cocktail glass.

WOODWARD COCKTAIL

1½ oz. Scotch
½ oz. Dry Vermouth
1 tbsp. Grapefruit Juice

Shake with ice and strain into cocktail glass.

EX-RAY EYES COIN TRICK

Tell a person that, without seeing the numbers, you can tell him whether a serial number on any amount of paper currency (United States) is odd or even. Have him fold the bill in half, putting his thumb over the serial number, but leaving the rest of the bill exposed. Then, merely by looking at the letter printed on the bill, as in fig. 1, you can determine whether or not the serial number is odd or even. Figure the letter A as Odd and B as Even and so on through the alphabet. While looking at the bill determine whether the letter is odd or even.

Tequila

P robably Mexico's most famous export, tequila is produced in only two designated regions in the country,
one near the town of Tequila, the other near Tepati-
tlán. Tequila is distilled from the sap of the mature
blue agave plant, also called the century plant. There are
other varieties of agave, from which mezcal is produced, but
by Mexican law, only the blue agave can be used for tequila.
Mexican law also dictates that tequila must contain 51 percent blue agave, with the remainder coming from cane or
other sugars. Tequila made from 100 percent blue agaze requires government inspection to certify its authenticity.

"White" tequila is ready for export immediately after distillation, requiring no aging. "Gold" tequila is usually aged in
white oak casks for two to four years, although Mexican regulations do not stipulate a minimum aging period. Tequila añejo,
however, must be aged for a minimum of one year. *Montezuma*
tequila comes from the Jalisco province where it is distilled
under strict Mexican supervision. Availability in both "white"
and the more complex "gold" makes *Montezuma* tequila a natural in Margaritas, mixed drinks, or straight up as a "shooter."

Tequila's popularity has exploded in the last few years and
the Margarita is, without question, the most popular way
tequila is consumed. Fueled by Americans' ever-growing taste
for Mexican and Southwestern cuisine, the Margarita is the
specialty drink most often ordered in bars and restaurants
across the country. Plain, salted, or sugared, straight up, on
the rocks, or frozen, Margaritas are now made in a mind-
boggling array of flavors and colors.

Margaritas are also the third most popular drink consumed
at home. *El Toro Tequila,* topped by a distinctive red sombrero
cap, is available in both white and gold versions to use in any
Margarita recipe. Though the drink is simple to make, many

consumers enjoy the convenience of already prepared Margaritas for home consumption. *Chi-Chi's Margaritas*, with tequila already in it, requires only blending with ice to make a refreshing, frosty drink. Best of all, *Chi-Chi's Margaritas* are available in several authentic flavors such as original, strawberry, and premium gold.

Mezcal is a close relative of tequila, distilled from the blue agave plant in the state of Oaxaca, Mexico. *Monte Alban* still distills its Mexcal in accordance to centuries-old tradition and technique—which includes placing an actual agave worm inside each bottle to certify the authenticity of the product. The mystique of this unusual occupant has provoked many a dare, bet, and even a *Monte Alban's* Worm Worshipers club. The trademark "worm," along with a unique taste and premium quality, have made *Monte Alban* the number one Mezcal brand not only in the U.S., but throughout the world. *Ole!*

The ancient Aztec Indians made a special low-alcohol drink called *pulque* from the fermented sap of agave plants. Apparently polite even to invaders, the Aztec emperor Montezuma supposedly presented hollowed-out gourds filled with this concoction to the Spanish explorer Cortez and his men. The Spaniards must have liked it, for they began to experiment, and discovered that the blue agaze produced the smoothest and most flavorful drink—the ancestor of today's tequila.

ALAMO SPLASH

1½ oz. Tequila
1 oz. Orange Juice
½ oz. Pineapple Juice
1 splash Lemon-lime Soda

Mix with cracked ice, strain into collins glass.

BIG RED HOOTER

1 oz. Tequila
¾ oz. Amaretto
Pineapple Juice
1 oz. Grenadine

Pour tequila and amaretto over ice into collins glass. Fill with pineapple juice and top with grenadine. Garnish with a cherry and serve with a straw.

BLOODY MARIA

1 oz. Tequila
2 oz. Tomato Juice
1 dash Lemon Juice
1 dash Tabasco Sauce
1 dash Celery Salt

Shake all ingredients with cracked ice. Strain into old-fashioned glass over ice cubes. Add a slice of lemon.

BLUE MARGARITA

1½ oz. Tequila
½ oz. Blue Curaçao
1 oz. Lime Juice

Rub rim of cocktail glass with lime juice. Dip rim in coarse salt. Shake ingredients with ice and strain into glass.

BRAVE BULL

1½ oz. Tequila
1 oz. Coffee Liqueur

Pour over ice cubes into old-fashioned glass and stir. Add a twist of lemon.

CACTUS BERRY

1¼ oz. Tequila
1¼ oz. Red Wine
1 oz. Triple Sec
6½ oz. Sour Mix
1 splash Lemon-lime Soda
1 dash Lime Juice

Shake with ice and pour into large salt-rimmed cocktail or margarita glass.

CATALINA MARGARITA

1½ oz. Tequila
1 oz. Peach Schnapps
1 oz. Blue Curaçao
4 oz. Sour Mix

Shake with cracked ice and strain into chilled cocktail or margarita glass.

CHAPALA

1½ oz. Tequila
1 tbsp. Orange Juice
1 tbsp. Lemon Juice
1 dash Triple Sec
2 tsps. Grenadine

Shake with ice and strain into old-fashioned glass over ice cubes. Add a slice of orange.

HAIRY SUNRISE

¾ oz.	Tequila
¾ oz.	Vodka
½ oz.	Triple Sec
3 oz.	Orange Juice
2–3 dashes	Grenadine

Mix all ingredients in blender except grenadine. Pour into collins glass. Float grenadine on top and garnish with a lime slice.

HOT PANTS

1½ oz.	Tequila
½ oz.	Peppermint Schnapps
1 tbsp.	Grapefruit Juice
1 tsp.	Powdered Sugar

Shake with ice cubes and pour into old-fashioned glass rimmed with salt.

LA BOMBA

1¼ oz.	Gold Tequila
¾ oz.	Cointreau
1½ oz.	Pineapple Juice
1½ oz.	Orange Juice
2 dashes	Grenadine

Shake all ingredients except grenadine with ice, three times only. Pour into sugar-rimmed cocktail glass. Add grenadine and garnish with a lime wheel.

Salud
   —a Spanish toast

MARGARITA

1½ oz.	Tequila
½ oz.	Triple Sec
1 oz.	Lemon or Lime Juice

Rub rim of cocktail glass with rind of lemon or lime, dip rim in salt. Shake ingredients with ice and strain into salt-rimmed glass.

MEXICANA

1½ oz.	Tequila
1 oz.	Lemon Juice
1 tbsp.	Pineapple Juice
1 tsp.	Grenadine

Shake with ice and strain into cocktail glass.

MEXICAN MADRAS

3 oz.	Cranberry Juice
½ oz.	Orange Juice
1 oz.	Gold Tequila
1 dash	Lime Juice

Pour juices and tequila into shaker half-filled with ice. Shake well and strain into old-fashioned glass. Garnish with an orange slice.

MEXICOLA

| 2 oz. | Tequila |
| Juice of ½ Lime |
| Cola |

Fill collins glass with ice cubes. Add tequila and lime juice, fill with cola, and stir.

PACIFIC SUNSHINE
1½ oz. Tequila
1½ oz. Blue Curaçao
1½ oz. Sour Mix
1 dash Bitters

Mix with cracked ice and pour, with ice, into chilled parfait or hurricane glass with a salted rim. Garnish with a lemon wheel.

PURPLE GECKO
1½ oz. Tequila
½ oz. Blue Curaçao
½ oz. Red Curaçao
1 oz. Cranberry Juice
1 oz. Sour Mix
½ oz. Lime Juice

Shake with ice and pour into salt-rimmed cocktail or margarita glass. Garnish with a lime wedge.

PURPLE PANCHO
1 oz. Tequila
½ oz. Blue Curaçao
½ oz. Sloe Gin
2 oz. Lime Juice
2 oz. Sour Mix

Shake with ice and pour into salt-rimmed cocktail or margarita glass. Garnish with a lime wheel.

ROSITA
1 oz. Tequila
½ oz. Dry Vermouth
½ oz. Sweet Vermouth
1 oz. Campari

Stir in old-fashioned glass with cracked ice. Add a twist of lemon peel and serve with short straws.

SHADY LADY
1 oz. Tequila
1 oz. Melon Liqueur
4 oz. Grapefruit Juice

Combine ingredients over ice in highball glass. Ganish with a lime and a cherry.

SILK STOCKINGS
1½ oz. Tequila
1 oz. Crème de Cacao
1½ oz. Cream
1 dash Grenadine

Shake ingredients with crushed ice. Strain into cocktail glass. Sprinkle cinnamon on top.

SLOE TEQUILA
1 oz. Tequila
½ oz. Sloe Gin
1 tbsp. Lime Juice

Combine ingredients with a half-cup of crushed ice in blender. Blend at low speed and pour into old-fashioned glass. Add ice cubes and twist of cucumber peel.

SOUTH OF THE BORDER
1 oz. Tequila
¾ oz. Coffee-flavored Brandy
Juice of ½ Lime

Shake with ice and strain into sour glass. Add a lime slice.

STRAWBERRY MARGARITA

1 oz. Tequila
½ oz. Triple Sec
½ oz. Strawberry
        Schnapps
1 oz. Lemon or Lime
        Juice
1 oz. Fresh or Frozen
        Strawberries

If desired, rub rim of cocktail glass with a rind of lemon or lime, dip rim in salt. Shake ingredients with ice and strain into glass.

TEQUILA CANYON

1½ oz. Tequila
⅛ oz.   Triple Sec
4 oz.   Cranberry Juice
¼ oz.   Pineapple Juice
¼ oz.   Orange Juice

Pour first three ingredients over ice into collins glass and stir gently. Top with pineapple and orange juices. Garnish with a lime wheel. Serve with a straw.

TEQUILA COLLINS

Juice of ½ Lemon
1 tsp.   Powdered Sugar
2 oz.   Tequila
Club Soda

Shake with ice and strain into collins glass. Add several ice cubes, fill with club soda and stir. Decorate with slices of lemon and orange, and a cherry. Serve with a straw.

TEQUILA MANHATTAN

2 oz.   Tequila
1 oz.   Sweet Vermouth
1 dash   Lime Juice

Shake with ice and strain over ice cubes into old-fashioned glass. Add a cherry and an orange slice.

TEQUILA MATADOR

1½ oz. Tequila
3 oz.   Pineapple Juice
Juice of ½ Lime

Shake with crushed ice and strain into champagne flute.

TEQUILA MOCKINGBIRD

1½ oz. Tequila
¾ oz.   Crème de Menthe
        (Green)
Juice of 1 Lime

Shake with ice and strain into cocktail glass. Decorate with a lime slice.

TEQUILA OLD-FASHIONED

1½ oz.   Tequila
½ tsp.   Sugar
1 dash   Bitters
1 tsp.   Water
1 splash Club Soda

Mix sugar, bitters, and water in old-fashioned glass. Add tequila, ice, and club soda. Decorate with a pineapple stick.

TEQUILA PINK

1½ oz.   Tequila
1 oz.   Dry Vermouth
1 dash   Grenadine

Shake with ice and strain into cocktail glass.

TEQUILA SOUR

Juice of ½ Lemon
1 tsp.   Powdered Sugar
2 oz.   Tequila

Shake with ice and strain into sour glass. Decorate with a half-slice of lemon and a cherry.

TEQUILA STRAIGHT

¼   Lemon
1 pinch   Salt
1½ oz.   Tequila

Put salt between thumb and index finger on back of left hand. Hold jigger of tequila in same hand and lemon wedge in right hand. Taste salt, drink the tequila, and then suck the lemon.

TEQUILA SUNRISE

2 oz.   Tequila
4 oz.   Orange Juice
¾ oz.   Grenadine

Stir tequila and orange juice with ice and strain into highball glass. Add ice cubes. Pour in grenadine slowly and allow to settle. Before drinking, stir to complete your sunrise.

TEQUINI

1½ oz.   Tequila
½ oz.   Dry Vermouth
1 dash   Bitters (if desired)

Stir with ice and strain into cocktail glass. Serve with a twist of lemon peel and an olive.

TEQUONIC

2 oz.   Tequila
Juice of ½ Lemon or Lime
Tonic Water

Pour tequila over ice cubes into old-fashioned glass. Add fruit juice, fill with tonic water, and stir.

TIJUANA TAXI

2 oz.   Gold Tequila
1 oz.   Blue Curaçao
1 oz.   Tropical Fruit
          Schnapps
Lemon-lime Soda

Pour tequila, curaçao, and schnapps over ice into large highball glass. Fill with lemon-lime soda and garnish with orange slice and a cherry.

T.N.T. NO. 2

1 oz.   Tequila
Tonic Water

Mix with ice in old-fashioned glass.

TOREADOR

1½ oz.   Tequila
½ oz.   Crème de Cacao
1 tbsp.   Light Cream

Shake with ice and strain
into cocktail glass. Top with
a little whipped cream and
sprinkle lightly with cocoa.

TRAFFIC LIGHT COOLER

¾ oz.   Melon Liqueur
1 oz.   Gold Tequila
1 splash Sour Mix
2 oz.   Orange Juice
½ oz.   Sloe Gin

Into pilsner glass filled with
ice cubes, first pour the
melon liqueur, then the
tequila, to create a green
layer. Add sour mix. Slowly
pour orange juice against
side of glass to create the
yellow layer. Add a few more
ice cubes, if needed.
Carefully float the sloe gin
on top for the red layer.
Garnish with a cherry and
lemon and lime wheels. Stir
just before drinking.

VIVA VILLA

Juice of 1 Lime
1 tsp.   Sugar
1½ oz.   Tequila

Shake with ice and strain
over ice cubes into old-
fashioned glass rimmed with
salt.

WILD THING

1½ oz.   Tequila
1 oz.   Cranberry Juice
1 oz.   Club Soda
½ oz.   Lime Juice

Pour over ice into old-
fashioned glass. Garnish
with a lime wheel.

The agave, from which tequila is
distilled, is a member of the
amaryllis family but is a succulent
with spiny leaves, which is why
tequila is sometimes nicknamed
"cactus whiskey."

CORNER THE COIN

Place eight coins in the form of a right angle with five coins making one leg of the L and four coins the other. Bet that you can put five coins in each leg by moving only one coin. METHOD: Take the last coin in the line that has five coins and place it on the coin at the angle as shown.

Vodka

Vodka has humility. By law, vodkas produced in the United States must be colorless, tasteless, and odorless. Because of its purity, vodka will graciously assume the characteristics of whatever it is mixed with. It is this mixability that has made vodka the most popular distilled spirit of all. The Bloody Mary and Screwdriver have been perennial favorites, and vodka-based specialty drinks, such as the White Russian, Black Russian, Cape Codder, and Seabreeze repeatedly make the top ten list. Vodka has even established itself in a number of traditional gin drinks: Vodka and Tonic, Vodka Martini, and Vodka Collins.

Vodka means "little water," a diminutive of the Russian word water, *voda*. It is commonly believed that the spirit originated in Russia sometime in the fourteenth century. In the days of the czars, Russian vodka was made from potatoes, whereas today's version is made from grain. Vodka was introduced in the United States during the 1930s and, in this country, is made from pure grain neutral spirits distilled from fermented corn, rye, or wheat. The higher the proof, the less flavor. Vodka is also filtered through charcoal to remove any remaining hint of flavor. Top-quality grains and pure spring water give *Barton Vodka* an unusually clean and natural quality. However *Fleischmann's Vodka* remains a favorite within the vodka category.

There are also vodkas that are specially flavored with lemon, lime, or other fruit, mint, pepper, and even buffalo grass. Flavored vodkas, especially lemon, are usually served straight and icy cold as an aperitif or mixed with juices or tonic water. The subtlety of the vodka flavors are becoming particularly appealing to consumers looking for lighter-tasting mixed drinks.

ALFIE COCKTAIL

1½ oz.   Lemon Vodka
1 tbsp.   Pineapple Juice
1 dash   Triple Sec

Shake with ice and strain
into cocktail glass.

AQUEDUCT

1½ oz.   Vodka
1½ tsps.   Curaçao (White)
1½ tsps.   Apricot-flavored
　　　　　　Brandy
1 tbsp.   Lime Juice

Combine and shake all
ingredients with ice and
strain into cocktail glass.
Add a twist of orange peel.

BANANA PUNCH

2 oz.   Vodka
1½ tsps.   Apricot-flavored
　　　　　Brandy
Juice of ½ Lime
Club Soda

Pour into collins glass filled
with crushed ice. Add club
soda and top with slices of
banana and sprigs of mint.

BEER BUSTER

1½ oz.   100-proof Vodka
Chilled Beer or Ale
2 dashes Tabasco Sauce

Put vodka into highball glass
and fill with beer or ale. Add
Tabasco sauce and stir
lightly.

BIKINI

2 oz.   Vodka
1 oz.   Light Rum
½ oz.   Milk
1 tsp.   Sugar
Juice of ½ Lemon

Shake with ice and strain
into cocktail glass. Garnish
with a lemon twist.

BLACK MAGIC

1½ oz.   Vodka
¾ oz.   Coffee Liqueur
1 dash   Lemon Juice

Stir and serve in old-
fashioned glass over ice
cubes. Add a twist of lemon
peel.

BLACK RUSSIAN

1½ oz.   Vodka
¾ oz.   Coffee Liqueur

Pour over ice cubes into old-
fashioned glass.

BLOODY BULL

1 oz.   Vodka
2 oz.   Tomato Juice
2 oz.   Beef Bouillon

Add all ingredients in
highball glass over ice. Stir,
and add a squeeze of lemon
and a slice of lime.

Bloody Mary, Twister

BLOODY MARY

1½ oz. Vodka
3 oz. Tomato Juice
1 dash Lemon Juice
½ tsp. Worcestershire Sauce
2–3 drops Tabasco Sauce
Salt and Pepper to taste

Shake with ice and strain into old-fashioned glass over ice cubes. A wedge of lime may be added.

BLUE LAGOON

1 oz. Vodka
1 oz. Blue Curaçao
Lemonade

Pour first two ingredients over ice in highball glass. Fill with lemonade. Garnish with a cherry.

BLUE MONDAY COCKTAIL

1½ oz. Vodka
¾ oz. Triple Sec
1 dash Blue Food Coloring

Stir with ice and strain into cocktail glass.

BOLSHOI PUNCH

1 oz. Vodka
2½ oz. Lemon Juice
1 tsp. Powdered Sugar
¼ oz. Rum
¼ oz. Crème de Cassis

Shake and pour over ice in old-fashioned glass.

BOSTON GOLD

1 oz. Vodka
½ oz. Crème de Banana
Orange Juice

Pour vodka and banana liqueur over ice cubes in highball glass. Fill with orange juice and stir.

BULL FROG

1½ oz. Vodka
5 oz. Lemonade

Pour over ice in collins glass and garnish with a slice of lime.

BULL SHOT

1½ oz. Vodka
3 oz. Chilled Beef Bouillon
1 dash Worcestershire Sauce
1 dash Salt
1 dash Pepper

Shake with cracked ice and strain into old-fashioned glass.

CAPE CODDER

1½ oz. Vodka
5 oz. Cranberry Juice

Pour into highball glass over ice. Stir well. Garnish with a wedge of lime.

CAPPUCCINO COCKTAIL

¾ oz. Coffee-flavored Brandy
¾ oz. Vodka
¾ oz. Light Cream

Shake well with ice. Strain into cocktail glass.

CARIBBEAN CRUISE

1 oz.	Vodka
¼ oz.	Light Rum
¼ oz.	Coconut Rum
4 oz.	Pineapple Juice
1 splash	Grenadine

Shake all ingredients except juice with ice and pour into collins glass filled with ice. Fill with pineapple juice. Garnish with a pineapple wedge and a cherry.

CASCO BAY LEMONADE

1½ oz.	Citrus Vodka
4 oz.	Sour Mix
1 splash	Cranberry Juice
1 splash	Lemon-lime Soda

Shake vodka, sour mix, and cranberry juice. Pour into collins glass filled with ice. Add lemon-lime soda. Float a lemon slice on top.

CITRONELLA COOLER

1 oz.	Citrus Vodka
1 dash	Lime Juice
2 oz.	Lemonade
1 oz.	Cranberry Juice

Pour over ice in collins glass. Top with a squeeze of fresh lime.

CLAMATO COCKTAIL

1½ oz.	Vodka
1 oz.	Clam Juice
3 oz.	Tomato Juice

Shake with ice, strain, and serve over ice cubes in old-fashioned glass.

CROCODILE COOLER

1½ oz.	Citrus Vodka
1 oz.	Melon Liqueur
¾ oz.	Triple Sec
2 oz.	Sour Mix
Lemon-lime Soda	

Place first four ingredients in parfait or hurricane glass filled with ice cubes. Fill with soda and stir well. Garnish with a pineapple wedge and a cherry or lime wheel. Serve with a straw.

DESERT SUNRISE

1¼ oz.	Vodka
1½ oz.	Orange Juice
1½ oz.	Pineapple Juice
1 dash	Grenadine

Pour over crushed ice in collins glass. Top with grenadine.

ELECTRIC JAM

1¼ oz.	Vodka
½ oz.	Blue Curaçao
2 oz.	Sour Mix
Lemon-lime Soda	

Pour over ice into collins glass and stir.

FRENCH MARTINI

| 1½ oz. | Vodka |
| 1 oz. | Black Raspberry Liqueur |

Pour over ice in mixing glass. Stir and strain into cocktail glass.

FRISKY WITCH

1 oz.	Vodka
1 oz.	Sambuca

Pour over ice in old-fashioned glass, stir. Garnish with a black licorice stick.

GABLES COLLINS

1½ oz.	Vodka
1 oz.	Crème de Noyaux
1 tbsp.	Lemon Juice
1 tbsp.	Pineapple Juice
Club Soda	

Shake with ice and strain into collins glass over ice cubes. Fill with club soda. Decorate with a slice of lemon and a pineapple chunk.

GENTLE BEN

1 oz.	Vodka
1 oz.	Gin
1 oz.	Tequila
Orange Juice	

Shake all ingredients with ice and pour into collins glass over ice cubes. Fill with orange juice and stir. Decorate with an orange slice and a cherry.

GEORGIA PEACH

1½ oz.	Vodka
½ oz.	Peach Schnapps
1 dash	Grenadine
Lemonade	

Pour first three ingredients into ice-filled collins glass. Fill with lemonade.

GLASS TOWER

1 oz.	Vodka
1 oz.	Peach Schnapps
1 oz.	Rum
1 oz.	Triple Sec
½ oz.	Sambuca
Lemon-lime Soda	

Pour ingredients into ice-filled collins glass. Fill with lemon-lime soda and garnish with an orange slice and a cherry.

GODCHILD

1 oz.	Amaretto
1 oz.	Vodka
1 oz.	Heavy Cream

Shake well with cracked ice. Strain and serve in champagne flute.

GODMOTHER

1½ oz.	Vodka
¾ oz.	Amaretto

Serve in old-fashioned glass over ice.

HANDBALL COOLER

1½ oz.	Vodka
Club Soda	
1 splash	Orange Juice

Pour vodka into highball glass filled with ice. Fill almost to top with club soda. Top with orange juice. Garnish with a lime wedge.

Na Zdorovia
    —a Russian toast

HARVEY WALLBANGER

1 oz.	Vodka
4 oz.	Orange Juice
½ oz.	Galliano

Pour vodka and orange juice into collins glass filled with ice cubes. Stir. Float Galliano on top.

HEADLESS HORSEMAN

2 oz.   Vodka
3 dashes Bitters
Ginger Ale

Pour into collins glass and add several ice cubes. Fill with ginger ale and stir. Decorate with a slice of orange.

HUNTSMAN COCKTAIL

1½ oz.   Vodka
½ oz.   Jamaica Rum
Juice of ½ Lime
Powdered Sugar to taste

Shake with ice and strain into cocktail glass.

ITALIAN SCREWDRIVER

1½ oz.   Citrus Vodka
3 oz.   Orange Juice
2 oz.   Grapefruit Juice
1 splash Ginger Ale

Mix and pour over ice into sugar-rimmed hurricane or parfait glass. Garnish with a lime wheel.

JERICHO'S BREEZE

1 oz.   Vodka
¾ oz.   Blue Curaçao
2½ oz.   Sour Mix
1 splash Lemon-lime Soda
1 splash Orange Juice

Combine ingredients in shaker, shake with ice until frothy. Strain into stemmed goblet. Garnish with a pineapple spear and a cherry.

JUNGLE JUICE

1 oz.   Vodka
1 oz.   Rum
½ oz.   Triple Sec
1 splash Sour Mix
1 oz.   Cranberry Juice
1 oz.   Orange Juice
1 oz.   Pineapple Juice

Pour over ice into collins glass. Garnish with an orange slice and a cherry.

KANGAROO COCKTAIL

1½ oz.   Vodka
¾ oz.   Dry Vermouth

Shake with ice and strain into cocktail glass. Serve with a twist of lemon peel.

KRETCHMA COCKTAIL

1 oz.   Vodka
1 oz.   Crème de Cacao
          (White)
1 tbsp.   Lemon Juice
1 dash   Grenadine

Shake with ice and strain into cocktail glass.

L.A. SUNRISE

1 oz.	Vodka
½ oz.	Crème de Banana
2 oz.	Orange Juice
2 oz.	Pineapple Juice
¼ oz.	Rum

Pour all ingredients except rum into hurricane or parfait glass filled with ice cubes. Float rum on top, garnish with a lime wheel and a cherry.

LONG ISLAND TEA

½ oz.	Vodka
½ oz.	Gin
½ oz.	Light Rum
½ oz.	Tequila
Juice of ½ Lemon	
1 dash	Cola

Combine ingredients and pour over ice in highball glass. Add cola for color. Garnish with slice of lemon.

MADRAS

1½ oz.	Vodka
4 oz.	Cranberry Juice
1 oz.	Orange Juice

Pour into highball glass over ice. Garnish with a wedge of lime.

MOSCOW MULE

1½ oz.	Vodka
Juice of ½ Lime	
Ginger Beer	

Pour vodka and lime juice into coffee mug. Add ice cubes and fill with ginger beer. Drop lime wedge in mug for decoration.

NAKED PRETZEL

¾ oz.	Vodka
1 oz.	Melon Liqueur
½ oz.	Crème de Cassis
2 oz.	Pineapple Juice

Stir and pour over ice in old-fashioned glass.

NIJINSKI BLINI

1 oz.	Vodka
2 oz.	Pureed Peaches
½ oz.	Lemon Juice
1 splash	Peach Schnapps
1 splash	Chilled Champagne

Pour into champagne flute and stir gently.

NINOTCHKA COCKTAIL

1½ oz.	Vodka
½ oz.	Crème de Cacao (White)
1 tbsp.	Lemon Juice

Shake with ice and strain into cocktail glass.

ORANG-A-TANG

1 oz.	Vodka
½ oz.	Triple Sec
1 splash	Grenadine
6 oz.	Orange Juice
1 splash	Sour Mix
1 oz.	151-proof Rum

Lightly blend all ingredients except rum. Strain into large snifter half-filled with ice cubes. Float rum on top. Garnish with tropical fruits.

PAVLOVA SUPREME

2 oz.   Chilled Vodka
½ oz.   Crème de Cassis

Mix in red-wine glass filled with crushed ice.

PINK LEMONADE

1½ oz.   Citrus Vodka
1 splash Triple Sec
1 splash Lime Juice
2 oz.   Sour Mix
2 oz.   Cranberry Juice

Shake and pour into ice-filled collins glass. Garnish with a lemon wheel.

PINK PUSSY CAT

1½ oz.   Vodka
Pineapple or Grapefruit Juice
1 dash   Grenadine

Pour vodka into highball glass filled with ice. Fill with juice. Add grenadine for color and stir.

POLYNESIAN COCKTAIL

1½ oz.   Vodka
¾ oz.   Cherry-flavored
         Brandy
Juice of 1 Lime

Rub rim of cocktail glass with lime and dip into powdered sugar. Shake ingredients with ice and strain into the prepared glass.

PURPLE MASK

1 oz.   Vodka
1 oz.   Grape Juice
½ oz.   Crème de Cacao
         (White)

Shake with ice and strain into cocktail glass.

PURPLE PASSION

1½ oz.   Vodka
3 oz.   Grapefruit Juice
3 oz.   Grape Juice
Sugar

Chill, stir, add sugar to taste, and serve in collins glass.

PURPLE PASSION TEA

¼ oz.   Vodka
¼ oz.   Rum
¼ oz.   Gin
½ oz.   Black Raspberry
         Liqueur
4 oz.   Sour Mix
3 oz.   Lemon-lime Soda

Pour into highball glass with ice, stir. Garnish with a lemon twist.

RED APPLE

1 oz.   100-proof Vodka
1 oz.   Apple Juice
1 tbsp. Lemon Juice
1 tsp.   Grenadine

Shake with ice and strain into cocktail glass.

ROBIN'S NEST

1 oz.   Vodka
1 oz.   Cranberry Juice
½ oz.   Crème de Cacao
         (White)

Shake with ice and strain into cocktail glass.

RUSSIAN BEAR COCKTAIL

1 oz.   Vodka
½ oz.   Crème de Cacao
         (White)
1 tbsp. Light Cream

Stir with ice and strain into cocktail glass.

RUSSIAN COCKTAIL

¾ oz.   Crème de Cacao
         (White)
¾ oz.   Gin
¾ oz.   Vodka

Shake with ice and strain into cocktail glass.

SAM-TINI

1¼ oz. Vodka
1 splash Sambuca
1 dash Blue Curaçao

Pour over ice in mixing glass. Stir and strain into cocktail glass. Garnish with a twist of orange.

SCREWDRIVER

1½ oz. Vodka
5 oz.   Orange Juice

Pour into highball glass over ice cubes. Stir well.

SEABREEZE

1½ oz. Vodka
4 oz.   Cranberry Juice
1 oz.   Grapefruit Juice

Pour into highball glass over ice cubes. Garnish with a wedge of lime.

SHALOM

1½ oz. 100-proof Vodka
1 oz.   Madeira
1 tbsp. Orange Juice

Shake with ice and strain into old-fashioned glass over ice cubes. Add an orange slice.

SIBERIAN SLEIGHRIDE

1¼ oz. Vodka
¾ oz.   Crème de Cacao
         (White)
½ oz.   Crème de Menthe
         (White)
3 oz.   Light Cream

Shake with ice and strain into snifter. Sprinkle with chocolate shavings.

SINO-SOVIET SPLIT

2 oz.   Vodka
1 oz.   Amaretto
Milk or Light Cream

Combine vodka and amaretto over ice in old-fashioned glass. Fill with milk or cream.

SONIC BLASTER

½ oz.   Vodka
½ oz.   Light Rum
½ oz.   Banana Liqueur
1 oz.   Pineapple Juice
1 oz.   Orange Juice
1 oz.   Cranberry Juice

Shake and pour over ice into collins glass. Garnish with orange and lime slices.

SOVIET

1½ oz.   Vodka
½ oz.   Amontillado Sherry
½ oz.   Dry Vermouth

Shake with ice and strain into old-fashioned glass over ice cubes. Add a twist of lemon peel.

SPUTNIK

1¼ oz.   Vodka
1¼ oz.   Peach Schnapps
3 oz.   Orange Juice
3 oz.   Light Cream

Mix all ingredients in shaker. Add ice, shake until frothy. Pour into stemmed goblet and garnish with slice of fresh peach.

STOCKHOLM 75

¾ oz.   Citrus Vodka
¾ oz.   Simple Syrup
¾ oz.   Lemon Juice
3 oz.   Chilled Champagne

Shake vodka, syrup, and juice with ice. Strain into oversized cocktail glass with sugared rim. Fill with champagne.

STUPID CUPID

2 oz.   Citrus Vodka
½ oz.   Sloe Gin
1 splash Sour Mix

Pour into mixing glass with crushed ice. Stir and strain into chilled cocktail glass. Garnish with a cherry.

SURF RIDER

3 oz.   Vodka
1 oz.   Sweet Vermouth
½ cup   Orange Juice
Juice of ½ Lemon
½ tsp.   Grenadine

Shake with ice and strain into cocktail glass. Garnish with an orange slice and a cherry.

SWEET MARIA

1 tbsp.   Light Cream
½ oz.   Amaretto
1 oz.   Vodka

Shake with cracked ice and strain into cocktail glass.

TOP BANANA

1 oz.   Vodka
1 oz.   Crème de Banana
Juice of ½ Orange

Shake with ice and strain into old-fashioned glass over ice cubes.

TROPICAL ICED TEA

½ oz.   Vodka
½ oz.   Rum
½ oz.   Gin
½ oz.   Triple Sec
1 oz.   Sour Mix
1 oz.   Pineapple Juice
1 oz.   Cranberry Juice
½ oz.   Grenadine

Combine all ingredients in mixing glass and pour over ice in collins glass. Garnish with seasonal fruits.

TWISTER

2 oz.   Vodka
Juice of 1/3 Lime
Lemon Soda

Pour vodka and lime into collins glass. Add several ice cubes and drop a lime twist into glass. Fill with lemon soda and stir.

VELVET HAMMER

1 1/2 oz.   Vodka
1 tbsp.   Crème de Cacao
1 tbsp.   Light Cream

Shake with ice and strain into cocktail glass.

VELVET PEACH HAMMER

1 3/4 oz.   Vodka
3/4 oz.   Peach Schnapps
1 splash Sour Mix

Pour vodka and schnapps over ice into old-fashioned glass. Stir and top with sour mix. Garnish with a slice of fresh peach.

VICTORY COLLINS

1 1/2 oz.   Vodka
3 oz.   Unsweetened Grape Juice
3 oz.   Lemon Juice
1 tsp.   Powdered Sugar

Shake with ice and strain into collins glass with ice cubes. Add a slice of orange.

VODKA AND APPLE JUICE

2 oz.   Vodka
Apple Juice

Pour vodka over ice into highball glass. Fill with apple juice and stir.

VODKA COLLINS

Juice of 1/2 Lemon
1 tsp.   Powdered Sugar
2 oz.   Vodka
Club Soda

Shake with ice and strain into collins glass. Add several ice cubes, fill with club soda, and stir. Decorate with slices of lemon and orange and a cherry. Serve with a straw.

VODKA COOLER

1/2 tsp.   Powdered Sugar
2 oz.   Vodka
2 oz.   Club Soda
Club Soda or Ginger Ale

In collins glass stir sugar with 2 oz. club soda. Fill glass with ice and add vodka. Fill with club soda or ginger ale and stir again. Insert a spiral of orange or lemon peel and dangle end over rim of glass.

VODKA DAISY

Juice of ½ Lemon
½ tsp.   Powdered Sugar
1 tsp.   Grenadine
2 oz.   Vodka

Shake with ice and strain into stein or metal cup. Add ice cubes and decorate with fruits.

VODKA GIMLET

1 oz.   Lime Juice
1 tsp.   Powdered Sugar
1½ oz.   Vodka

Shake with ice and strain into cocktail glass.

VODKA GRASSHOPPER

¾ oz.   Vodka
¾ oz.   Crème de Menthe (Green)
¾ oz.   Crème de Cacao (White)

Shake with ice and strain into cocktail glass.

VODKA ON THE ROCKS

2 oz.   Vodka

Put two or three ice cubes in old-fashioned glass and add vodka. Serve with a twist of lemon peel.

VODKA SALTY DOG

1½ oz.   Vodka
5 oz.   Grapefruit Juice
¼ tsp.   Salt

Pour into highball glass over ice cubes. Stir well.

VODKA "7"

2 oz.   Vodka
Juice of ½ Lime
Lemon-lime Soda

Pour lime juice and vodka into collins glass over ice cubes. Drop a twist of lime in glass, fill with lemon-lime soda, and stir.

VODKA SLING

1 tsp.   Powdered Sugar
1 tsp.   Water
Juice of ½ Lemon
2 oz.   Vodka

Dissolve sugar in water and lemon. Add vodka. Pour into old-fashioned glass over ice cubes and stir. Add a twist of orange peel.

VODKA SOUR

Juice of ½ Lemon
½ tsp.   Powdered Sugar
2 oz.   Vodka

Shake with ice and strain into sour glass. Decorate with a half-slice of lemon and a cherry.

VODKA STINGER

1 oz.   Vodka
1 oz.   Crème de Menthe (White)

Shake with ice and strain into cocktail glass.

VODKA AND TONIC

2 oz.   Vodka
Tonic Water

Pour vodka into highball glass over ice. Add tonic and stir. Garnish with a lemon wedge.

WARSAW COCKTAIL

1½ oz.   Vodka
½ oz.   Blackberry-flavored Brandy
½ oz.   Dry Vermouth
1 tsp.   Lemon Juice

Shake with ice and strain into cocktail glass.

WHITE RUSSIAN

1 oz.   Coffee Liqueur
2 oz.   Vodka
Milk or Cream

Pour coffee liqueur and vodka in old-fashioned glass over ice cubes and fill with milk or cream.

Legend has it that celery became known as a substitute for a swizzle stick in the 1960s at The Pump Room in Chicago's Ambassador East Hotel. A celebrity ingenue was served a Bloody Mary without a stirrer, so she took a celery stalk from the relish tray and mixed her drink. The maitre d'hôtel noticed and so the celery stalk swizzler was born!

THREE COINS ON THE TABLE

Lay two coins on a table some distance apart. Lay a third coin *exactly* midway between them. Then ask the others present to estimate which coins are farthest apart. Some will say the middle and the left end; others will say the middle and the right end coin. But then you tell them they are all wrong. The *two end coins* are farthest apart.

A Congressman was once asked by a constituent to explain his attitude toward whiskey.

"If you mean the demon drink that poisons the mind, pollutes the body, desecrates family life, and inflames sinners, then I'm against it," the Congressman said.

"But if you mean the elixir of Christmas cheer, the shield against winter chill, the taxable potion that puts needed funds into public coffers to comfort little crippled children, then I'm for it. This is my position, and I will not compromise."

—*Traditional anecdote,*
original source unknown

Whiskey is distilled from a fermented mash of grain (usually corn, rye, barley, or wheat) and then aged in oak barrels. In the United States, whiskey must be distilled at less than 190 proof (although whiskey with a special designation such as bourbon or rye cannot be distilled above 160 proof) and bottled at no less than 80 proof.

Whiskey, when placed in barrels to age, is a clear liquid. It is during the aging period that whiskey obtains its characteristic amber color, flavor, and aroma.

The major whiskey-producing countries are the United States, Canada, Scotland, and Ireland. Special grain characteristics, recipes, and distillation processes make the whiskey of each country distinct from that of the others.

Bourbon and Tennessee whiskey, as well as Scotch, are described in their own sections in this book. Here we'll cover some of the other commonly known whiskey types.

American whiskeys fall into two major categories—straight whiskey and blended whiskey. Straight whiskey is distilled from a 51 percent base of a single grain and not blended with neutral grain spirits or any other whiskey. Straight whiskeys are aged in charred oak barrels for a minimum of two years. Bourbon, described earlier, is a straight whiskey. Rye whiskey is distilled from a mash of grain containing not less than 51 percent rye. It is much like bourbon in color, but is different in taste and heavier in flavor. Corn whiskey is distilled from a mash of grain containing not less than 80 percent corn and commonly aged in reused charred oak barrels.

Blended whiskey is a blend of one or more straight whiskeys and neutral grain spirits, containing at least 20 percent straight whiskey bottled at no less than 80 proof.

Like Scotch, Canadian whisky is spelled without the "e." Canadian whiskies are blended whiskies, usually distilled from rye, corn, and barley. Produced only in Canada, under government supervision, most Canadian whisky sold in the United States is at least three years old. Canadian whisky, generally lighter-bodied than American whiskey, is usually sold at 80 proof. More than a century of distilling skill has been used to give *Northern Light Canadian Whisky* its smooth, light character. *Canadian LTD,* blended in Canada and bottled domestically, is another popular brand, ranking fifth in the country among popularly priced Canadian whiskies.

Irish whiskey, produced only in Ireland, is, like Scotch, a blended product containing both barley malt whiskies and grain whiskies. Unlike Scotch, however, the malt is dried in coal-fired kilns and the aroma of the fires does not reach the malt. Generally aged for a minimum of five years in used sherry casks, Irish whiskey is lighter in flavor and less smoky than Scotch.

OVER YOUR HEAD

Tell someone that you will cut a regular 2" x 3½" business or calling card so that you will be able to put your head through it. METHOD: Fold the card the long way so that the two wide edges meet. Then cut a series of slits on the folded side about ¼" apart and about ⅛" from the opposite side. Then, reverse the card and cut another series of slits in the opposite direction from the first series and between them ending about ⅛" from the opposite margin. Next, cut along the long fold from A to B as shown. Unfold the card, open it gently, and it will fit over your head with room to spare.

ALGONQUIN

1½ oz. Blended Whiskey
1 oz. Dry Vermouth
1 oz. Pineapple Juice

Shake with ice and strain into cocktail glass.

AQUARIUS

1½ oz. Blended Whiskey
½ oz. Cherry-flavored Brandy
1 oz. Cranberry Juice

Shake with ice and strain into old-fashioned glass over ice.

BLACK HAWK

1¼ oz. Blended Whiskey
1¼ oz. Sloe Gin

Stir with ice and strain into cocktail glass. Serve with a cherry.

BLARNEY STONE COCKTAIL

2 oz. Irish Whiskey
½ tsp. Anisette
½ tsp. Triple Sec
¼ tsp. Maraschino
1 dash Bitters

Shake with ice and strain into cocktail glass. Add a twist of orange peel and an olive.

CABLEGRAM

Juice of ½ Lemon
1 tsp. Powdered Sugar
2 oz. Blended Whiskey
Ginger Ale

Stir with ice cubes in highball glass and fill with ginger ale.

CALIFORNIA LEMONADE

Juice of 1 Lemon
Juice of 1 Lime
1 tbsp. Powdered Sugar
2 oz. Blended Whiskey
¼ tsp. Grenadine
Club Soda

Shake with ice and strain into collins glass over shaved ice. Fill with club soda and decorate with slices of orange and lemon, and a cherry. Serve with straws.

CANADIAN BREEZE

1½ oz. Canadian Whisky
1 tsp. Pineapple Juice
1 tbsp. Lemon Juice
½ tsp. Maraschino

Shake with ice and strain into old-fashioned glass over ice cubes. Garnish with a pineapple wedge or spear and a cherry.

CANADIAN CHERRY

1½ oz. Canadian Whisky
½ oz. Cherry-flavored Brandy
1½ tsps. Lemon Juice
1½ tsps. Orange Juice

Shake all ingredients and strain into old-fashioned glass over ice cubes. Moisten glass rim with cherry brandy.

CANADIAN COCKTAIL
1½ oz. Canadian Whisky
1 dash Bitters
1½ tsps. Triple Sec
1 tsp. Powdered Sugar

Shake with ice and strain into cocktail glass.

CANADIAN PINEAPPLE
1½ oz. Canadian Whisky
1 tsp. Pineapple Juice
1 tbsp. Lemon Juice
½ tsp. Maraschino

Shake with ice and strain into old-fashioned glass over ice cubes. Add a stick of pineapple.

CANAL STREET DAISY
Juice of ¼ Lemon
Juice of ¼ Orange
1 oz. Blended Whiskey
Club Soda

Pour all ingredients into collins glass over ice cubes. Add club soda and an orange slice.

COMMODORE COCKTAIL
Juice of ½ Lime or
        ¼ Lemon
1 tsp. Powdered Sugar
2 dashes Orange Bitters
1½ oz. Blended Whiskey

Shake with ice and strain into cocktail glass.

COWBOY COCKTAIL
1½ oz. Blended Whiskey
1 tbsp. Light Cream

Shake with ice and strain into cocktail glass.

DINAH COCKTAIL
Juice of ¼ Lemon
½ tsp. Powdered Sugar
1½ oz. Blended Whiskey

Shake well with ice and strain into cocktail glass. Serve with a mint leaf.

DOUBLE STANDARD SOUR
Juice of ½ Lemon or
        1 Lime
½ tsp. Powdered Sugar
¾ oz. Blended Whiskey
¾ oz. Gin
½ tsp. Grenadine

Shake with ice and strain into sour glass. Decorate with a half-slice of lemon and a cherry.

EVERYBODY'S IRISH COCKTAIL
1 tsp. Crème de Menthe
        (Green)
1 tsp. Chartreuse (Green)
2 oz. Irish Whiskey

Stir with ice and strain into cocktail glass. Serve with a green olive.

FANCY WHISKEY
2 oz. Blended Whiskey
1 dash Bitters
¼ tsp. Triple Sec
¼ tsp. Powdered Sugar

Shake with ice and strain into cocktail glass. Add a twist of lemon peel.

FOX RIVER COCKTAIL

1 tbsp.	Crème de Cacao (Brown)
2 oz.	Blended Whiskey
4 dashes	Bitters

Stir with ice and strain into cocktail glass.

FRISCO SOUR

Juice of	¼ Lemon
Juice of	½ Lime
½ oz.	Benedictine
2 oz.	Blended Whiskey

Shake with ice and strain into sour glass. Decorate with slices of lemon and lime.

HORSE'S NECK (WITH A KICK)

2 oz.	Blended Whiskey
	Ginger Ale

Peel rind of whole lemon in spiral fashion and put in collins glass with one end hanging over the rim. Fill glass with ice cubes. Add blended whiskey. Then fill with ginger ale and stir well.

IMPERIAL FIZZ

Juice of	½ Lemon
½ oz.	Light Rum
1½ oz.	Blended Whiskey
1 tsp.	Powdered Sugar
	Club Soda

Shake with ice and strain into highball glass. Add two ice cubes. Fill with club soda and stir.

INCIDER COCKTAIL

1½ oz.	Blended Whiskey
	Apple Cider

Mix blended whiskey with a generous helping of apple cider. Serve over ice in old-fashioned glass and garnish with a slice of apple.

IRISH RICKEY

Juice of	½ Lime
1½ oz.	Irish Whiskey
	Club Soda

Pour lime juice and whiskey into highball glass over ice cubes. Fill with club soda and stir. Add a piece of lime.

IRISH SHILLELAGH

Juice of	½ Lemon
1 tsp.	Powdered Sugar
1½ oz.	Irish Whiskey
1 tbsp.	Sloe Gin
1 tbsp.	Light Rum

Shake with ice and strain into punch cup. Decorate with fresh raspberries, strawberries, a cherry, and two peach slices.

IRISH WHISKEY

½ tsp.	Triple Sec
½ tsp.	Anisette
¼ tsp.	Maraschino
1 dash	Bitters
2 oz.	Irish Whiskey

Stir with ice and strain into cocktail glass. Serve with an olive.

IRISH WHISKEY HIGHBALL

2 oz.   Irish Whiskey
Ginger Ale or Club Soda

Pour Irish whiskey into highball glass over ice cubes and fill with ginger ale or club soda. Add a twist of lemon peel, if desired, and stir.

JOHN COLLINS

Juice of ½ Lemon
1 tsp.   Powdered Sugar
2 oz.   Blended Whiskey
Club Soda

Shake with ice and strain into collins glass. Add several cubes of ice, fill with club soda, and stir. Decorate with slices of orange and lemon, and a cherry. Serve with straws.

KING COLE COCKTAIL

1 slice   Orange
1 slice   Pineapple
½ tsp.   Powdered Sugar
2 oz.   Blended Whiskey
2   Ice Cubes

Muddle first three ingredients well in old-fashioned glass and add whiskey and ice cubes. Stir well.

Abraham Lincoln once replied to a Prohibitionist's complaint that General Grant was overly fond of his bottle.
"Find out the brand of whiskey the General uses," Lincoln said. "I would like to furnish the same brand to my other generals."

KLONDIKE COOLER

½ tsp.   Powdered Sugar
2 oz.   Club Soda
2 oz.   Blended Whiskey
Club Soda or Ginger Ale

In collins glass, mix powdered sugar and club soda. Fill glass with ice and add whiskey. Fill with club soda or ginger ale and stir again. Insert a spiral of orange or lemon peel (or both) and dangle end over rim of glass.

LADIES' COCKTAIL

1¾ oz.   Blended Whiskey
½ tsp.   Anisette
2 dashes Bitters

Stir with ice and strain into cocktail glass. Serve with a pineapple stick on top.

LAWHILL COCKTAIL

¾ oz.   Dry Vermouth
1½ oz.   Blended Whiskey
¼ tsp.   Anisette
¼ tsp.   Maraschino
1 dash   Bitters

Stir with ice and strain into cocktail glass.

LINSTEAD COCKTAIL

1 oz.   Blended Whiskey
1 oz.   Pineapple Juice
½ tsp.   Powdered Sugar
¼ tsp.   Anisette
¼ tsp.   Lemon Juice

Shake with ice and strain into cocktail glass.

MANHASSET

1½ oz. Blended Whiskey
1½ tsp. Dry Vermouth
1½ tsp. Sweet Vermouth
1 tbsp. Lemon Juice

Shake with ice and strain
into cocktail glass.

MANHATTAN

¾ oz. Sweet Vermouth
1½ oz. Blended Whiskey

Stir with ice and strain into
cocktail glass. Serve with a
cherry.

MANHATTAN (DRY)

¾ oz. Dry Vermouth
1½ oz. Blended Whiskey

Stir with ice and strain into
cocktail glass. Serve with an
olive.

MILK PUNCH

1 tsp. Powdered Sugar
2 oz. Blended Whiskey
1 cup Milk

Shake with ice and strain
into collins glass. Sprinkle
nutmeg on top.

MONTANA STUMP PULLER*

2 oz. Canadian Whisky
1 oz. Crème de Menthe
 (White)

Stir with ice and strain into
shot glass.

*Ronald Sperry, Winner, Boston
"Shake Up the World" Contest

NEW YORK COCKTAIL

Juice of 1 Lime or
 ½ Lemon
1 tsp. Powdered Sugar
1½ oz. Blended Whiskey
½ tsp. Grenadine

Shake with ice and strain
into cocktail glass. Add a
twist of lemon peel.

NEW YORK SOUR

Juice of ½ Lemon
1 tsp. Powdered Sugar
2 oz. Blended Whiskey
Claret

Shake first three ingredients
with ice and strain into sour
glass, leaving about half-inch
on which to float claret.
Decorate with a half-slice of
lemon and a cherry.

OLD-FASHIONED

1 cube Sugar
1 dash Bitters
1 tsp. Water
2 oz. Blended Whiskey

In old-fashioned glass, put
sugar cube, bitters, and
water and muddle well. Add
whiskey, stir. Add a twist of
lemon peel and ice cubes.
Decorate with slices of
orange and lemon and a
cherry. Serve with a swizzle
stick.

OLD PAL COCKTAIL

½ oz. Grenadine
½ oz. Sweet Vermouth
1¼ oz. Blended Whiskey

Stir with ice and strain into
cocktail glass.

OPENING COCKTAIL
▽ ½ oz.   Grenadine
½ oz.   Sweet Vermouth
1½ oz.   Blended Whiskey

Stir with ice and strain into cocktail glass.

ORIENTAL COCKTAIL
▽ 1 oz.   Blended Whiskey
½ oz.   Sweet Vermouth
½ oz.   Triple Sec
Juice of ½ Lime

Shake with ice and strain into cocktail glass.

PADDY COCKTAIL
▽ 1½ oz.   Irish Whiskey
1½ oz.   Sweet Vermouth
1 dash   Bitters

Stir with ice and strain into cocktail glass.

PALMER COCKTAIL
▽ 2 oz.   Blended Whiskey
1 dash   Bitters
½ tsp.   Lemon Juice

Stir with ice and strain into cocktail glass.

PREAKNESS COCKTAIL
▽ ¾ oz.   Sweet Vermouth
1½ oz.   Blended Whiskey
1 dash   Bitters
½ tsp.   Benedictine

Stir with ice and strain into cocktail glass. Add a twist of lemon peel.

Slainte
   —an Irish toast

QUEBEC
▽ 1½ oz.   Canadian Whisky
½ oz.   Dry Vermouth
1½ tsps.   Amer Picon
1½ tsps.   Maraschino

Shake with ice and strain into cocktail glass rimmed with sugar.

RORY O'MORE
▽ ¾ oz.   Sweet Vermouth
1½ oz.   Irish Whiskey
1 dash   Orange Bitters

Stir with ice and strain into cocktail glass.

RYE HIGHBALL
▯ 2 oz.   Rye Whiskey
Ginger Ale or Club Soda

Pour whiskey over ice into highball glass. Fill with ginger ale or club soda and ice cubes. Add a twist of lemon peel and stir.

RYE WHISKEY COCKTAIL
▽ 1 dash   Bitters
1 tsp.   Powdered Sugar
2 oz.   Rye Whiskey

Shake with ice and strain into cocktail glass. Serve with a cherry.

SEABOARD
▯ 1 oz.   Blended Whiskey
1 oz.   Gin
1 tbsp.   Lemon Juice
1 tsp.   Powdered Sugar

Shake with ice and strain into old-fashioned glass over ice cubes. Decorate with mint leaves.

SHAMROCK

1½ oz.	Irish Whiskey
½ oz.	Dry Vermouth
1 tsp.	Crème de Menthe (Green)

Stir with ice and strain into cocktail glass. Serve with an olive.

SWISS FAMILY COCKTAIL

½ tsp.	Anisette
2 dashes	Bitters
¾ oz.	Dry Vermouth
1½ oz.	Blended Whiskey

Stir with ice and strain into cocktail glass.

T-BIRD

1⅛ oz.	Canadian Whisky
¾ oz.	Amaretto
2 oz.	Pineapple Juice
1 oz.	Orange Juice
2 dashes	Grenadine

Shake with ice and strain into highball glass filled with ice. Garnish with an orange slice and a cherry. Serve with a straw.

T.N.T. NO. 1

| 1½ oz. | Blended Whiskey |
| 1½ oz. | Anisette |

Shake with ice and strain into cocktail glass.

TIPPERARY COCKTAIL

¾ oz.	Irish Whiskey
¾ oz.	Chartreuse (Green)
¾ oz.	Sweet Vermouth

Stir with ice and strain into cocktail glass.

TWIN HILLS

1½ oz.	Blended Whiskey
2 tsps.	Benedictine
1½ tsps.	Lemon Juice
1½ tsps.	Lime Juice
1 tsp.	Sugar

Shake with ice and strain into sour glass. Add a slice of lime and a slice of lemon.

WARD EIGHT

Juice of ½ Lemon	
1 tsp.	Powdered Sugar
1 tsp.	Grenadine
2 oz.	Blended Whiskey

Shake with ice and strain into red-wine glass filled with cracked ice. Add slices of orange, lemon, and a cherry. Serve with straws.

WHISKEY COBBLER

1 tsp.	Powdered Sugar
2 oz.	Club Soda
2 oz.	Blended Whiskey

Dissolve sugar in club soda in red-wine glass. Fill with shaved ice and add whiskey. Stir and decorate with seasonal fruit. Serve with a straw.

WHISKEY COCKTAIL

1 dash	Bitters
1 tsp.	Simple Syrup
2 oz.	Blended Whiskey

Stir with ice and strain into cocktail glass. Serve with a cherry.

WHISKEY COLLINS

Juice of ½ Lemon
1 tsp.   Powdered Sugar
2 oz.   Blended Whiskey
Club Soda

Shake with ice and strain into collins glass. Add several ice cubes, fill with club soda, and stir. Decorate with slices of lemon and orange and a cherry. Serve with straw.

WHISKEY DAISY

Juice of ½ Lemon
½ tsp.   Powdered Sugar
1 tsp.   Grenadine
2 oz.   Blended Whiskey

Shake with ice and strain into beer mug or metal cup. Add one ice cube and decorate with fruit.

WHISKEY FIX

Juice of ½ Lemon
1 tsp.   Powdered Sugar
2½ oz.   Blended Whiskey

Shake juice and sugar with ice and strain into highball glass. Fill glass with ice and whiskey. Stir and add a slice of lemon. Serve with straws.

WHISKEY HIGHBALL

2 oz.   Blended Whiskey
Ginger Ale or Club Soda

Pour whiskey over ice into highball glass. Fill with ginger ale or club soda. Add a twist of lemon peel and stir.

WHISKEY MILK PUNCH

1 tsp.   Powdered Sugar
2 oz.   Blended Whiskey
8 oz.   Milk

Shake with ice and strain into collins glass, and sprinkle nutmeg on top.

WHISKEY ORANGE

Juice of ½ Orange
1 tsp.   Powdered Sugar
½ tsp.   Anisette
1½ oz.   Blended Whiskey

Shake with ice and strain into highball glass over ice cubes. Decorate with slices of orange and lemon.

WHISKEY RICKEY

Juice of ½ Lime
1½ oz.   Blended Whiskey
Club Soda

Pour into highball glass over ice cubes and fill with club soda. Stir. Drop the lime rind into glass.

WHISKEY SANGAREE

½ tsp.   Powdered Sugar
1 tsp.   Water
2 oz.   Blended Whiskey
1 splash Club Soda
1 tbsp.   Port

Dissolve sugar in water in old-fashioned glass. Add whiskey, ice cubes, and club soda. Stir and float port on top. Sprinkle lightly with nutmeg.

WHISKEY SLING

1 tsp.   Powdered Sugar
1 tsp.   Water
Juice of ½ Lemon
2 oz.   Blended Whiskey

In old-fashioned glass, dissolve sugar in water and lemon juice. Add ice cubes and whiskey. Stir and add a twist of lemon peel.

WHISKEY SMASH

1 cube   Sugar
1 oz.   Club Soda
4 sprigs   Mint
2 oz.   Blended Whiskey

Muddle sugar with club soda and mint in old-fashioned glass. Add whiskey, then ice cubes. Stir and decorate with a slice of orange and a cherry. Add a twist of lemon peel.

WHISKEY SOUR

Juice of ½ Lemon
½ tsp.   Powdered Sugar
2 oz.   Blended Whiskey

Shake with ice and strain into sour glass. Decorate with a half-slice of lemon and a cherry.

WHISKEY SQUIRT

1½ oz.   Blended Whiskey
1 tbsp.   Powdered Sugar
1 tbsp.   Grenadine
Club Soda

Shake with ice and strain into highball glass. Fill with club soda and ice cubes. Decorate with cubes of pineapple and strawberries.

WHISKEY SWIZZLE

Juice of 1 Lime
1 tsp.   Powdered Sugar
2 oz.   Club Soda
2 dashes Bitters
2 oz.   Blended Whiskey

Put lime juice, sugar, and club soda into collins glass. Fill glass with ice and stir. Add bitters and whiskey. Fill with club soda and serve with a swizzle stick.

WHISPERS-OF-THE-FROST COCKTAIL

¾ oz.   Blended Whiskey
¾ oz.   Cream Sherry
¾ oz.   Port
1 tsp.   Powdered Sugar

Stir with ice and strain into cocktail glass. Serve with slices of lemon and orange.

WHITE PLUSH

2 oz.   Blended Whiskey
1 cup   Milk
1 tsp.   Powdered Sugar

Shake with ice and strain into collins glass.

The Prohibition era gave rise to a number of colloquial expressions. The practice of smuggling bottles of whiskey in one's boots led to the word *bootlegger* entering the English language. Because clandestine whiskey-makers operated their stills at night, their product became known as "moonshine." The lack of charred oak barrels also gave their product the name "white lightning."

Cordials and Liqueurs

What puts the fuzz in a Fuzzy Navel? What turns a Grasshopper green? What makes a Pink Squirrel nutty? And what makes a Banshee wail? Give up? Surprise—it's liqueurs!

In European countries, liqueurs have long been savored as after-dinner drinks, bringing a delightful end to a leisurely repast. In the United States, perhaps because Americans seem to do everything at a breakneck pace, lingering over a liqueur served straight up is not quite the tradition it is in Europe. Americans have always tended to enjoy liqueurs mixed with other ingredients, evidenced by the popularity of classic cocktails such as the Grasshopper and the Pink Squirrel. Hot drinks also often get their kick from liqueurs—you'll find a whole section of tummy-warmers in a separate chapter!

Americans inevitably put their own spin on things and are quick to launch or latch on to trends. Schnapps, derived from the German word meaning gulp or mouthful, took the country by storm in the mid-1980s and was produced in virtually every flavor you could imagine—and some you'd never think of! The Fuzzy Navel, born during the schnapps phenomenon, remains an often-requested drink.

Today, while still sipped and savored on their own, liqueurs are most often used in a variety of frozen and ice cream-based drinks (fear not, there's a section devoted to these, too) and the newest sensation to rock the nation—shooters. (Do we have recipes? You bet—in another section of course!) Romantic occasions call for the eponymous amaretto of love— *Amaretto di Amore*—the ideal spirit of sharing. Feeling hospitable? Warm your guests' spirit with the delicate Scottish cream flavor of *Heather Cream*. This specially blended cream cordial features a high-quality, matured, single malt Scotch combined with fresh, rich dairy cream. Want to experiment with shooters or tropical drinks? You'll find virtually every flavor of liqueur and schnapps in the venerable *Mr. Boston* line.

Most people use the terms *cordial* and *liqueur* interchangeably. Though both describe liquors made by combining or redistilling spirits with one or more aromatic flavorings and are usually highly sweetened, there are subtle differences. Liqueurs are flavored with flowers, herbs, seeds, roots, plants, barks, or any number of species, while cordials are generally prepared with fruit pulp or juices. *Sabroso Coffee Liqueur* is well known for its rich coffee flavor and aroma. This versatile liqueur can be enjoyed in coffee, straight up, on the rocks, and mixed with cream or other mixers.

Regardless of what you call them, however, liqueurs date back centuries and were originally formulated as medicinal elixirs to "cure" a variety of ills. Made in every country of the world, nearly all liqueurs are quite sweet, with a highly concentrated, dessert-like flavor. Several, made from closely guarded secret recipes and processes, are known throughout the world by their proprietary brand names.

Here are brief descriptions of the most well-known liqueurs. In addition to these, there are numerous other flavored liqueurs, including coffee, hazelnut, melon, strawberry, and black raspberry.

Amaretto	Made from apricot pits, with an almond flavor
Amer Picon	Bitter, orange-flavored French aperitif cordial made from quinine and spices
Anisette or Anis	Flavored with anise seed, producing a licorice flavor
Benedictine	Secret herb formula first produced by Benedictine monks over 400 years ago
Chartreuse	Yellow and green herb liqueurs developed by Carthusian monks
Cointreau	Made from brandy and orange peel; similar to curaçao and triple sec, but sweeter

Peppermint Twist, Twin Peach, Chilled Butterscotch Schnapps

Crème de Banana	Made with artificial banana flavoring
Crème de Cacao	Flavored with cacao and vanilla beans
Crème de Cassis	Flavored with black currants
Crème de Menthe	Flavored with mint; in both green and white colors
Crème de Noyeaux	Flavored with apricot and peach pits and almonds
Curaçao	Orange-flavored, made from dried orange peel; in both orange and blue colors
Galliano	Flavored with herbs, roots, and spices
Kümmel	Flavored with caraway, anise seed, and other herb flavors
Malibu	Rum-based, flavored with coconut
Mandarine Napoléon	Rich and aromatic, flavored with mandarine orange peel
Maraschino	Made from cherries grown in Dalmatia, in the former Yugoslavia
Rock and Rye	Sweetened rye whiskey, sometimes bottled with rock candy or fruit slices
Sambuca	Licorice-flavored, made from white flowers of elderberry bush; predominantly produced in Italy
Sloe Gin	Made from sloe berries produced by the blackthorn bush
Southern Comfort	Blend of bourbon and peach liqueur
Strega	Italian liqueur, made from herbs, spices, and plants
Triple Sec	Highly refined form of curaçao

ABSINTHE SPECIAL COCKTAIL

1½ oz.   Anisette
1 oz.   Water
¼ tsp.   Powdered Sugar
1 dash   Orange Bitters

Shake with ice and strain into cocktail glass.

AMARETTO AND CREAM

1½ oz.   Amaretto
1½ oz.   Light Cream

Shake well with cracked ice. Strain and serve in cocktail glass.

AMARETTO MIST

1½ oz.   Amaretto

Serve in old-fashioned glass over crushed ice with a twist of lemon or a wedge of lime, if desired.

AMARETTO ROSE

1½ oz.   Amaretto
½ oz.   Rose's Lime Juice
Club Soda

Pour amaretto and lime juice over ice in collins glass and fill with club soda.

AMARETTO SOUR

1½ oz.   Amaretto
¾ oz.   Lemon Juice

Shake well with cracked ice and strain into sour glass. Garnish with a slice of orange.

AMARETTO STINGER

1½ oz.   Amaretto
¾ oz.   Crème de Menthe (White)

Shake with ice and strain into cocktail glass.

AMBER AMOUR

1½ oz.   Amaretto
½ oz.   Sour Mix
Club Soda

Pour over ice into collins glass. Top with club soda and stir. Garnish with a cherry.

AMORE-ADE

1¼ oz.   Amaretto
¾ oz.   Triple Sec
3 oz.   Club Soda

Combine ingredients in oversized red-wine glass. Add ice and garnish with a lemon wedge.

APPLE PIE NO. 2

3 oz.   Apple Schnapps
1 splash   Cinnamon Schnapps

Pour into old-fashioned glass over ice and garnish with an apple slice and a sprinkle of cinnamon.

ARISE MY LOVE

1 tsp.   Crème de Menthe (Green)
Chilled Champagne

Put crème de menthe into champagne flute. Fill with champagne.

BANSHEE

1 oz.	Crème de Banana
½ oz.	Crème de Cacao (White)
½ oz.	Light Cream

Shake with cracked ice and strain into cocktail glass.

BLACKJACK

1 oz.	Kirschwasser
½ oz.	Brandy
1 oz.	Coffee

Shake with cracked ice and strain into old-fashioned glass over ice cubes.

BLACKTHORN

| 1½ oz. | Sloe Gin |
| 1 oz. | Sweet Vermouth |

Stir with ice and strain into cocktail glass. Add a twist of lemon peel.

BLANCHE

1 oz.	Anisette
1 oz.	Triple Sec
½ oz.	Curaçao (White)

Shake with cracked ice and strain into cocktail glass.

BOCCIE BALL

1½ oz.	Amaretto
1½ oz.	Orange Juice
2 oz.	Club Soda

Serve in highball glass over ice.

Alla Tua Salute
—an Italian toast

BOSTON ICED COFFEE*

6 oz.	Coffee, cooled
1 oz.	Crème de Menthe (White)
1 oz.	Crème de Cacao (White)
1 oz.	Brandy

Pour over ice in highball glass, stir. Garnish with a lemon twist.

*Dorothy Colquhoun, Winner, Boston "Shake Up the World" Contest

BURNING SUN

| 1½ oz. | Strawberry Schnapps |
| 4 oz. | Pineapple Juice |

Pour over ice in highball glass, stir. Garnish with a fresh strawberry.

BUSHWACKER

½ oz.	Coffee Liqueur
½ oz.	Amaretto
½ oz.	Light Rum
½ oz.	Irish Cream Liqueur
2 oz.	Light Cream

Blend and pour over ice in old-fashioned glass.

CAFÉ CABANA

| 1 oz. | Coffee Liqueur |
| 3 oz. | Club Soda |

Pour into collins glass over ice. Stir and garnish with a lime wedge.

CHOCOLATE-COVERED STRAWBERRY*

1 oz.	Strawberry Schnapps
¼ oz.	Crème de Cacao (White)
½ oz.	Cream

Stir with ice and serve over ice in red-wine glass. Garnish with a fresh strawberry.

Roberta Lewis, Winner, Boston "Shake Up the World" Contest

CRÈME DE MENTHE FRAPPÉ

Fill cocktail glass up to brim with shaved ice. Add Crème de Menthe (Green). Serve with two short straws.

DEPTH CHARGE

Shot of any flavor of schnapps in a glass of beer.

DIANA COCKTAIL

Crème de Menthe (White)
Brandy

Fill cocktail glass with ice, then fill ¼ full with crème de menthe and float brandy on top.

DUCHESS

1½ oz.	Anisette
½ oz.	Dry Vermouth
½ oz.	Sweet Vermouth

Shake with ice and strain into cocktail glass.

FERRARI

1 oz.	Amaretto
2 oz.	Dry Vermouth

Mix in old-fashioned glass with ice cubes and add a lemon twist.

FRENCH CONNECTION

1½ oz.	Cognac
¼ oz.	Amaretto

Serve in old-fashioned glass over ice.

FRENCH FANTASY

1 oz.	Black Raspberry Liqueur
1 oz.	Mandarine Napoléon
2 oz.	Cranberry Juice
2 oz.	Orange Juice

Pour over ice into highball glass and stir. Garnish with an orange slice and a cherry.

FUZZY NAVEL

3 oz.	48-proof Peach Schnapps
3 oz.	Orange Juice

Combine orange juice and schnapps and pour over ice in highball glass. Garnish with an orange slice.

GOLDEN CADILLAC

1 oz.	Galliano
2 oz.	Crème de Cacao (White)
1 oz.	Light Cream

Combine with a half-cup of crushed ice in blender at low speed for ten seconds. Strain into champagne flute.

GOLDEN DREAM

1 tbsp.	Orange Juice
½ oz.	Triple Sec
1 oz.	Galliano
1 tbsp.	Light Cream

Shake with ice and strain into cocktail glass.

GOOBER

1½ oz.	Vodka
1½ oz.	Black Raspberry Liqueur
1½ oz.	Melon Liqueur
1 oz.	Triple Sec
1 oz.	Grenadine
3 oz.	Pineapple Juice
4 oz.	Orange Juice

Shake with ice and strain into collins glass filled with ice. Garnish with an orange slice and a cherry. Serve with a straw.

GRASSHOPPER

¾ oz.	Crème de Menthe (Green)
¾ oz.	Crème de Cacao (White)
¾ oz.	Light Cream

Shake with ice and strain into cocktail glass.

The Arabs produced a cosmetic through distillation, which harem women used as eye makeup. This was called *al-kohl* from which the word alcohol is derived.

HEAT WAVE

1¼ oz.	Coconut Rum
½ oz.	Peach Schnapps
3 oz.	Pineapple Juice
3 oz.	Orange Juice
½ oz.	Grenadine

Pour all ingredients except grenadine over ice in hurricane or parfait glass. Top with grenadine and garnish with a fresh peach slice.

ITALIAN SOMBRERO

1½ oz.	Amaretto
3 oz.	Light Cream

Put ingredients in blender or shake well. Serve over ice cubes or straight up in champagne flute.

ITALIAN SURFER

1 oz.	Amaretto
1 oz.	Brandy
	Pineapple Juice

Fill a collins glass with ice. Add amaretto and brandy. Fill with pineapple juice. Garnish with a pineapple spear and a cherry.

JOHNNIE COCKTAIL

¾ oz.	Triple Sec
1½ oz.	Sloe Gin
1 tsp.	Anisette

Shake with ice and strain into cocktail glass.

LOVER'S KISS

½ oz.	Amaretto
⅓ oz.	Cherry Brandy
½ oz.	Crème de Cacao (Brown)
1 oz.	Cream

Shake with ice and strain into parfait glass. Top with whipped cream. Sprinkle with chocolate shavings and top with a cherry.

LSC RUGBY ELECTRIC GELATIN*

1 box	Lemon-lime Gelatin
2 cups	Peppermint Schnapps

Mix ingredients together, pour into collins glasses and chill for 1½ hours. Serve with a straw. Makes 4–5 servings.

Dorrie Lynn Faulkner, Winner, Boston "Shake Up the World" Contest

MARMALADE

1½ oz.	Curaçao
Tonic Water	

Pour curaçao over ice in highball glass and fill with tonic water. Garnish with an orange slice.

McCLELLAND COCKTAIL

¾ oz.	Triple Sec
1½ oz.	Sloe Gin
1 dash	Orange Bitters

Shake with ice and strain into cocktail glass.

MELON COOLER

1 oz.	Melon Liqueur
½ oz.	Peach Schnapps
½ oz.	Raspberry Schnapps
2 oz.	Pineapple Juice

Shake with cracked ice and pour into margarita or cocktail glass. Garnish with a lime wheel and a cherry.

MINT HIGHBALL

2 oz.	Crème de Menthe (Green)
Ginger Ale or Club Soda	

Pour into highball glass over ice cubes and fill with ginger ale or club soda. Add a twist of lemon peel, if desired, and stir.

MINT ON ROCKS

2 oz.	Crème de Menthe (Green)

Pour over ice cubes in old-fashioned glass.

MOULIN ROUGE

1½ oz.	Sloe Gin
¾ oz.	Sweet Vermouth
1 dash	Bitters

Stir with ice and strain into cocktail glass.

PANAMA COCKTAIL

1 oz.	Crème de Cacao (White)
1 oz.	Light Cream
1 oz.	Brandy

Shake with ice and strain into cocktail glass.

PEACH MELBA

1 oz.   Peach Schnapps
½ oz.   Black Raspberry
         Liqueur
3 oz.   Cream

Shake with ice and pour into old-fashioned glass. Garnish with a peach slice. Serve with a short straw.

PEPPERMINT ICEBERG

2 oz.   Peppermint
         Schnapps

Pour over ice cubes into old-fashioned glass. Stir and serve with a peppermint candy swizzle stick.

PEPPERMINT STICK

1 oz.   Peppermint
         Schnapps
1½ oz.   Crème de Cacao
         (White)
1 oz.   Light Cream

Shake with ice and strain into champagne flute.

PEPPERMINT TWIST

1½ oz.   Peppermint
         Schnapps
½ oz.   Crème de Cacao
         (White)
3 scoops Vanilla Ice Cream

Blend and pour into large parfait glass. Garnish with a mint sprig and a peppermint candy stick. Serve with a straw.

PINK SQUIRREL

1 oz.   Crème de Noyaux
1 tbsp. Crème de Cacao
         (White)
1 tbsp. Light Cream

Shake with ice and strain into cocktail glass.

PORT AND STARBOARD

1 tbsp. Grenadine
½ oz.   Crème de Menthe
         (Green)

Pour carefully into pousse café glass, so that crème de menthe floats on grenadine.

POUSSE CAFÉ

Equal parts:
Grenadine
Chartreuse (Yellow)
Crème de Cassis
Crème de Menthe (White)
Chartreuse (Green)
Brandy

Pour carefully, in order given, into pousse café glass so that each ingredient floats on preceding one.

QUAALUDE

1 oz.   Vodka
1 oz.   Hazelnut Liqueur
1 oz.   Coffee Liqueur
1 splash Milk

Pour over ice in old-fashioned glass.

RASPBERRY ROMANCE

¾ oz.   Coffee Liqueur
¾ oz.   Black Raspberry
         Liqueur
1¼ oz.   Irish Cream
         Liqueur
Club Soda

Pour liqueurs over ice in
parfait glass. Fill with club
soda and stir.

RITZ FIZZ

Chilled Champagne
1 dash   Lemon Juice
1 dash   Blue Curaçao
1 dash   Amaretto

Fill flute with champagne.
Add remaining ingredients
and stir. Garnish with a
lemon twist.

ROAD RUNNER

1 oz.   Vodka
½ oz.   Amaretto
½ oz.   Coconut Cream

Combine in blender with
half-scoop of crushed ice for
15 seconds. Rim edge of a
chilled champagne flute with
a slice of orange. Dip rim in
a sugar and nutmeg mixture.
Pour cocktail into the
prepared glass. Top with a
dash of nutmeg.

ROCKY MOUNTAIN COOLER

1½ oz.   Peach Schnapps
4 oz.   Pineapple Juice
2 oz.   Lemon-lime Soda

Pour over ice in collins glass
and stir.

ST. PATRICK'S DAY

¾ oz.   Crème de Menthe
         (Green)
¾ oz.   Chartreuse (Green)
¾ oz.   Irish Whiskey
1 dash   Bitters

Stir with ice and strain into
cocktail glass.

SAMBUCA STRAIGHT

2 oz.   Sambuca
3   Coffee Beans

Pour sambuca into snifter
and float coffee beans on
top. According to Italian
tradition, an odd number of
beans shows the guest is
welcome.

SAN FRANCISCO COCKTAIL

¾ oz.   Sloe Gin
¾ oz.   Sweet Vermouth
¾ oz.   Dry Vermouth
1 dash   Bitters
1 dash   Orange Bitters

Shake with ice and strain
into cocktail glass. Serve
with a cherry.

SANTINI'S POUSSE CAFÉ

½ oz.   Brandy
1 tbsp. Maraschino
½ oz.   Triple Sec
½ oz.   Rum

Pour in order given into
pousse café glass.

SHEER ELEGANCE

1½ oz.   Amaretto
1½ oz.   Black Raspberry
           Liqueur
½ oz.   Vodka

Shake with ice and strain
into cocktail glass.

SLOEBERRY COCKTAIL

1 dash   Bitters
2 oz.   Sloe Gin

Stir with ice and strain into
cocktail glass.

SLOE DRIVER

1½ oz.   Sloe gin
5 oz.   Orange Juice

Pour ingredients over ice
into highball glass and stir.

SLOE GIN COCKTAIL

2 oz.   Sloe Gin
1 dash   Orange Bitters
¼ tsp.   Dry Vermouth

Stir with ice and strain into
cocktail glass.

SLOE GIN COLLINS

Juice of ½ Lemon
2 oz.   Sloe Gin
Club Soda

Shake lemon juice and sloe
gin with ice and strain into
collins glass. Add several ice
cubes, fill with club soda,
and stir. Decorate with slices
of lemon and orange and a
cherry. Serve with straws.

SLOE GIN FIZZ

Juice of ½ Lemon
1 tsp.   Powdered Sugar
2 oz.   Sloe Gin
Club Soda

Shake with ice and strain
into highball glass with two
ice cubes. Fill with club soda
and stir. Decorate with a
slice of lemon.

SLOE GIN RICKEY

Juice of ½ Lime
2 oz.   Sloe Gin
Club Soda

Pour into highball glass over
ice cubes. Stir. Drop a lime
rind into glass.

SLOE VERMOUTH

1 oz.   Sloe Gin
1 oz.   Dry Vermouth
1 tbsp. Lemon Juice

Shake with ice and strain
into cocktail glass.

SOMETHING DIFFERENT

1 oz.   Peach Schnapps
1 oz.   Amaretto
2 oz.   Pineapple Juice
2 oz.   Cranberry Juice

Shake with ice and pour into
highball glass filled with ice
cubes.

SPLASH & CRASH

2 oz.   Amaretto
6 oz.   Cranberry Juice
2 oz.   Orange Juice
½ oz.   151-proof Rum

Pour amaretto and juices over ice in collins glass. Top with rum and garnish with a lime wheel.

STRAWBERRY FIELDS FOREVER

2 oz.   Strawberry
          Schnapps
½ oz.   Brandy
Club Soda

Pour over ice in highball glass. Fill with club soda. Garnish with a fresh strawberry.

STRAWBERRY SUNRISE

2 oz.   Strawberry
          Schnapps
½ oz.   Grenadine
Orange Juice

Pour over ice in highball glass. Fill with orange juice. Garnish with a fresh strawberry.

SUN KISS

2 oz.   Amaretto
4 oz.   Orange Juice

Combine amaretto and orange juice in collins glass filled with ice. Garnish with a lime wedge.

THUNDER CLOUD

½ oz.   Crème de
          Noyaux
½ oz.   Blue Curaçao
½ oz.   Amaretto
¾ oz.   Vodka
2 oz.   Sour Mix
1 oz.   Lemon-lime Soda

Fill hurricane or parfait glass with ice. Layer ingredients in order given. Whirl gently with a large straw.

TIKKI DREAM

¾ oz.   Melon Liqueur
4¼ oz.   Cranberry Juice

Pour over ice into sugar-rimmed highball glass. Garnish with a wedge of watermelon.

TOASTED ALMOND

1½ oz.   Coffee Liqueur
1 oz.   Amaretto
1½ oz.   Cream or Milk

Add all ingredients over ice in old-fashioned glass.

TROPICAL COCKTAIL

¾ oz.   Crème de Cacao
          (White)
¾ oz.   Maraschino
¾ oz.   Dry Vermouth
1 dash   Bitters

Stir with ice and strain into cocktail glass.

TWIN PEACH

2 oz.   Peach Schnapps
Cranberry Juice

Fill highball glass with ice.
Add schnapps, fill with
cranberry juice, and stir.
Garnish with an orange or
peach slice.

In the late 1500s, Queen Eliza-
beth of England was said to have
substituted a strong ale for orange juice as her breakfast beverage of choice.

WATERMELON

1 oz.   Strawberry Liqueur
1 oz.   Vodka
1 oz.   Sour Mix
1 oz.   Orange Juice

Pour over ice in collins glass.
Garnish with an orange slice
and serve with a straw.

YELLOW PARROT COCKTAIL

¾ oz.   Anisette
¾ oz.   Chartreuse (Yellow)
¾ oz.   Apricot-flavored
            Brandy

Shake with ice and strain
into cocktail glass.

ZERO MIST

2 oz.   Crème de Menthe
1 oz.   Water

For each serving, chill
liqueur and water in freezer
compartment of refrigerator
for 2 hours or longer (does
not have to be frozen solid).
Serve in cocktail glasses.

SIX OF A KIND MAKE FOUR

Arrange six coins on a table as in fig. 1. Ask someone to rearrange them so that they form two straight rows of four coins each. When he says, "I give up" get ready to run before placing coin 4 on coin 2 as in fig. 2.

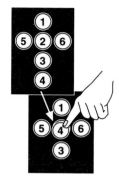

Shooters

"**D**own the hatch!" Another B-52 bites the dust!
"Bottoms up!" Anyone for a Sex on the Beach?
"Bonzai!" It's a Kamikaze!

Just *what* is going on here? Welcome to the wacky world of shooters—the hottest craze to hit the bar scene in years.

Gone are the days when a shot was two ounces of straight whiskey knocked back in a single swallow. (Remember the saloon scenes in those dusty old Westerns?) Shooters, slammers, and tooters, tagged with usually fanciful names, are concocted with virtually any spirit and mixer handy in a well-stocked bar.

The raging popularity of shooters is attributable partly to the fact that many are fairly low in alcohol content, appealing to the lighter tastes of today's young adults. Frequently made with several juices, as well as lower-proof liqueurs, the small size of the shooter limits the amount of spirit contained in a single drink. Some, like the Rattlesnake, are skillfully layered works of art, similar to a pousse café. Others, like the Bloody Caesar, incorporate surprising ingredients such as clams or oysters.

Mostly, however, shooters are fun. As colorful and creative as their sometimes bizarre names, shooters not only taste good, but have become integral to unique and entertaining promotions in bars around the country, many of which have developed signature drinks and themed libations for special occasions. These are often made up in large batches, rather than by individual servings.

Another appealing feature of this latest drink sensation is the often innovative glassware in which they're served, such as shot glasses ranging in shape from cowboy boots to animals,

173

like bears and hogs. There are even shot glasses that can be worn on a string like a necklace. Perhaps the most original development in this phenomenon, however, is the "tooter," a test tube-shaped glass. Racked just like the laboratory test tubes you remember from your high school chemistry class, tooters filled with colorful concoctions (sometimes complete with mini garnishes) make appetite-appealing displays. There are special server trays, too, including holsters resembling old Western gun belts, where the tubes are secured in small loops not unlike those that held extra bullets (a creative approach no doubt inspired by the "shooter" name).

Of course, the granddaddy of shooters—a lick of salt, washed down with a shot of straight tequila, followed by a suck on a wedge of lime and the obligatory shudder—is not only still around and kicking energetically, but has inspired similar drinks like the Lemon Drop and the Cordless Screwdriver. *99 Bananas* is a 99-proof schnapps with the *apeeling* flavor of real bananas. Try a shot of *99 Bananas Schnapps* with a beer on the side, or mixed with your favorite fruit juice.

On the pages that follow, you'll find recipes for all the drinks already mentioned, plus a multitude of others. Remember, though, that one of the most fun things about shooters is that their composition is limited only by your own creativity. So go ahead, experiment—turn the page and have a ball—a Melonball, that is!

Three slightly deaf men were driving from the north of England to London in an old, noisy car, and hearing was difficult. As they were nearing the city, one asked, "Is this Wembley?"

"No," replied the second, "this is Thursday."

"So am I," put in the third. "Let's stop and have one."

AFFAIR

1 oz.	Strawberry Schnapps
1 oz.	Cranberry Juice
1 oz.	Orange Juice

Stir with ice and strain into cordial glass.

ALABAMA SLAMMER

1 oz.	Amaretto
1 oz.	Southern Comfort
1/2 oz.	Sloe Gin
1 splash	Lemon Juice

Stir with ice and strain into shot glass. Add lemon juice.

ANGEL'S DELIGHT

1 1/2 tsps.	Grenadine
1 1/2 tsps.	Triple Sec
1 1/2 tsps.	Sloe Gin
1 1/2 tsps.	Light Cream

Pour carefully, in order given, into cordial glass so that each ingredient floats on preceding one without mixing.

ANGEL'S KISS

1/4 oz.	Crème de Cacao (White)
1/4 oz.	Sloe Gin
1/4 oz.	Brandy
1/4 oz.	Light Cream

Pour ingredients carefully, in order given, so that they do not mix. Use cordial glass.

ANGEL'S TIP

| 3/4 oz. | Crème de Cacao (White) |
| 1/4 oz. | Light Cream |

Float cream and insert toothpick in cherry and put on top. Use cordial glass.

ANGEL'S WING

1/2 oz.	Crème de Cacao (White)
1/2 oz.	Brandy
1 tbsp.	Light Cream

Pour ingredients carefully, in order given, so that they do not mix. Use cordial glass.

B-52

1/2 oz.	Coffee Liqueur
1/2 oz.	Irish Cream Liqueur
1/2 oz.	Mandarine Napoléon

In shot glass, pour carefully, in order given, so each ingredient floats on preceding one.

BANANA SLIP

| 1 1/2 oz. | Crème de Banana |
| 1 1/2 oz. | Irish Cream Liqueur |

Pour carefully, in order given, into cordial glass, to form 2 layers.

BETWEEN-THE-SHEETS

Juice of 1/4 Lemon	
1/2 oz.	Brandy
1/2 oz.	Triple Sec
1/2 oz.	Light Rum

Shake with ice and strain into shot glass.

BLOODY CAESAR SHOOTER

1   Littleneck Clam
1 oz.   Vodka
1½ oz.   Tomato Juice
2 drops   Worcestershire
          Sauce
2 drops   Tabasco Sauce
1 dash   Horseradish
Celery Salt

Put the clam in the bottom of a shot glass. Add Worcestershire sauce, Tabasco, and horseradish. Add vodka and tomato juice. Sprinkle with celery salt and garnish with a small lime wedge.

BLUE MARLIN

1 oz.   Light Rum
½ oz.   Blue Curaçao
1 oz.   Lime Juice

Stir with ice and strain into shot glass.

BONZAI PIPELINE

½ oz.   Vodka
1 oz.   Tropical Fruit
          Schnapps

Stir with ice and strain into shot glass.

BUZZARD'S BREATH

½ oz.   Amaretto
½ oz.   Peppermint
          Schnapps
½ oz.   Coffee Liqueur

Stir with ice and strain into shot glass.

C.C. KAZI

1⅛ oz.   Tequila
2 oz.   Cranberry Juice
1 tsp.   Lime Juice

Shake with ice and strain into cordial glass.

CAPRI

¾ oz.   Crème de Cacao
          (White)
¾ oz.   Crème de Banana
¾ oz.   Light Cream

Shake with ice and strain into cordial glass.

CHARLIE CHAPLIN

1 oz.   Sloe Gin
1 oz.   Apricot-flavored
          Brandy
1 oz.   Lemon Juice

Shake with ice and strain into cordial glass.

CORDLESS SCREWDRIVER

1¾ oz.   Vodka
Orange Wedge
Sugar

Chill vodka and strain into shot glass. Dip orange wedge in sugar. To drink, shoot the vodka and immediately take a draw on the orange.

COSMOS

1½ oz.   Vodka
½ oz.   Lime Juice

Shake with ice and strain into shot glass.

FIFTH AVENUE

½ oz.	Crème de Cacao (Brown)
½ oz.	Apricot-flavored Brandy
1 tbsp.	Light Cream

Pour carefully, in order given, into cordial glass, so that each ingredient floats on preceding one.

FLYING GRASSHOPPER

¾ oz.	Crème de Menthe (Green)
¾ oz.	Crème de Cacao (White)
¾ oz.	Vodka

Stir with ice and strain into cordial glass.

4TH OF JULY TOOTER

1 oz.	Grenadine
1 oz.	Vodka
1 oz.	Blue Curaçao

In cordial or shot glass, pour carefully, in order given, so that each ingredient floats on preceding one.

FOXY LADY

1 oz.	Amaretto
½ oz.	Crème de Cacao (Brown)
1 oz.	Heavy Cream

Shake with ice and strain into cordial glass.

GALACTIC ALE

1¼ oz.	Vodka
1¼ oz.	Blue Curaçao
1 oz.	Lime Juice
½ oz.	Black Raspberry Liqueur

Shake with ice and strain into shot glass. Makes 2 servings.

GREEN DEMON

½ oz.	Vodka
½ oz.	Rum
½ oz.	Melon Liqueur
½ oz.	Lemonade

Shake with ice and strain into shot glass.

INTERNATIONAL INCIDENT

¼ oz.	Vodka
¼ oz.	Coffee Liqueur
¼ oz.	Amaretto
¼ oz.	Hazelnut Liqueur
½ oz.	Irish Cream Liqueur

Shake with ice and strain into shot glass.

IRISH CHARLIE

| 1 oz. | Irish Cream Liqueur |
| 1 oz. | Crème de Menthe (White) |

Stir with ice and strain into cordial glass.

I go from stool to stool in singles bars hoping to get lucky, but there's never any gum under any of them.

—*Emo Phillips*

IRISH FLAG

1 oz.   Crème de Menthe
        (Green)
1 oz.   Irish Cream
        Liqueur
1 oz.   Mandarine Napoléon

In cordial glass, pour
carefully, in order given, so
that each ingredient floats on
preceding one.

JOHNNY ON THE BEACH

1½ oz. Vodka
1 oz.   Melon Liqueur
1 oz.   Black Raspberry
        Liqueur
½ oz.   Pineapple Juice
½ oz.   Orange Juice
½ oz.   Grapefruit Juice
½ oz.   Cranberry Juice

Stir with ice and strain into
shot glasses. Makes 2
servings.

KAMIKAZE

½ oz.   Lime Juice
½ oz.   Triple Sec
½ oz.   Vodka

Shake with ice and strain
into shot glass.

LEMON DROP

1½ oz. Vodka
Lemon wedge
Sugar

Chill vodka and strain into
shot glass. Dip lemon wedge
in sugar. To drink, shoot the
vodka and immediately take
a draw on the lemon.

MELON BALL

1 oz.   Melon Liqueur
1 oz.   Vodka
1 oz.   Pineapple Juice

Shake with ice and strain
into cordial glass.

MOCHA MINT

¾ oz.   Coffee-flavored
        Brandy
¾ oz.   Crème de Cacao
        (White)
¾ oz.   Crème de Menthe
        (White)

Shake with ice and strain
into cordial glass.

MONKEY SHINE SHOOTER

½ oz.   Bourbon Liqueur
½ oz.   Crème de Banana
½ oz.   Irish Cream
        Liqueur

Shake with ice and strain
into cordial glass.

NUTTY PROFESSOR

½ oz.   Mandarine Napoléon
½ oz.   Hazelnut Liqueur
½ oz.   Irish Cream Liqueur

Stir and strain into shot
glass.

OH MY GOSH

1 oz.   Amaretto
1 oz.   Peach Schnapps

Stir with ice and strain into
shot glass.

PARISIAN BLONDE

¾ oz.　Light Rum
¾ oz.　Triple Sec
¾ oz.　Jamaica Rum

Shake with ice and strain into cordial glass.

PEACH BUNNY

¾ oz.　Peach-flavored Brandy
¾ oz.　Crème de Cacao (White)
¾ oz.　Light Cream

Shake with ice and strain into cordial glass.

PEACH TART

1 oz.　Peach Schnapps
½ oz.　Lime Juice

Stir with ice and strain into shot glass.

PEPPERMINT PATTIE

1 oz.　Crème de Cacao (White)
1 oz.　Crème de Menthe (White)

Shake with ice and strain into cordial glass.

PIGSKIN SHOT

1 oz.　Vodka
1 oz.　Melon Liqueur
½ oz.　Sour Mix

Shake with ice and strain into chilled shot glass.

PINEAPPLE UPSIDE DOWN CAKE

½ oz.　Irish Cream Liqueur
½ oz.　Vodka
½ oz.　Butterscotch Schnapps
½ oz.　Pineapple Juice

Stir and strain into shot glass.

PURPLE HOOTER

1½ oz.　Citrus Vodka
½ oz.　Triple Sec
¼ oz.　Black Raspberry Liqueur

Shake with ice and strain into chilled shot glass.

RATTLESNAKE

1 oz.　Coffee Liqueur
1 oz.　Crème de Cacao (White)
1 oz.　Irish Cream Liqueur

In cordial or shot glass, pour carefully, in order given, so that each ingredient floats on preceding one.

ROCKY MOUNTAIN

1 oz.　Southern Comfort
1 oz.　Amaretto
½ oz.　Lime Juice

Shake with ice and strain into shot glass.

Ooogy Wawa
　　　　—a Zulu toast

SAMBUCA SLIDE

1 oz.   Sambuca
½ oz.   Vodka
½ oz.   Light Cream

Stir with ice and strain into shot glass.

SCOOTER

1 oz.   Amaretto
1 oz.   Brandy
1 oz.   Light Cream

Combine in blender or shake well with cracked ice. Strain into cordial glass.

SEX ON THE BEACH

½ oz.   Black Raspberry
              Liqueur
½ oz.   Melon Liqueur
½ oz.   Vodka
1 oz.   Pineapple Juice
Cranberry Juice

Stir with ice and strain into cordial or shot glass. Top with cranberry juice.

SHAVETAIL

1½ oz.   Peppermint
              Schnapps
1 oz.   Pineapple Juice
1 oz.   Light Cream

Shake with ice and strain into cordial glass.

SILVER SPIDER

½ oz.   Vodka
½ oz.   Rum
½ oz.   Triple Sec
½ oz.   Crème de Menthe
              (White)

Stir with ice and strain into shot glass.

SOUR APPLE

¼ oz.   Vodka
¼ oz.   Apple Liqueur
½ oz.   Melon Liqueur
½ oz.   Lemon-lime Soda

Shake and strain into cordial glass.

STALACTITE

1⅛ oz.   Sambuca
¼ oz.   Irish Cream Liqueur
¼ oz.   Black Raspberry
              Liqueur

Pour sambuca into cordial glass. Float Irish cream on top of sambuca. Carefully pour black raspberry liqueur, drop by drop, as top layer. The raspberry liqueur will pull the Irish cream through the sambuca and will settle on bottom.

STARS AND STRIPES

⅓ oz.   Grenadine
⅓ oz.   Heavy Cream
⅓ oz.   Blue Curaçao

Pour carefully, in order given, into cordial glass, so that each ingredient floats on preceding one.

TERMINATOR

½ oz.   Coffee Liqueur
½ oz.   Irish Cream Liqueur
½ oz.   Sambuca
½ oz.   Mandarine Napoléon
½ oz.   Vodka

In cordial glass, pour carefully, in order given, so that each layer floats on preceding one.

TO THE MOON

½ oz.   Coffee Liqueur
½ oz.   Amaretto
½ oz.   Irish Cream Liqueur
½ oz.   151-proof Rum

Stir with ice and strain into shot glass.

TRAFFIC LIGHT

½ oz.   Crème de Noyaux
½ oz.   Galliano
½ oz.   Melon Liqueur

Layer liqueurs in order given in cordial glass.

WOO WOO

½ oz.   Peach Schnapps
½ oz.   Vodka
1 oz.   Cranberry Juice

Shake with ice and strain into shot glass.

THREE GLASS TRICK

Put 3 glasses on a table, inverting the middle one as shown in fig. 1. Ask someone to turn the glasses three times, turning two glasses each time and ending with all three glasses bottom sides up. METHOD: Turn over A&B as in fig. 2; then turn over A&C as in fig. 3; then turn over A and B as in fig. 4; and the glasses are all facedown. Then turn up the middle glass, and rush someone into doing the trick, which he will not be able to do since he will be starting in a different position from the one in which you started (fig.5).

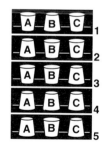

Feeling parched and dry, overcome by the summer heat? Or does your sweet tooth need satisfying but you don't want a heavy dessert? Versatile frozen drinks are the answer to both.

Frozen drinks are perfect summertime quaffs. Refreshingly frosty, these glacial sippers can make you feel almost cool with just their frigid-sounding names: The Blizzard, The Big Chill, or Frosty Noggin. Some are tropical in nature, combining spirits or liqueurs with fruit juices, and blended with ice. Served in tall, generous glasses and garnished with an assortment of seasonal fruits, they're best slowly sipped through a straw while envisioning sugar-white beaches and swaying palms. Others are creamy concoctions made with ice cream, bringing back sweet memories of long-ago summertime treats.

Ice cream–based frozen drinks, often mixed with liqueurs such as crème de cacao, amaretto, or Irish cream and topped with whipped cream, also make delicious dessert substitutes. Just imagine sipping a Strawberry Shortcake or Raspberry Cheesecake after a satisfying meal. Or how about savoring the classic blend of peach and raspberry flavors in a Peach Melba Freeze?

You'll find plenty of luscious recipes in this section, for both summertime and year-round enjoyment. Next time it's ninety in the shade, with a little help from your blender, you can quickly catch a Tidal Wave or feel a Maui Breeze. Or grab your Inner Tube and float out Over the Rainbow. And when you're hankering for a creamy treat, any time of year, you'll find a recipe that's sure to put you on Cloud Nine.

APPLE COLADA

2 oz.	Apple Schnapps
1 oz.	Cream of Coconut
1 oz.	Half-and-Half

Blend all ingredients with 2 cups of crushed ice in blender at high speed. Pour into highball glass and serve with a straw. Garnish with an apple slice and a cherry.

APPLE GRANNY CRISP

1 oz.	Apple Schnapps
½ oz.	Brandy
½ oz.	Irish Cream Liqueur
2 scoops	Vanilla Ice Cream
	Graham Cracker Crumbs

Combine ingredients in blender and blend until smooth. Serve topped with whipped cream and cinnamon.

APPLE RIVER INNER TUBE

1 oz.	Brandy
1 oz.	Crème de Cacao (Brown)
1½ scoops	Vanilla Ice Cream

Combine ingredients in blender with crushed ice and blend until smooth. Pour into parfait glass. Garnish with half a spiced apple ring.

APRICOT CREAM SPRITZ

¾ cup	Milk
½ cup	Apricot Nectar
¼ cup	Crushed Ice
2 tbsps.	Apricot-flavored Brandy
2 cups	Sparkling Wine

Place first 4 ingredients in blender and blend until smooth. Pour equal amounts into 6 large, red-wine glasses. Add about ⅓ cup wine to each glass. Stir gently. Makes 6 servings.

BANANA DAIQUIRI

1½ oz.	Light Rum
1 tbsp.	Triple Sec
1½ oz.	Lime Juice
1 tsp.	Sugar
1	Medium Banana, sliced

Combine ingredients in blender with 1 cup crushed ice and blend until smooth. Pour into champagne flute. Garnish with a cherry.

BANANA DI AMORE

1 oz.	Amaretto
1 oz.	Crème de Banana Liqueur
2 oz.	Orange Juice
1 oz.	Sour Mix

Blend with 1 cup crushed ice until frozen. Serve in red-wine glass, garnished with orange and banana slices.

Sköl
—a Norwegian and Swedish toast

BANANA FOSTER

2 scoops	Vanilla Ice Cream
1½ oz.	Spiced Rum
½ oz.	Banana Liqueur
1	medium Banana

Combine ingredients in blender and blend until smooth. Pour into large brandy snifter and sprinkle with cinnamon.

BAY CITY BOMBER

½ oz.	Vodka
½ oz.	Rum
½ oz.	Tequila
½ oz.	Gin
½ oz.	Triple Sec
1 oz.	Orange Juice
1 oz.	Pineapple Juice
1 oz.	Cranberry Juice
1 oz.	Sour Mix
¼ oz.	151-proof Rum

Combine ingredients in blender with 1 cup crushed ice and blend until smooth. Pour into parfait glass. Float rum on top. Garnish with cherry and orange slice.

BEACH BUM'S COOLER

1¼ oz.	Irish Cream
¼ oz.	Banana Liqueur
1½ oz.	Piña Colada Mix
¾ oz.	Light Rum
¼	Banana
2 scoops	Vanilla Ice Cream
1 splash	Cream

Combine ingredients in blender and blend until smooth. Pour into parfait glass and garnish with a pineapple slice and a paper umbrella.

BLUE CLOUD COCKTAIL

1 oz.	Amaretto
½ oz.	Blue Curaçao
2 oz.	Vanilla Ice Cream

Combine ingredients in blender and blend until smooth. Pour into brandy snifter. Top with whipped cream and a cherry.

BLUE VELVET

1 oz.	Black Raspberry Liqueur
1 oz.	Melon Liqueur
4 oz.	Vanilla Ice Cream
Blue Curaçao	

Combine ingredients in blender with crushed ice and blend until smooth. Pour into parfait glass. Top with whipped cream and drizzle with blue curaçao. Garnish with a cherry.

BLUSHIN' RUSSIAN

1 oz.	Coffee Liqueur
¾ oz.	Vodka
1 scoop	Vanilla Ice Cream
4	Large fresh Strawberries

Combine ingredients in blender and blend until smooth. Pour into parfait glass. Garnish with a chocolate-covered strawberry.

BUNKY PUNCH

1½ oz.   Vodka
1 oz.   Melon Liqueur
1 oz.   Peach Schnapps
1½ oz.   Cranberry Juice
2 oz.   Orange Juice
½ oz.   Grape Juice

Combine ingredients in blender with ice and blend until smooth. Serve in parfait glass and garnish with slice of lime.

CANYON QUAKE

¾ oz.   Irish Cream
         Liqueur
¾ oz.   Brandy
1 oz.   Amaretto
2 oz.   Light Cream

Combine ingredients in blender and blend with ice until smooth. Pour into large snifter.

CAVANAUGH'S SPECIAL

1 oz.   Coffee Liqueur
1 oz.   Crème de Cacao
         (White)
1 oz.   Amaretto
2 scoops Vanilla Ice Cream

In snifter, pour coffee liqueur and set aside. In blender, blend next three ingredients with ice cubes. When the mixture reaches milk shake consistency, pour on top of coffee liqueur. Top with whipped cream and chocolate sprinkles.

CHAMPAGNE CORNUCOPIA

1 oz.   Cranberry Juice
2 scoops Rainbow Sherbet
1 oz.   Vodka
¾ oz.   Peach Schnapps
1 oz.   Champagne

Pour cranberry juice into oversized red-wine glass. Combine sherbet, vodka, and schnapps in blender and blend until smooth. Pour blended mixture over cranberry juice to produce a swirl effect and layer champagne on top. Garnish with an orange slice.

CHERRY REPAIR KIT

½ oz.   Half and Half
½ oz.   Crème de Cacao
         (White)
½ oz.   Amaretto
6   Maraschino
         Cherries
½ oz.   Maraschino Cherry
         Juice

Combine ingredients in blender with ice and blend until smooth. Garnish with a cherry and serve with a straw.

CHI-CHI

1½ oz.   Vodka
1 oz.   Cream of Coconut
4 oz.   Pineapple Juice

Blend ingredients with 1 cup of crushed ice in blender at high speed. Pour into red-wine glass. Garnish with a slice of pineapple and a cherry.

CHILLY IRISHMAN

3 oz.	Cold Espresso
1 oz.	Irish Whiskey
½ oz.	Coffee Liqueur
½ oz.	Irish Cream Liqueur
1 scoop	Vanilla Ice Cream
1 dash	Simple Syrup

Combine ingredients in blender with 4 cups of crushed ice and blend until smooth. Pour into parfait glass. Garnish with a 3- or 4-leaf clover.

CHOCO-BANANA SMASH

1¼ oz.	Irish Cream Liqueur
¼ oz.	Vanilla Extract
½ oz.	Light Cream
½ scoop	Vanilla Ice Cream
½	Medium Banana

Combine ingredients in blender with a small scoop of crushed ice and blend until smooth. Pour into parfait glass. Garnish with a cherry and 1-inch banana slice on a cocktail pick. Top with whipped cream and chocolate sprinkles.

The man stood at the bar for hours telling the bartender about all his great exploits.

"Now," said the bartender, "tell me something you can't do."

"Well," said the man," for one thing, I can't pay the check."

CHOCOLATE ALMOND CREAM

1 qt.	Vanilla Ice Cream
½ cup	Amaretto
½ cup	Crème de Cacao (White)

Combine ingredients in blender and blend until smooth. Pour into parfait glasses. Garnish with shaved chocolate. Makes 4–6 servings.

CITRUS BANANA FLIP

1	Medium Banana, cut in pieces
10 oz.	Club Soda
⅔ cup	Orange Juice Concentrate
⅔ cup	Milk
½ cup	Dark Rum
½ cup	Lime Juice
3 tbsps.	Brown Sugar

Combine ingredients in blender with ½ cup crushed ice and blend until smooth. Pour into collins glasses. Makes 4–6 servings.

CLOUD 9

8 oz.	Vanilla Ice Cream
1 oz.	Irish Cream Liqueur
½ oz.	Black Raspberry Liqueur
1 oz.	Amaretto

Combine ingredients in blender and blend until smooth. Pour into 16-oz. parfait glass. Top with whipped cream and a chocolate peanut-butter cup, split in half.

COOL OPERATOR

1 oz.	Melon Liqueur
½ oz.	Lime Juice
½ oz.	Vodka
½ oz.	Light Rum
4 oz.	Grapefruit Juice
2 oz.	Orange Juice

Combine ingredients in blender, fill halfway with ice, and blend until thick. Pour into parfait glass. Garnish with a melon wedge and a cherry.

CRANBERRY COOLER

1½ oz.	Bourbon
1½ oz.	Cranberry Juice
½ oz.	Lime Juice
1 tsp.	Sugar

Combine ingredients in blender with 1 cup of crushed ice and blend until smooth. Pour into parfait glass.

CREAMY GIN SOUR

½ cup	Gin
½ cup	Lime Juice
½ cup	Lemon Juice
½ cup	Heavy Cream
¼ cup	Triple Sec
1 tbsp.	Sugar
10 oz.	Club Soda

Combine ingredients in blender with ¾ cup of crushed ice and blend until frothy. Pour into large red-wine glasses. Makes 4–6 servings.

DEATH BY CHOCOLATE

1 oz.	Irish Cream Liqueur
½ oz.	Crème de Cacao (Brown)
½ oz.	Vodka
1 scoop	Chocolate Ice Cream

Combine ingredients in blender with 1 cup of crushed ice and blend until smooth. Pour into parfait glass. Garnish with whipped cream and chocolate curls. Serve with a straw.

DEVIL'S TAIL

1½ oz.	Light Rum
1 oz.	Vodka
1 tbsp.	Lime Juice
1½ tsps.	Grenadine
1½ tsps.	Apricot-flavored Brandy

Combine all ingredients with ½ cup of crushed ice in blender. Blend at low speed and pour into champagne flute. Add a twist of lime peel.

DI AMORE DREAM

1½ oz.	Amaretto di Amore
¾ oz.	Crème de Cacao (White)
2 oz.	Orange Juice
2 scoops	Vanilla Ice Cream

Combine ingredients in blender and blend until smooth. Pour into parfait glass. Garnish with an orange slice.

DREAMY MONKEY

1 oz.	Vodka
½ oz.	Crème de Banana
½ oz.	Crème de Cacao (Brown)
1	Banana
2 scoops	Vanilla Ice Cream
1 oz.	Light Cream

Combine ingredients in blender (use half of the banana) and blend until smooth. Pour into parfait glass. Top with whipped cream and garnish with remaining banana half.

FROSTY NOGGIN

1½ oz.	Rum
¾ oz.	Crème de Menthe (White)
3 oz.	Prepared Dairy Eggnog
3 cups	Vanilla Ice Cream

Combine ingredients in blender and blend until smooth. Pour into parfait glass. Top with whipped cream decorated with a few drops of green crème de menthe. Garnish with a rolled cookie.

FROZEN BERKELEY

1½ oz.	Light Rum
½ oz.	Brandy
1 tbsp.	Passion Fruit Syrup
1 tbsp.	Lemon Juice

Combine ingredients with ½ cup of crushed ice in blender and blend at low speed. Pour into champagne flute.

FROZEN CAPPUCCINO

½ oz.	Irish Cream Liqueur
½ oz.	Coffee Liqueur
½ oz.	Hazelnut Liqueur
1 scoop	Vanilla Ice Cream
1 dash	Light Cream

Combine ingredients in blender with ½ cup crushed ice and blend until smooth. Serve in parfait glass, rimmed with cinnamon sugar. Garnish with a cinnamon stick and an 8-inch straw.

FROZEN CITRON NEON

1½ oz.	Citrus Vodka
1 oz.	Melon Liqueur
½ oz.	Blue Curaçao
½ oz.	Lime Juice
1 oz.	Sour Mix

Combine ingredients in blender with ice and blend until smooth. Pour into parfait glass. Garnish with a lemon slice and a cherry.

FROZEN DAIQUIRI

1½ oz.	Light Rum
1 tbsp.	Triple Sec
1½ oz.	Lime Juice
1 tsp.	Sugar

Combine ingredients in blender with 1 cup crushed ice and blend at low speed for five seconds. Then blend at high speed until firm. Pour into champagne flute. Top with a cherry.

FROZEN FUZZY

1 oz.	Peach Schnapps
½ oz.	Triple Sec
½ oz.	Lime Juice
½ oz.	Grenadine
1 splash Lemon-lime Soda	

Combine ingredients in blender. Fill with enough ice to reach the level of the liquid and blend. Pour into champagne flute. Garnish with a lime wedge.

FROZEN MARGARITA

1½ oz.	Tequila
½ oz.	Triple Sec
1 oz.	Lemon or Lime Juice

Combine ingredients with 1 cup of crushed ice in blender at low speed for five seconds. Then blend at high speed until firm. Pour into cocktail glass. Garnish with a slice of lemon or lime.

FROZEN MATADOR

1½ oz.	Tequila
2 oz.	Pineapple Juice
1 tbsp.	Lime Juice

Combine all ingredients with 1 cup of crushed ice in blender. Blend at low speed and pour into old-fashioned glass. Add a pineapple stick.

FROZEN MINT DAIQUIRI

2 oz.	Light Rum
1 tbsp.	Lime Juice
6	Mint Leaves
1 tsp.	Sugar

Combine all ingredients with 1 cup of crushed ice in blender at low speed and pour into old-fashioned glass.

FROZEN PINEAPPLE DAIQUIRI

1½ oz.	Light Rum
4	Pineapple Chunks
1 tbsp.	Lime Juice
½ tsp.	Sugar

Combine all ingredients with 1 cup of crushed ice in blender. Blend at low speed and pour into champagne flute.

FRUITY SMASH

1 pint	Vanilla Ice Cream
⅓ cup	Cherry-flavored Brandy
⅓ cup	Crème de Banana

Combine ingredients in blender and blend until smooth. Pour into large cocktail glasses. Garnish with cherries. Makes 4–6 servings.

GAELIC COFFEE

¾ oz.	Irish Whiskey
¾ oz.	Irish Cream Liqueur
1½ oz.	Crème de Cacao (Brown)
2 oz.	Milk
1 tsp.	Instant Coffee

Combine ingredients in blender with ice and blend until smooth. Pour into Irish coffee cup. Top with whipped cream and sprinkle with green crème de menthe for color.

GEORGIO

2 oz.	Coffee Liqueur
2 oz.	Irish Cream Liqueur
1	Banana, ripe
½ cup	Light Cream

Combine ingredients in blender with 1 cup ice and blend until smooth. Pour equal amounts into parfait glasses. Top with whipped cream and a light dusting of cocoa. Add a mint sprig for color. Makes 2 servings.

GULF STREAM

1 oz.	Blue Curaçao
3 oz.	Champagne
½ oz.	Light Rum
½ oz.	Brandy
6 oz.	Lemonade
1 oz.	Lime Juice

Combine ingredients in blender with ice and blend until smooth. Pour into sugar-rimmed parfait glass. Garnish with a whole strawberry.

HUMMER

1 oz.	Coffee Liqueur
1 oz.	Light Rum
2 large scoops	Vanilla Ice Cream

Combine ingredients in blender and blend briefly. Serve in highball glass.

ICED COFFEE À L'ORANGE

1 qt.	Vanilla Ice Cream
4 tsps.	Instant Coffee
1 cup	Triple Sec

Combine ingredients in blender and blend until smooth. Pour into parfait glasses. Garnish with orange slices. Makes 5–6 servings.

ICY RUMMED CACAO

1 qt.	Vanilla Ice Cream
½ cup	Dark Rum
½ cup	Crème de Cacao (Brown)

Combine ingredients in blender and blend until smooth. Pour into parfait glasses. Garnish with shaved chocolate. Makes 4–6 servings.

When Teddy Roosevelt went on an African safari in 1909, he made sure his hunting party wouldn't run out of beer—he brought more than 500 gallons with him!

IRISH DREAM

½ oz.   Hazelnut Liqueur
½ oz.   Irish Cream
          Liqueur
¾ oz.   Crème de Cacao
          (Brown)
4 oz.   Vanilla Ice Cream

Combine ingredients in blender with ice and blend until smooth. Pour into frosted pilsner glass. Top with whipped cream and chocolate sprinkles.

ITALIAN DREAM

1½ oz.   Irish Cream
          Liqueur
½ oz.   Amaretto
2 oz.   Light Cream

Combine ingredients in blender with ice and blend until smooth. Serve in parfait glass.

JACK'S JAM

½ oz.   Peach Schnapps
½ oz.   Apple Schnapps
½ oz.   Strawberry Liqueur
¼ oz.   Banana Liqueur
2 oz.   Lemon Juice
1 oz.   Orange Juice
2 tbsps. Powdered Sugar

Combine ingredients in blender with crushed ice and blend until smooth. Pour into parfait glass. Garnish with a sprig of fresh mint and a maraschino cherry.

JAMAICAN BANANA

½ oz.   Light Rum
½ oz.   Crème de Cacao
          (White)
½ oz.   Crème de Banana
2 scoops Vanilla Ice Cream
1 oz.   Half-and-Half
1   Whole Banana

Blend, then garnish with 2 slices banana, a strawberry, and nutmeg, and serve in large brandy snifter.

KOKOMO JOE

1 oz.   Light Rum
1 oz.   Banana Liqueur
5 oz.   Orange Juice
3 oz.   Piña Colada Mix
½   Banana

Combine ingredients in blender with 1 cup of ice and blend until smooth. Garnish with a slice of orange.

LEBANESE SNOW

1½ oz.   Strawberry Liqueur
1 oz.   Crème de Banana
1 oz.   Light Cream

Combine ingredients in blender with crushed ice and blend until smooth. Garnish with a strawberry.

LICORICE MIST

1¼ oz.   Sambuca
½ oz.   Coconut Liqueur
2 oz.   Light Cream

Combine ingredients in blender with ice and blend until smooth. Pour into parfait glass. Cut off ends of licorice stick and use it as a straw/garnish.

LONELY NIGHT

¾ oz.	Coffee Liqueur
1¼ oz.	Irish Cream Liqueur
1¼ oz.	Hazelnut Liqueur
1 scoop	Vanilla Ice Cream

Combine ingredients in blender with ice and blend until smooth. Pour into parfait glass. Top with whipped cream and shaved chocolate.

MARASCHINO CHERRY

1 oz.	Rum
½ oz.	Amaretto
½ oz.	Peach Schnapps
1 oz.	Cranberry Juice
1 oz.	Pineapple Juice
1 dash	Grenadine

Combine ingredients in blender with 2–3 cups ice and blend until smooth. Garnish with whipped cream and a cherry.

MAUI BREEZE

½ oz.	Amaretto
½ oz.	Triple Sec
½ oz.	Brandy
1 oz.	Sour Mix
2 oz.	Orange Juice
2 oz.	Guava Juice

Combine ingredients in blender with ice and blend until smooth. Serve in parfait glass garnished with a pineapple spear, a cherry, and an orchid.

MISSISSIPPI MUD

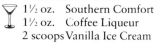

1½ oz.	Southern Comfort
1½ oz.	Coffee Liqueur
2 scoops	Vanilla Ice Cream

Combine ice cream and liqueurs in blender and blend until smooth. Spoon into cocktail glass. Top with shaved chocolate.

MONT BLANC

1 oz.	Black Raspberry Liqueur
1 oz.	Vodka
1 oz.	Light Cream
1 scoop	Vanilla Ice Cream

Combine ingredients in blender and blend until smooth. Pour into oversized red-wine glass.

NUTTY COLADA

3 oz.	Amaretto
3 tbsps.	Coconut Milk
3 tbsps.	Crushed Pineapple

Put ingredients in blender with 2 cups crushed ice and blend at high speed for a short time. Pour into collins glass and serve with a straw.

ORANGE BLOSSOM SPECIAL

1 oz.	Peach Schnapps
2½ oz.	Lemon-lime Soda
3 oz.	Orange Sherbet
1½ oz.	Vanilla Ice Cream
2½ oz.	Light Cream

Combine ingredients in blender with 6 ice cubes and blend until smooth. Pour into parfait glass. Garnish with a cherry and an orange slice.

ORANGE TREE

1½ oz.	Amaretto
¾ oz.	Crème de Noyaux
1½ oz.	Orange Juice
¾ oz.	Vanilla Ice Cream

Combine ingredients in blender and blend until smooth. Pour into parfait glass. Top with whipped cream and garnish with a thin slice of orange.

OVER THE RAINBOW

2 oz.	Spiced Rum
1 oz.	Orange Curaçao
2 scoops	Rainbow Sherbet
4 slices	Fresh Peach, peeled
2	Strawberries

Combine ingredients in blender with 1 cup ice and blend until smooth. Pour into parfait glass. Garnish with a strawberry and a peach slice.

PEACH MELBA FREEZE

¾ oz.	Peach Schnapps
¾ oz.	Black Raspberry Liqueur
¾ oz.	Hazelnut Liqueur
4 oz.	Vanilla Ice Cream
¾ oz.	Light Cream
1 oz.	Melba Sauce (or Raspberry Jam)

Combine ingredients in blender and blend until smooth. Pour into chilled 8-oz. glass. Garnish with a peach slice.

PEACHY AMARETTO

1 cup	Vanilla Ice Cream
1 cup	Peaches
1 cup	Amaretto

Combine ingredients in blender and blend until smooth. Pour into parfait glasses. Makes 3–4 servings.

PEPPERMINT PENGUIN

½ oz.	Crème de Menthe (Green)
½ oz.	Chocolate Mint Liqueur
3	Chocolate Sandwich Cookies
3 oz.	Light Cream

Combine ingredients in blender with 1 scoop of ice and blend until all ice is crushed. Pour into hurricane or parfait glass. Top with whipped cream. Garnish with a cookie and a cherry.

PINEAPPLE BANANA REFRESHER

2 cups	Pineapple Juice
1 cup	Pineapple Sherbet
½ cup	Crème de Banana
½ cup	Dark Rum

Combine ingredients in blender and blend until smooth. Pour into highball glasses. Garnish with a pineapple wedge and a banana slice. Makes 4–5 servings.

PISTACHIO MINT ICE CREAM

1 oz.	Hazelnut Liqueur
½ oz.	Crème de Menthe (Green)
1 oz.	Vodka
2 oz.	Heavy Cream

Combine ingredients in blender and blend until smooth. Pour into cocktail glass and garnish with a mint leaf.

RASPBERRY CHEESECAKE

1 tbsp.	Cream Cheese, softened
1 oz.	Crème de Cacao (White)
1 oz.	Black Raspberry Liqueur
2 scoops	Vanilla Ice Cream

Combine ingredients in blender with ½ scoop crushed ice and blend. Pour into parfait glass.

SMOOTH MOVE

1 oz.	Rum
2 oz.	Pineapple Juice
2 oz.	Prune Juice
2 oz.	Sour Mix

Combine ingredients in blender with 1 scoop of ice and blend. Pour into sugar-rimmed parfait glass. Garnish with a pineapple spear and a cherry.

SPARKLING STRAWBERRY MIMOSA

2 oz.	Frozen Sliced Strawberries in Syrup, partially thawed
2 oz.	Orange Juice
4 oz.	Chilled Champagne

Combine sliced berries and juice in blender and blend until smooth. Pour over ice into a parfait glass. Fill with champagne and garnish with a whole strawberry and an orange slice.

STRAWBERRIES AND CREAM

1 oz.	Strawberry Schnapps
1½ tbsps.	Sugar
2 oz.	Half-and-Half
2 whole	Strawberries

Place ingredients except strawberries in blender with 2 cups crushed ice and blend at high speed. Add strawberries and blend for 10 seconds. Pour into parfait glass and serve with a straw. Garnish with a fresh strawberry.

STRAWBERRY ALEXANDRA

5 oz.   Frozen Sliced
         Strawberries in
         Syrup, partially
         thawed
1 scoop Vanilla Ice Cream
1 oz.   Crème de Cacao
         (White)
1 oz.   Brandy

Combine ingredients in
blender and blend until
smooth. Pour into stemmed
glass. Top with sweetened
whipped cream. Garnish
with chocolate curls. Serve
with straw and spoon.

STRAWBERRY BANANA SPRITZ

1 pint   Vanilla Ice Cream
1 cup   Strawberries, fresh
         or frozen
1 cup   Crème de Banana
10 oz.   Club Soda

Combine ingredients in
blender and blend until
smooth. Pour into parfait
glasses. Garnish with whole
strawberries. Makes 4–6
servings.

STRAWBERRY DAWN

1 oz.   Gin
1 oz.   Cream of Coconut
4   Fresh Strawberries
         or ⅓ cup Frozen
         Strawberries

Blend ingredients with 1 cup
ice in blender at high speed.
Pour into cocktail glass.
Garnish with a strawberry
slice and a mint sprig.

STRAWBERRY SHORTCAKE

1 oz.   Amaretto
¾ oz.   Crème de Cacao
         (White)
3 oz.   Strawberries in
         Syrup
5 oz.   Vanilla Ice Cream

Combine ingredients in
blender and blend until
smooth. Pour into oversized
red-wine glass. Top with
whipped cream and garnish
with a fresh strawberry.

SURF'S UP

½ oz.   Crème de Banana
½ oz.   Crème de Cacao
         (White)
5 oz.   Pineapple Juice
1 oz.   Light Cream

Combine ingredients in
blender and blend until
smooth. Pour into parfait
glass. Garnish with an
orange slice and a cherry.

SWEET-TART

2 oz.	Vodka
3 oz.	Cranberry Juice
3 oz.	Pineapple Juice
1 dash	Lime Juice

Combine ingredients in blender with 1 scoop ice and blend until smooth. Garnish with a lime wheel.

TENNESSEE WALTZ

1¼ oz.	Peach Schnapps
2 oz.	Pineapple Juice
1 oz.	Passion Fruit Juice
4 oz.	Vanilla Ice Cream

Combine ingredients in blender and blend until smooth. Pour into parfait glass. Garnish with whipped cream and a strawberry.

TEQUILA FROST

1¼ oz.	Tequila
1¼ oz.	Pineapple Juice
1¼ oz.	Grapefruit Juice
½ oz.	Honey
½ oz.	Grenadine
2 oz.	Vanilla Ice Milk

Combine ingredients in blender and blend until smooth. Pour into parfait glass. Garnish with an orange slice and a cherry.

THE ALL-AMERICAN DAIQUIRI

Blue Layer:

¾ oz.	Light Rum or Vodka
1½ oz.	Sour Mix
½ oz.	Blueberry Flavoring

Red Layer:

| ¾ oz. | Light Rum or Vodka |
| 2 oz. | Strawberry Daiquiri Mix |

White Layer:
Whipped Cream

For red and blue layers, combine ingredients in blender with 1 cup crushed ice and blend until very thick. Layer frozen colors—blue, red, and white—in parfait glass. Top with a cherry and an American flag frill pick.

THE BIG CHILL

1½ oz.	Dark Rum
1 oz.	Pineapple Juice
1 oz.	Orange Juice
1 oz.	Cranberry Juice
1 oz.	Cream of Coconut

Combine ingredients in blender with 1 scoop ice and blend until smooth. Serve in 12-oz. pilsner glass and garnish with a pineapple wedge and a cherry.

THE BLIZZARD

1 oz.   Brandy
1 oz.   Irish Cream
              Liqueur
1 oz.   Coffee Liqueur
1 oz.   Light Rum
2 scoops Vanilla Ice Cream
1 splash Light Cream

Combine ingredients in
blender and blend until
smooth. Pour into a large
snifter and garnish with a
sprinkle of nutmeg.

THE BRASS FIDDLE

2 oz.   Peach Schnapps
¼ oz.   Tennessee Whisky
2 oz.   Pineapple Juice
1 oz.   Orange Juice
1 oz.   Grenadine

Combine first 4 ingredients
in blender with ice and blend
until smooth. Pour frozen
mixture into a parfait glass
that has been swirled with
grenadine. Garnish with a
pineapple slice and a cherry.

TIDAL WAVE

1¼ oz.   Melon Liqueur
1 oz.   Pineapple Juice
1 oz.   Orange Juice
½ oz.   Coconut Syrup
1½ oz.   Sour Mix
½ oz.   Light Rum

Combine ingredients in
blender with ice and blend
until smooth. Pour into
parfait glass. Garnish with a
lime wheel and a cherry.

TIDBIT

1 oz.   Gin
1 scoop Vanilla Ice Cream
1 dash   Dry Sherry

Blend ingredients in blender
at low speed and pour into
highball glass.

TROLLEY CAR

1¼ oz.   Amaretto
2 oz.   Fresh Strawberries
2 scoops Vanilla Ice Cream

Combine ingredients in
blender and blend until
smooth. Pour into parfait
glass and garnish with a
fresh strawberry.

LIFT A BOTTLE WITH A STRAW

Offer to lift an 8-ounce bottle with a straw! A remarkable feat but easy to do. Bend the straw into one short and one long segment. Push the short end in and it will spring out to act as a lever by which the bottle is lifted.

Hot Drinks

Chilly days and frosty nights are made for snuggling in front of a roaring fire, hands wrapped around a hot drink that warms you down to your toes.

Even if you don't have a fireplace, you can enjoy the very special warmth of the hot drinks found on the following pages, from the classic Irish Coffee to the spectacular Capriccio and the deliciously different Hot Gold.

Hot toddies, simple mixtures of hot water, sugar, and a single spirit such as whiskey, rum, brandy, and even gin, are remembered by many as old-fashioned cold remedies. While it was the heat, not the spirit, that seemed to make you feel better, toddies are one of those classic comforts we are loath to abandon even today.

Many hot drinks use coffee as their base, laced with either whiskey, rum, brandy or liqueurs, or a combination of several of these. However, virtually any heated beverage can make a delightful drink, and in this section you'll find recipes made with hot chocolate, tea, cider, steamed milk, and even orange juice.

Whichever you choose, remember that the best hot drinks are made with high-quality ingredients: piping hot, freshly brewed coffee or tea, old-fashioned hot chocolate made with real cocoa and milk instead of a mix, cream you've whipped yourself, and fresh spices.

Most important of all, remember that a hot drink can be a tantalizing experience. Don't rush it. Let the mug warm your hands. Savor the aroma before taking that first sip. Relish the comforting feeling. By the time you're done, you'll have warmed not only your body, but your soul.

AMARETTO TEA

6 oz.   Hot Tea
1½–2 oz. Amaretto

Pour hot tea into parfait glass, putting a spoon in the glass to prevent cracking. Add amaretto but do not stir. Top with whipped cream.

AMERICAN GROG

1 cube   Sugar
Juice of ¼ Lemon
1½ oz.   Light Rum

Pour ingredients into hot mug and fill with hot water. Stir.

APRIHOT

3 oz.   Apricot-flavored Brandy
3 oz.   Boiling Water

Combine in coffee mug with a dash of cinnamon, and garnish with an orange or lemon slice.

BLACK GOLD

4 oz.   Hot Coffee
¼ oz.   Triple Sec
¼ oz.   Amaretto
¼ oz.   Irish Cream Liqueur
¼ oz.   Hazelnut Liqueur
1 dash   Cinnamon Schnapps

Pour all ingredients except coffee and cinnamon schnapps into Irish coffee glass. Add coffee and schnapps and stir. Top with whipped cream and shaved chocolate. Serve with a cinnamon stick as a stirrer.

BLUE BLAZER

2½ oz.   Blended Whiskey
2½ oz.   Boiling Water
1 tsp.   Powdered Sugar

Use two large silver-plated mugs with handles. Put the whiskey into one mug and the boiling water into the other. Ignite the whiskey and, while it is blazing, mix both ingredients by pouring them four or five times from one mug to the other. If done well, this will have the appearance of a continuous stream of liquid fire. Sweeten with powdered sugar and serve with a twist of lemon peel. Serve in 4-oz. punch cup.

BOSTON CARIBBEAN COFFEE*

1 oz.   Crème de Cacao (Brown)
1 oz.   Dark Rum
Hot Coffee

Dip rim of Irish coffee glass in lime juice, then in sugar. Pour liqueur and rum into the glass. Fill with freshly brewed coffee. Top with whipped cream and sprinkle with cinnamon. Garnish with a cinnamon stick as a stirrer.

Niki Lamont, Winner, Boston "Shake Up the World" Contest

BRANDY BLAZER

1 cube   Sugar
1 piece   Orange Peel
2 oz.   Brandy

Combine ingredients in old-fashioned glass. Light the liquid with match, stir with long spoon for a few seconds, and strain into hot punch cup.

CAFFÈ DI AMARETTO

1 oz.   Amaretto
1 cup   Hot Coffee

Add amaretto to a cup of hot black coffee. Serve in an Irish coffee glass. Top with whipped cream.

CAFÉ L'ORANGE

½ oz.   Cognac
½ oz.   Cointreau
1 oz.   Mandarine Napoléon
4 oz.   Hot Coffee

Pour cognac and liqueurs into Irish coffee glass. Add coffee. Top with whipped cream and garnish with finely chopped orange rind.

The Americans are a funny lot. They drink whiskey to keep them warm; then they put some ice in it to make it cool. They put sugar in it to make it sweet, and then they put a slice of lemon in it to make it sour. Then they say "Here's to you" and drink it themselves.

—*B.N. Chakravarty*
India Speaks to America, 1966

CAPRICCIO

1 tbsp.   Sugar
½ oz.   Brandy
½ oz.   Crème de Café
1 oz.   Amaretto
Hot Coffee

Put sugar in bottom of Irish coffee glass that has had its rim moistened and dipped in cinnamon sugar. Add brandy and liqueurs. Fill ¾ full with coffee. Top with whipped cream, toasted almond slices, and a cherry.

CHOCOLATE COFFEE KISS

¼ oz.   Coffee Liqueur
¼ oz.   Irish Cream
          Liqueur
1 splash Crème de Cocoa
          (Brown)
1 splash Mandarine Napoléon
1½ oz.   Chocolate Syrup
Hot Coffee

Pour liqueurs and syrup into Irish coffee glass, and fill with coffee. Top with whipped cream and garnish with shaved chocolate and a cherry.

DOUBLEMINT

1 oz.   Spearmint
          Schnapps
Hot Coffee
1 dash   Crème de Menthe
          (Green)

Pour schnapps into Irish coffee glass. Add coffee and stir. Top with whipped cream. Add crème de menthe for color.

GIN TODDY (HOT)

1 cube   Sugar
Boiling Water
2 oz.   Gin

Put sugar into punch cup and fill two-thirds full with boiling water. Add gin. Stir and decorate with a slice of lemon. Sprinkle nutmeg on top.

HANDICAPPER'S CHOICE

1 oz.   Irish Whiskey
1 oz.   Amaretto
5 oz.   Hot Coffee

Pour whiskey and amaretto into Irish coffee glass and fill with hot coffee. Top with whipped cream.

HOT BRANDY ALEXANDER

¾ oz.   Brandy
¾ oz.   Crème de Cacao
           (Brown)
4 oz.   Steamed Milk

Pour ingredients into heated mug. Top with whipped cream and chocolate shavings.

HOT BRANDY TODDY

1 cube   Sugar
Boiling Water
2 oz.   Brandy

Put sugar in coffee mug and fill two-thirds full with boiling water. Add brandy and stir. Decorate with a slice of lemon and sprinkle with nutmeg.

HOT BRICK TODDY

1 tsp.   Butter
1 tsp.   Powdered Sugar
3 pinches Cinnamon
1 oz.   Hot Water

Put all ingredients except whiskey into punch cup. Dissolve thoroughly. Add whiskey. Fill with boiling water and stir.

HOT BUTTERED RUM

1 tsp.   Brown Sugar
Boiling Water
1 tbsp.   Butter
2 oz.   Dark Rum

Put sugar into punch cup and fill two-thirds full with boiling water. Add butter and rum. Stir and sprinkle nutmeg on top.

HOT BUTTERED WINE

½ cup   Muscatel
¼ cup   Water
1 tsp.   Butter
2 tsps.   Maple Syrup

Heat wine and water just to simmering; do not boil. Preheat Irish coffee glass with boiling water. Pour heated wine mixture into glass and add butter and maple syrup. Stir and sprinkle with nutmeg. Serve at once.

Gam Bay
   —a Chinese toast

HOT CINNAMON ROLL

1½ oz. Cinnamon
Schnapps
Hot Apple Cider

Pour hot cider into Irish
coffee glass. Add schnapps.
Top with whipped cream.
Add a cinnamon stick as a
stirrer.

HOT GOLD

6 oz. Very Warm Orange
Juice
3 oz. Amaretto

Pour orange juice into red-
wine glass or mug. Add
amaretto and garnish with
cinnamon stick as stirrer.

HOT KISS

6 oz. Hot Coffee
½ oz. Crème de Menthe
(White)
1 oz. Irish Whiskey
½ oz. Crème de Cacao
(White)

Pour liqueurs and whiskey
into Irish coffee glass. Add
coffee and stir. Top with
whipped cream and garnish
with a chocolate-covered
mint.

INDIAN SUMMER

2 oz. Apple Schnapps
Hot Apple Cider

Wet rim of sour glass and
dip in cinnamon. Add
schnapps and top off with
cider. Add a cinnamon stick,
if desired.

IRISH COFFEE

 1½ oz. Irish Whiskey
Hot Coffee

Into Irish coffee glass
rimmed with sugar, pour
Irish whiskey. Fill to within
half an inch of top with
coffee. Cover surface to brim
with whipped cream.

ITALIAN COFFEE

 ½ oz. Amaretto
Hot Coffee
1½ tbsps.Coffee Ice Cream

Pour amaretto into Irish
coffee glass. Fill with hot
coffee. Top with coffee ice
cream and sprinkle with
ground coriander.

JAMAICA COFFEE

 1 oz. Coffee-flavored
Brandy
¾ oz. Light Rum
Hot Coffee

Pour brandy and rum into
coffee mug. Fill with hot
coffee. Sweeten to taste. Top
with whipped cream and
sprinkle with nutmeg.

MEXICAN COFFEE

1 oz. Coffee Liqueur
½ oz. Tequila
5 oz. Hot Coffee

Stir coffee liqueur and
tequila in coffee cup, add
coffee, and top with
whipped cream.

MEXITALY COFFEE

¾ oz.   Coffee Liqueur
¾ oz.   Amaretto
Hot Coffee

Dip rim of Irish coffee glass
in cherry juice, then in
cinnamon sugar. Pour
liqueurs into glass and add
coffee. Top with whipped
cream and shaved chocolate.

MULLED CLARET

1 cube   Sugar
Juice of ½ Lemon
1 dash   Bitters
1 tsp.   Mixed Cinnamon
          and Nutmeg
5 oz.   Claret or Red Wine

Put all ingredients into a
metal mug. Heat poker red-
hot and hold in liquid until
boiling and serve; or warm
on a stove.

RAZZMATAZZ

1 oz.   Black Raspberry
          Liqueur
½ oz.   Crème de Cassis
½ oz.   Coffee Liqueur
Hot Coffee

Pour liqueurs into Irish
coffee glass. Add coffee. Top
with whipped cream and
garnish with berries in
season.

A Scotsman was playing golf one
bitter cold day. At the end of the
round he slipped something into
the caddie's hand and said kind-
ly, "That's for a glass of hot
whiskey, my man."

The caddie opened his hand
and discovered a lump of sugar!

RUEDESHEIM KAFFE

3 cubes   Sugar
1½ oz.   Asbach Uralt
          Brandy
Hot Coffee

Place sugar cubes in heat-
proof coffee cup. Add
brandy and set aflame.
Allow to burn for a good
minute, then fill with coffee.
Top with whipped cream
and sprinkle with grated
chocolate.

RUM TODDY (HOT)

1 cube   Sugar
Boiling Water
2 oz.   Light or Dark Rum

Put sugar into Irish coffee
cup and fill two-thirds full
with boiling water. Add rum
and stir. Decorate with a
slice of lemon and sprinkle
with nutmeg.

RUSSIAN COFFEE

½ oz.   Coffee Liqueur
½ oz.   Hazelnut Liqueur
¼ oz.   Vodka
Hot Coffee

Pour liqueurs and vodka into
Irish coffee glass. Add coffee.
Top with whipped cream.

SNOW BUNNY

1½ oz.   Triple Sec
Hot Chocolate

Pour triple sec into a heavy
mug. Fill with hot chocolate.
Garnish with a stick of
cinnamon for flavoring and
to use as a stirrer.

SPANISH COFFEE

1 oz.   Spanish Brandy
Hot Coffee

Add coffee to brandy in mug and top with whipped cream.

STEAMING PEACH

2 oz.   Peach Schnapps
4 oz.   Hot Water

Pour schnapps into snifter. Add hot water and stir. Float an orange slice as a garnish.

WHISKEY TODDY (HOT)

1 cube   Sugar
Boiling Water
2 oz.   Blended Whiskey

Put sugar into Irish coffee glass and fill two-thirds full with boiling water. Add whiskey and stir. Decorate with a slice of lemon and sprinkle with nutmeg.

THE IRON FIST TRICK

Tell someone to hold his fists one on top of the other and you will knock them apart with only your two index fingers. Clench your fingers into fists, leaving your forefingers free; then, strike his top fist with your left finger, moving with a strong horizontal motion. You will be able to do this every time. He will then believe he can do the same to you, but he can't because, when you place one fist on top of the other, secretly slip the thumb of your bottom fist inside the top one.

Eggnogs and Punches

A well-established holiday tradition, eggnog first became popular during colonial times. Basically a combination of milk, eggs, and liquor (historically rum, but whiskey and brandy are also used), the name eggnog is probably derived from the word *noggin,* meaning a small drinking cup. Eggnog can be made from scratch, but since those recipes use raw eggs, which may carry the risk of salmonella poisoning, only recipes using commercially prepared eggnog are included here. *Mr. Boston Egg Nog,* made with a blended whiskey, offers ready-to-serve convenience, requiring only chilling. Dairy eggnogs, which do no contain any alcohol, can be found in the refrigerated dairy case of most larger groceries. Eggnogs are most often served in quantity, but the following pages also contain some interesting variations for single servings.

Punches are an ideal way to serve a large number of guests without making individual drinks. Since they usually are made with only a single spirit, punches are also a great budget-conscious party beverage. Punch can be made with virtually any spirit, as well as wine, champagne, and even beer. Cold punches are popular any time of year, while hot punches are especially appropriate for winter get-togethers. Recipes for both can be found under separate headings within this section, serving anywhere from six guests to more than forty. Also included are several nonalcoholic punch recipes.

While cold punches in smaller quantities can be mixed in and served from a pitcher, larger recipes are usually served in a punch bowl from which guests can help themselves. Use a block office, not ice cubes, to keep punch chilled. Ice blocks can be elaborately decorative, frozen in gelatin molds with embedded fruits, or made simply by freezing water in a plastic freezer container.

Eggnogs

AMBASSADOR'S MORNING LIFT

32 oz.	Prepared Dairy Eggnog
6 oz.	Cognac
3 oz.	Jamaica Rum
3 oz.	Crème de Cacao (Brown)

Combine ingredients in large punch bowl and serve. Sprinkle nutmeg on top of each serving. Brandy or bourbon may be substituted for cognac. Makes 10–12 servings.

BALTIMORE EGGNOG

32 oz.	Prepared Dairy Eggnog
5 oz.	Brandy
5 oz.	Jamaica Rum
5 oz.	Madeira Wine

Combine ingredients in large punch bowl and serve. Sprinkle nutmeg on top of each serving. Makes 10–12 servings.

BRANDY EGGNOG

32 oz.	Prepared Dairy Eggnog
12 oz.	Brandy

Combine ingredients in large punch bowl and serve. Sprinkle nutmeg on top of each serving. Makes 10–12 servings.

BREAKFAST EGGNOG

32 oz.	Prepared Dairy Eggnog
10 oz.	Apricot-flavored Brandy
2½ oz.	Triple Sec

Combine ingredients in large punch bowl and serve. Sprinkle nutmeg on top of each serving. Makes 10–12 servings.

CHRISTMAS YULE EGGNOG

32 oz.	Prepared Dairy Eggnog
12 oz.	Blended Whiskey
1½ oz.	Light Rum

Combine ingredients in large punch bowl and serve. Sprinkle nutmeg on top of each serving. Makes 10–12 servings.

EGG CRUSHER*

8 oz.	Mr. Boston Egg Nog
1 oz.	Light Rum
1 oz.	Coffee Liqueur

Stir with ice and strain into oversized snifter. Sprinkle with nutmeg.

*Martin Stevens, Winner, Boston "Shake Up the World" Contest

FROSTY NOG

½ cup   Mr. Boston Egg Nog
2 tbsps. Sugar

Combine eggnog and sugar in blender. Slowly add up to three cups of ice, blending at medium speed. Continue to blend until smooth and frosty. Pour into parfait glass. Garnish with almond slivers and nutmeg.

IMPERIAL EGGNOG

32 oz.   Prepared Dairy Eggnog
10 oz.   Brandy
2 oz.   Apricot-flavored Brandy

Combine ingredients in large punch bowl and serve. Sprinkle nutmeg on top of each serving. Makes 10–12 servings.

MAPLE EGGNOG

32 oz.   Prepared Dairy Eggnog
½ cup   Maple Syrup

Combine ingredients in large pitcher and chill. Stir before serving. Garnish with nutmeg, if desired. Refrigerate leftovers. Makes 8 servings.

NASHVILLE EGGNOG

32 oz.   Prepared Dairy Eggnog
6 oz.   Bourbon
3 oz.   Brandy
3 oz.   Jamaica Rum

Combine ingredients in large punch bowl and serve. Sprinkle nutmeg on top of each serving. Makes 10–12 servings.

NOG DE CACAO

1½ oz.   Crème de Cacao
1½ oz.   Mr. Boston Egg Nog

Pour over ice in old-fashioned glass and stir.

PORT WINE EGGNOG

32 oz.   Prepared Dairy Eggnog
18 oz.   Port Wine

Combine ingredients in large punch bowl and serve. Sprinkle nutmeg on top of each serving. Makes 10–12 servings.

RUM EGGNOG

32 oz.   Prepared Dairy Eggnog
12 oz.   Light Rum

Combine ingredients in large punch bowl and serve. Sprinkle nutmeg on top of each serving. Makes 10–12 servings.

RUSSIAN NOG

1 oz.   Vodka
1 oz.   Coffee Liqueur
1 oz.   Mr. Boston
          Egg Nog

Pour over ice in old-fashioned glass and stir.

SHERRY EGGNOG

32 oz.   Prepared Dairy
           Eggnog
18 oz.   Cream Sherry

Combine ingredients in large punch bowl and serve. Sprinkle nutmeg on top of each serving. Makes 10–12 servings.

WHISKEY EGGNOG

32 oz.   Prepared Dairy
           Eggnog
12 oz.   Blended Whiskey

Combine ingredients in large punch bowl and serve. Sprinkle nutmeg on top of each serving. Makes 10–12 servings.

Kampai
      —a Japanese toast

Cold Punches

APRICOT ORANGE FIZZ

1½ cups Orange Juice
½ cup   Light Rum
¼ cup   Apricot Brandy
2 tbsps. Lime Juice
Club Soda

In pitcher, stir together orange juice, rum, brandy, and lime juice. Pour into ice-filled collins glasses about two-thirds full. Top with club soda. Stir and garnish with lime slices. Makes 6 servings.

BOMBAY PUNCH

Juice of 12 Lemons
Powdered Sugar
32 oz.   Brandy
32 oz.   Dry Sherry
½ cup   Maraschino
½ cup   Triple Sec
4   750-ml. bottles
          Chilled
          Champagne
64 oz.   Chilled Club Soda

Add enough powdered sugar to sweeten lemon juice. Pour over a large block of ice in punch bowl and stir. Then add remaining ingredients. Stir well and decorate with fruits in season. Serve in punch cups. Makes 60 servings.

BOOM BOOM PUNCH

64 oz.	Light Rum
32 oz.	Orange Juice
1	750-ml. bottle Sweet Vermouth
1	750-ml. bottle Chilled Champagne

Pour all ingredients except champagne into punch bowl over large block of ice. Stir. Top with champagne. Decorate with sliced bananas. Makes 36 servings.

BRANDY PUNCH

Juice of	1 dozen Lemons
Juice of	4 Oranges
Sugar	
1 cup	Grenadine
32 oz.	Club Soda
1 cup	Triple Sec
1.75 liters	Brandy
2 cups	Tea (optional)

Add enough sugar to sweeten lemon and orange juice and mix with grenadine and club soda. Pour over large block of ice in punch bowl and stir well. Then add triple sec, brandy, and tea, if desired. Stir well and decorate with fruits in season. Makes 35 servings.

BRUNCH PUNCH

3 qts.	Tomato Juice, chilled
1 liter	Light or Dark Rum
2½ tsps.	Worcestershire Sauce
5 oz.	Lemon or Lime Juice

Salt and Pepper to taste

Combine all ingredients in large container and stir. Pour over block of ice in punch bowl and garnish with thinly sliced lemons or limes. Makes 40 servings.

CAPE CODDER PUNCH

3	32-oz. bottles Cranberry-apple Drink
3 cups	Vodka
2 cups	Orange Juice
⅔ cup	Lemon Juice
½ cup	Sugar
1	28-oz. bottle Mineral Water, chilled

Combine first 5 ingredients, stirring until sugar dissolves and chill. Stir in mineral water just before serving. Makes 40 servings.

CARDINAL PUNCH

Juice of 1 dozen Lemons
Powdered Sugar

16 oz.	Brandy
16 oz.	Light Rum
1 split	Chilled Champagne
64 oz.	Claret or Red Wine
32 oz.	Club Soda
8 oz.	Sweet Vermouth
16 oz.	Strong Tea (optional)

Add enough powdered sugar to sweeten lemon juice. Pour over large block of ice in punch bowl and stir well. Then add remaining ingredients. Stir well and decorate with fruits in season. Makes 42 servings.

CHAMPAGNE CUP

4 tsps.	Powdered Sugar
6 oz.	Club Soda
1 oz.	Triple Sec
2 oz.	Brandy
16 oz.	Chilled Champagne

Fill large glass pitcher with cubes of ice and all ingredients except champagne. Add champagne. Stir well and decorate with fruits in season and rind of cucumber inserted on each side of pitcher. Top with a small bunch of mint. Serve in red-wine glasses. Makes 6 servings.

CHAMPAGNE PUNCH

Juice of 1 dozen Lemons
Powdered Sugar

1 cup	Maraschino
1 cup	Triple Sec
16 oz.	Brandy
2	750-ml. bottles Chilled Champagne
16 oz.	Club Soda
16 oz.	Strong Tea (optional)

Add enough powdered sugar to sweeten lemon juice. Pour over large block of ice in punch bowl and stir well. Then add remaining ingredients. Stir well and decorate with fruits in season. Makes 32 servings.

CHAMPAGNE SHERBET PUNCH

3 cups	Chilled Pineapple Juice
¼ cup	Lemon Juice
1 qt.	Pineapple Sherbet
1	750-ml. bottle Chilled Champagne

In a punch bowl, combine juices. Just before serving, scoop sherbet into punch bowl; add champagne. Stir gently. Makes 20 servings.

CIDER CUP

4 tsps.	Powdered Sugar
6 oz.	Club Soda
1 oz.	Triple Sec
2 oz.	Brandy
16 oz.	Apple Cider

Fill large glass pitcher with ice. Stir in the ingredients and decorate with fruits in season and a rind of cucumber inserted on each side of pitcher. Top with a small bunch of mint. Serve in red-wine glasses. Makes 6 servings.

CITRUS-BEER PUNCH

6	Lemons
2 cups	Sugar
2 cups	Water
1 cup	Chilled Grapefruit Juice
2	12-oz. cans Chilled Light Beer

Remove peel from lemons and set aside. Juice lemons (about 2 cups juice). In large saucepan, stir together sugar and water. Bring to boiling and add reserved lemon peel. Remove from heat. Cover and let stand 5 minutes. Remove and discard peel. Add lemon juice and grapefruit juice to sugar mixture. Transfer mixture to a 3-quart pitcher; cover and chill. Just before serving, add beer. Pour into glass mugs over cracked ice and garnish with lemon slices. Makes 8 servings.

CLARET CUP

4 tsps.	Powdered Sugar
6 oz.	Club Soda
1 oz.	Triple Sec
2 oz.	Brandy
16 oz.	Claret

Fill large glass pitcher with ice. Stir in the ingredients and decorate with fruits in season and a rind of cucumber inserted on each side of pitcher. Top with a small bunch of mint. Serve in red-wine glasses. Makes 6 servings.

CLARET PUNCH

Juice of 1 dozen Lemons	
Powdered Sugar	
1 cup	Triple Sec
16 oz.	Brandy
3	750-ml. bottles Claret
32 oz.	Club Soda
32 oz.	Strong Tea (optional)

Add enough powdered sugar to sweeten lemon juice. Pour over large block of ice in punch bowl and stir well. Then add remaining ingredients. Stir and decorate with fruits in season. Makes 40 servings.

EXTRA-KICK PUNCH

2 qts.	Water
1 cup	Brown Sugar
2 cups	Dark Rum
1 cup	Brandy
1 cup	Lemon Juice
1 cup	Pineapple Juice
¼ cup	Peach Brandy

Combine water and brown sugar, stirring until sugar dissolves. Add remaining ingredients; chill. Pour over block of ice in punch bowl. Makes 28 servings.

FISH HOUSE PUNCH

Juice of 1 dozen Lemons	
Powdered Sugar	
1½ liters	Brandy
1 liter	Peach-flavored Brandy
16 oz.	Light Rum
32 oz.	Club Soda
16 oz.	Strong Tea (optional)

Add enough powdered sugar to sweeten lemon juice. Pour over large block of ice in punch bowl and stir well. Then add remaining ingredients. Stir well and decorate with fruits in season. Makes 40 servings.

> Fish House Punch, made with rum and peach brandy, originated in Colonial times at the fishing and social club called State in Schuylkill in Pennsylvania.

KENTUCKY PUNCH

12 oz.	Frozen Orange Juice Concentrate, thawed and undiluted
12 oz.	Frozen Lemonade Concentrate, thawed and undiluted
1 cup	Lemon Juice
1 liter	Bourbon
1	2-liter bottle Lemon-lime Soda

Combine all ingredients except soda in large container and chill. Pour into punch bowl over large block of ice and stir in soda. Makes 32 servings.

LOVING CUP

4 tsps.	Powdered Sugar
6 oz.	Club Soda
1 oz.	Triple Sec
2 oz.	Brandy
16 oz.	Claret

Fill large glass pitcher with ice and stir in the ingredients. Decorate with fruits in season and rind of cucumber inserted on each side of the pitcher. Top with a small bunch of mint sprigs. Makes 6 servings.

MINT JULEP PUNCH

1 cup   Mint Jelly
4 cups   Water
3¼ cups Bourbon
6 cups   Pineapple Juice
½ cup   Lime Juice
7 cups   Lemon-lime Soda

Combine mint jelly and 2 cups of water in saucepan, stirring over low heat until jelly melts. Cool. Add bourbon, pineapple juice, remaining water, and lime juice; chill. To serve, pour mixture over a block of ice in punch bowl. Slowly pour in soda, stirring gently. Garnish with lime slices and fresh mint leaves, if desired. Makes 44 servings.

RHINE WINE CUP

4 tsps.   Powdered Sugar
6 oz.   Club Soda
1 oz.   Triple Sec
2 oz.   Brandy
16 oz.   White Wine

Mix ingredients and pour into large glass pitcher over cubes of ice. Stir and decorate with fruits in season. Insert rind of cucumber on each side of pitcher. Top with mint sprigs. Serve in red-wine glasses. Makes 6 servings.

SANGRIA

¼ cup   Sugar (or to taste)
1 cup   Water
1   Thinly Sliced Orange
1   Thinly Sliced Lime
1   750-ml. bottle Red or Rosé wine
6 oz.   Sparkling Water
Other Fruits as desired (bananas, strawberries, etc.)

Dissolve sugar in water in large pitcher. Add fruit and wine and 12 or more ice cubes. Stir until cold. Add sparkling water. Serve in red-wine glasses, putting some fruit in each glass. Makes 10 servings.

SAUTERNE CUP

4 tsps.   Powdered Sugar
6 oz.   Club Soda
1 tbsp.   Triple Sec
1 tbsp.   Curaçao
2 oz.   Brandy
16 oz.   Sauterne

Put all ingredients in large glass pitcher with ice. Stir and decorate with fruits in season and rind of cucumber inserted on each side of pitcher. Top with a small bunch of mint sprigs. Serve in white-wine glasses. Makes 6 servings.

TEQUILA PUNCH

1 liter	Chilled Tequila
1	750-ml. bottle Chilled Champagne
4	750-ml. bottles Chilled Sauterne
64 oz.	Fresh Fruits (cubes or balls)

Put all ingredients in large punch bowl and sweeten to taste with simple syrup. Add ice cubes just before serving. Makes 40 servings.

WEST INDIAN PUNCH

64 oz.	Light Rum
1	750-ml. bottle Crème de Banana
32 oz.	Pineapple Juice
32 oz.	Orange Juice
32 oz.	Lemon Juice
¾ cup	Powdered Sugar
1 tsp.	Grated Nutmeg
1 tsp.	Cinnamon
½ tsp.	Grated Cloves
6 oz.	Club Soda

Dissolve sugar and spices in club soda. Pour into large punch bowl over a block of ice and add rum, crème de banana, and juices. Stir and decorate with sliced bananas. Makes 48 servings.

WHISKEY SOUR PUNCH

3	6-oz. cans Frozen Lemonade Concentrate thawed and undiluted
4 cups	Bourbon
3 cups	Orange Juice
1	2-liter bottle Club Soda, chilled

Combine ingredients over block of ice in punch bowl. Stir gently. Garnish with orange slices. Makes 32 servings.

Hot Punches

HOT APPLE BRANDY

6 cups   Apple Juice
1½ cups Apricot Brandy
3   Cinnamon Sticks
½ tsp.   Ground Cloves

Simmer all ingredients over low heat for 30 minutes. Serve warm in brandy snifters. Makes 6–8 servings.

HOT BURGUNDY PUNCH

¼ cup   Sugar
1½ cups Boiling Water
Peel of ½ Lemon
1   3-inch Cinnamon
          Stick
5   Whole Cloves
½ tsp.   Ground Allspice
1 cup   Apple Juice
1   750-ml. bottle
          Burgundy Wine
½ tsp.   Nutmeg

In large saucepan, dissolve sugar in boiling water. Add lemon peel, cinnamon, cloves, allspice and apple juice. Cook over moderately high heat for 15 minutes. Strain into another saucepan and add wine. Simmer over low heat but do not boil. Serve hot in heat-proof cups with a sprinkle of nutmeg. Makes 16 servings.

HOT RUMMED CIDER

1½ qts. Apple Cider
6 tbsps. Brown Sugar
3 tbsps. Butter
1½ cups Light Rum

Bring cider and sugar to a boil in large saucepan. Reduce heat and add butter. When butter is melted, add rum. Serve in heat-proof punch bowl or pitcher. Makes 6–8 servings.

SMUGGLER'S BREW

1½ cups Dark Rum
1 qt.   Tea
3 tbsps. Butter
½ cup   Sugar
½ tsp.   Nutmeg
½ cup   Brandy

Heat all ingredients except brandy in large saucepan until boiling. Heat brandy in small saucepan until barely warm and add to rum mixture. Pour into heat-proof con-tainer to serve. Makes 8 servings.

WINTER CIDER

1½ cups Rum
1 cup   Peach Brandy
¾ cup   Peach Schnapps
6   Cinnamon Sticks
1 gal.   Apple Cider

In large saucepan, bring cider and cinnamon to a full boil over medium heat. Reduce heat and add rum, brandy, and schnapps, stirring until heated through. Serve in Irish coffee glasses, garnished with a cinnamon stick and an apple slice. Makes 18–20 servings.

Nonalcoholic Punches

BANANA PUNCH

1½ qts.   Water
3 cups   Sugar
12 oz.   Frozen Orange
          Juice Concentrate,
          thawed and
          undiluted
46 oz.   Pineapple-
          grapefruit Juice
4   Bananas, mashed
Club Soda

Mix water and sugar. Add juices and bananas. Pour into quart-size freezer containers and freeze overnight. About 1 hour before serving, remove from freezer and place mixture in punch bowl. Add 1 liter of club soda per 2 quarts of mix and stir gently. Makes 40 servings.

DOUBLE BERRY PUNCH

2 qts.   Cranberry Juice
3 cups   Raspberry-flavored
          Soda, chilled
10 oz.   Frozen Raspberries,
          thawed
1 qt.   Raspberry Sherbet

Chill cranberry juice in punch bowl. Just before serving, slowly pour in soda and stir gently. Serve over small scoops of sherbet in punch cups and garnish with raspberries. Makes 25–30 servings.

FUNSHINE FIZZ

2 cups   Orange Juice
2 cups   Pineapple Juice
1 pint   Orange Sherbet
1 cup   Club Soda

Combine first 3 ingredients in blender, blending until smooth. Pour mixture into pitcher and stir in club soda. Serve in collins glasses. Makes 6–8 servings.

TROPICAL CREAM PUNCH

14 oz.   Sweetened
          Condensed Milk
6 oz.   Frozen Orange Juice
          Concentrate,
          thawed and
          undiluted
6 oz.   Frozen Pineapple
          Juice Concentrate,
          thawed and
          undiluted
1   2-liter bottle Chilled
          Club Soda

In punch bowl, combine sweetened condensed milk and juice concentrates; mix well. Add club soda, stir gently. Add block of ice and garnish with orange slices. Makes 22 servings.

THE PAPER BRIDGE TRICK

Ask someone to support a glass on a paper bridge set on two other glasses. Of course, the person will not be able to do so, unless he is aware of the method, which is to pleat the paper as shown in the illustration, thus adding the necessary strength to support the glass.

"Beer" refers to all brewed and fermented beverages that are made from malted grains and hops. It is the third most popular beverage in the world, surpassed only by water and tea. Beer-making dates back many centuries. A 9,000-year-old Mesopotamian tablet mentions a recipe for beer, as do 8,000-year-old Babylonian clay tablets. Beer was brewed by the ancient Egyptians as early as 3000 B.C.

There are five major types of beer: lager, ale, stout, porter, and bock. For all of these, the stages of brewing are similar. The difference between light and dark beers comes from the amount of roasting, or "kilning," of the barley malt. The more roasting, the darker the color and the greater the caramelization of malt sugars.

Usually made from barley, beer begins with the germination of the grain. Once germinated, the barley is called "malt."

The malt is then dried in a hot kiln. The temperature and duration of roasting determines both the color and sweetness of the final product. The longer the roast, the darker and sweeter the beer.

Next, the roasted malt is mixed with other cereals and water and cooked.

After cooking, liquid from this pre-alcoholic mash is drained off. The liquid is called "wort." The wort is put into a brew kettle and infused with hops, a small, soft flower that adds a depth of flavor and a pleasantly bitter tang to beer.

After a few hours of boiling in the wort, the hops are strained out, the wort is cooled, and yeast is added, which "attacks" the malt sugar, causing fermentation.

Yeast converts wort to beer. The pedigree of the yeast, the secret formula so carefully perpetuated so that the beer will have the small flavor year after year, is the brewmaster's "magic wand."

Two different types of yeasts make all the differences among beers. When "bottom" yeast finishes eating the sugar, it settles to the bottom of the tank. Lager is a "bottom-fermented" beer. Practically all beers brewed in the United States are lagers.

Ale, on the other hand, is a "top-fermented" beverage. "Top" yeast floats on the top of the tank when it finishes eating the sugar.

The difference made by the two yeasts can be tasted. Ales tend to have a fruity/spicy aroma and a more robust and hoppier flavor than lagers.

The ideal serving temperature is 45°F for beer and 50°F for ale. Beer goes flat if served too cold.

Store bottled or canned beer in a cool, dark place. Extremely sensitive to sunlight, bottled beer must never be put in windows or it will acquire a "skunky" odor. At home, store cans or bottles in the lowest, coolest part of the refrigerator.

To serve beer, pour it so that the stream flows directly to the center of the glass, which should be stationary on the table. This produces a nice foam or "head." Beer naturally accompanies hamburgers, stews, sausage, cold cuts, pizza, and sharp cheeses.

Here are some definitions:

Beer—a generic term for all brewed and fermented beverages made from cereal grains.

Lager—bright, clear-bodied beer, effervescent. A "bottom-fermented" brew. Most of the world's beers are lagers. *St. Pauli Girl* beer from Germany, *Corona Extra* from Mexico, and *Point Special Beer* from the Stevens Point Brewery in Wisconsin, are all sparkling gold in color with a clean, rich taste.

Ale—aromatic malt brew usually fuller-bodied, darker, and more bitter than lager. A "top-fermented" brew. *Double Diamond Ale* from England and *Point Pale Ale* are two brews with similar ale characteristics.

Stout—a very dark beer, sometimes sweetish and quite strong with a pronounced hops taste.

Porter—a type of ale with a rich, heavy foam. Sweeter than ale. Not quite as strong as stout.

Pilsner—a term put on labels of many light beers around the world. These are bright, lagered beers in the style made famous by Pilsner Urquell from Pilsen, Bohemia.

Bock Beer—a strong style of lager beer, originally seasonal (spring). *Point Bock* is a rich and creamy bock made with roasted malt that gives it a genuine caramel color and flavor. It is only available for a short time during the winter/spring season.

Malt Liquor—a beer with considerable variation from light to dark color, and from a strong, hoppy flavor to very little flavor at all. Higher alcoholic content than most other beers.

Sweet Beer—a combination of fruit juice and beer. Yields a sweeter drink and higher alcoholic content than lagers.

Sake—actually a type of beer in that it is a refermented rice brew of high alcoholic content.

Light Beer—lagers, lower in alcohol and calories, mild in taste. *Corona Light* is an excellent light beer with the full taste of a regular-strength beer but contains fewer calories and less alcohol.

Low-alcohol Beer—similar to Light Beer, but contains even less alcohol and fewer calories.

Nonalcoholic Beer—by law, must contain less than .5 percent alcohol by volume. *St. Pauli N.A.,* which was introduced into the United States in 1991, has a pleasant hop aroma, a well-balanced malt flavor, crisp hop finish, and the taste of an imported beer.

Almost every country can lay claim to producing excellent beer products including China *(Tsingtao),* Germany *(St. Pauli Girl* lager, dark, and nonalcoholic), England (*Double Diamond),* Mexico *(Corona Extra, Corona Light, Modelo Especial, Negra Modelo, Pacifico),* Italy *(Peroni),* and the United States. In fact, there has been an explosion of microbreweries around the country, but it's generally the tried and true that will remain, including the *Stevens Point Brewery* in Stevens Point, Wisconsin, who produces such quality products as *Point Special, Point Bock, Point Classic Amber, Point Pale Ale, Point Winter Spice,* and *Point Maple Wheat.*

Wine

Wine, one of the oldest beverages known, is a natural product made entirely from grapes. Its probable Mediterranean origin predates written history, with the earliest known documents indicating that wine has been made since 4000 b.c. Wine, winemaking, and the cultivation of wine grapes gradually spread throughout the Western world via tradesmen, religious sects, and conquering armies. Today, almost every continent can enjoy wine from its own resources.

For many people, especially Europeans, wine is an integral part of life. It enhances the enjoyment of nearly every occasion. A bottle of wine on the table turns mere eating into dining.

But where to start? The world of wine can be overwhelming. The variety of labels seems endless, the terminology may appear confusing, and the customs related to serving it are varied and sometimes mystifying. Although becoming knowledgeable about wine has become a popular hobby in the United States in recent years, it is not essential to the enjoyment of the beverage. Wine is first and foremost a pleasant drink meant to accompany food. Wine appreciation is similar to the appreciation of food. It takes no special expertise, merely the enjoyment of harmonious and attractive flavors.

What makes the subject of wine fascinating, however, is that each wine has its own personality. Nature guarantees it will never have quite the same character every year, even if it comes from the same vineyard, winemaker, and process. This factor, combined with the ever-changing character of wine as it ages, results in a complex world of beverages that can satisfy nearly every taste and suit nearly every occasion and meal.

Covering the vast world of wines made all over the world could take up a book itself. Indeed, there are quite a few excellent references by numerous experts available at bookstores and libraries, which will not be duplicated here. On the following pages you'll find basic information about wine, including how it is made, some common terminology, how to store, serve, and taste wines, and suggestions about which types of wine complement different kinds of foods. In addition to the books on the market, many communities offer wine appreciation courses and even wine tastings. If you are interested in learning more about wines, we encourage you to take advantage of these resources.

HOW WINE IS MADE

Grapes are picked when ripe, usually from September to October (in the Northern Hemisphere), and put into a crusher-stemmer, which removes the stems and produces grape "must." Must is pumped through a press to separate the juice from the skins. The juice of virtually all wine grape varieties is white. The color of red wines comes from leaving the dark skins of red grapes in contact with their juice, which colors it during fermentation. The juice is pumped into a settling tank, then into a fermentation vat where the natural wine yeasts are augmented. When fermentation is complete, the wine is drawn off and placed in casks for aging, if desired. After aging, wine is filtered and bottled.

WINE APPRECIATION

There are only two things you need in order to become a discriminating wine connoisseur and a smart wine buyer: experience and a good memory. The more wines you experience, the better you'll be able to discriminate between what you do and don't like. Learning to assess high-quality wine is fun and can save you money. A twelve-dollar bottle may or may not be twice as good as a six-dollar bottle, but only your palate can make that decision.

Preferences in wine are subjective and everyone's taste differs. The guidelines that are commonly given for tasting, judging, and selecting wine are useful rules of thumb and often a help, but are only intended to enhance enjoyment. Such guidelines can be ignored whenever your taste dictates otherwise.

WINE TASTING

There are three criteria for judging wine: color, aroma, and taste. You must first examine the wine in a clear glass for color. The deeper the color, the fuller the flavor. The wine should be clear and appealing. Murkiness indicates something has happened to change the taste and quality of the wine.

Next, swirl the glass to aerate the wine. This helps release the bouquet, or aroma. Most of anyone's judgment of wine is based on the aroma because the sense of taste is dependent on smell. In a light white wine, a fruity, flowery, grapey perfume may arise. The big red wines may have a spicy berrylike character.

Now, taste it. Take some in your mouth and savor it before swallowing. Notice the components. Is it dry or sweet? Is it fruity or acidic? It is too heavy, too light, or well-balanced? And most important—do you like it? If you do, write down the type, producer, and vintage of the wine. It will be helpful to have a list of a few names you can rely on for your next trip to a wine and spirits store.

WINE STORAGE

After purchase, wines should be stored in a cool, dry place such as a basement or storeroom, away from heat and wide variations in temperature. Screw-top wines can be stored standing up, but wines that have corks should be stored on their sides so that the cork remains moist. If the cork dries out, air will enter the bottle and oxidize the wine. Once opened, keep the leftover wine corked tightly and place in the refrigerator. Most wines will keep like this for only a few days. After that, the wine absorbs oxygen and beings to turn to vinegar.

If wine, particularly red wine, has been stored for a number of years, a sediment may form on the side of the bottle. This is a natural side effect of aging and does not mean the wine has been spoiled. However, before serving, pour the wine slowly and carefully into a clean decanter or pitcher, holding the shoulder of the bottle over a flashlight, so you can stop pouring when the sediment reaches the neck. The wine in the decanter will be clear.

WINE SERVICE

When serving wine, as with serving food, it's usually better to serve lighter beverages before more substantial ones. Hence, white wine is normally served before red, light wine before heavy, and dry before sweet. Red wines should be served at room temperature (65°) or slightly cool to the touch. White wines, rosés, and light reds such as Beaujolais are best served with a slight chill. For maximum effervescence, champagne and sparkling wine are best served very cold (45°) but not so chilled that the delicate flavors are lost.

For each wine type there is a proper kind of glass that provides optimum enjoyment, but in practice only a couple of styles are necessary. The best all-purpose glass for both red and white wine is an eight-to-ten-ounce clear glass that has a large bowl at the base and is slightly tapered inward on the top. The bowl allows plenty of room for swirling and the tapered top concentrates the scent. For champagne, a tall, clear flute-shaped glass ensures that the wine will retain the long stream of bubbles the winemaker went to such great effort to offer you. Shallow, bowl-shaped glasses give the wine a broad surface area from which the bubbles dissipate rapidly and cause the wine to go flat, if not spill.

It is common to have more than one glass at a table setting if you're serving more than one kind of wine.

WINE AND FOOD

In deciding which wine to serve with a particular meal or dish, remember that ideally the wine and food should make each other taste better. Consider the occasion: A picnic calls for something simple, a holiday dinner something special. Consider regional affinities. Italian wines, not surprisingly, go very well with Italian dishes. Consider, too, the intensity of the dish: Subtle, mild food goes well with delicate wines. Rich, spicy foods are best paired with big, full-flavored wines. Wines can be chosen to harmonize with the dish—a red wine and a steak, for example—or provide a pleasant contrast, such as a lemon-sharp, crisp white with a rich, oily salmon steak.

Here are some suggested types of wine for various occasions, meals, dishes, and courses:

Aperitif hour—champagne and sparkling wine, crisp whites such as Macon, California, Fumé Blanc, dry Fino Sherry. These wines have crisp acidity and are pleasantly sharp and savory in taste, which stimulates the appetite and refreshes the palate. Their cutting flavor makes an attractive contrast to rich canapés, caviar, oysters, nuts.

Fish—normally, crisp whites are best, because their high acidity accents fish flavors in much the same way a squeeze of lemon does. Shellfish, for example, is excellent with sharper whites such as Muscadet. Lobster, however, has an affinity with rich, round whites such as Chardonnay or white Burgundy. But exceptionally rich fish dishes, such as salmon, will pair nicely with a light red or dry rosé.

Chicken, veal, pork, and mild cheeses—these lighter, versatile foods can be paired with lighter, less tannic reds, such as Beaujolais, Chianti, Pinot Noir, or flavorful whites such as Rieslings, Chenin Blanc, Chardonnay, and Gewürztraminer.

Lamb, game, and strong cheeses—these flavorful foods are best with Bordeaux, Cabernet Sauvignon, rich red Burgundies, Barolos, Riojas, Rhône wines, and other intense reds whose flavors naturally complement red meat and whose astringent tannins balance the fattiness of meats and cheeses.

Baked ham and turkey, sausages—best with fine dry rosés.

Beef and steak—excellent with Pinot Noirs, Cabernet Sauvignon, Merlots, Zinfandels, and other medium-bodied reds. Prime ribs call for an elegant, subtle red such as Pinot Noir; a charcoal-broiled steak with pepper sauce needs an equally assertive red, such as spicy Zinfandel.

Desserts—over-sugary desserts overpower fine sweet wines. Mild fruit tarts, cakes, berries, etc., are delicious with sweet Rieslings, Sauternes, and Muscats. Mild chocolate desserts are best paired with ruby Port.

A GLOSSARY OF BASIC WINE TERMS

Acidity—a term used to indicate pleasant tartness or sharpness to the taste due to the presence of fruit acids.

Aroma—that portion of the wine's odor derived from the grape variety and fermentation.

Balance—a tasting term denoting complete harmony among the main components of a wine.

Body—the weight or fullness of wine on the palate.

Bouquet—that portion of a wine's odor that develops after it is bottled.

Dry—a tasting term to denote the absence of sweetness in wine.

Enology—the study of winemaking.

Fermentation—the process of converting natural grape sugar into alcohol and carbon dioxide by the addition of yeast.

Generic Wine—wine blended with several grape varieties in which the character of any one variety does not dominate. These wines are labeled with a generalized term such as Chablis, Burgundy, or Rhine.

Nose—the total odor of wine composed of aroma, bouquet, and other factors.

Residual Sugar—the natural grape sugar that is left in a wine which determines the sweetness level.

Tannin—the components in a wine that have an astringent, puckery, and sometimes bitter quality, and a mouth-drying aftertaste.

Varietal Wine—Wine made from 75% of one grape variety, such as Chardonnay or Cabernet Sauvignon.

Vintage Wine—Wine made from grapes that are harvested in one given year. The wine must be at least 95% from the grapes and year started on the label. The remaining 5% is used to blend in different juice (wine) that will create a unique taste profile to that company's wine.

Bad men live that they may eat and drink, whereas good men eat and drink that they may live.

—*Socrates*

AMERICANO

2 oz.   Sweet Vermouth
2 oz.   Campari
Club Soda

Pour sweet vermouth and
Campari into highball glass
over ice cubes. Fill with club
soda and stir. Add a twist of
lemon peel.

ANDALUSIA

1½ oz.   Dry Sherry
½ oz.   Brandy
½ oz.   Light Rum

Stir well with cracked ice
and strain into cocktail
glass.

BISHOP

Juice of ¼ Lemon
Juice of ¼ Orange
1 tsp.   Powdered Sugar
Burgundy

Shake with ice and strain
into highball glass. Add two
ice cubes, fill with burgundy,
and stir well. Decorate with
fruits.

BRAZIL COCKTAIL

1½ oz.   Dry Vermouth
1½ oz.   Dry Sherry
1 dash   Bitters
¼ tsp.   Anisette

Stir with ice and strain into
cocktail glass.

BROKEN SPUR COCKTAIL

¼ oz.   Sweet Vermouth
1½ oz.   Port
¼ tsp.   Triple Sec

Stir with ice and strain into
cocktail glass.

CHAMPAGNE COCKTAIL

1 cube   Sugar
2 dashes Bitters
Chilled Champagne

Place sugar and bitters in
chilled champagne flute and
fill with champagne. Add a
twist of lemon peel.

CLARET COBBLER

1 tsp.   Powdered Sugar
2 oz.   Club Soda
3 oz.   Claret

Dissolve powdered sugar in
club soda and then add
claret. Fill red-wine glass
with ice and stir. Decorate
with fruits in season. Serve
with straws.

DIPLOMAT

1½ oz.   Dry Vermouth
½ oz.   Sweet Vermouth
2 dashes Bitters
½ tsp.   Maraschino

Stir with ice and strain into
cocktail glass. Serve with a
half-slice of lemon and a
cherry.

A Votre Santé
　　　　—a French toast

KIR ROYALE

6 oz.   Champagne
1 splash Crème de Cassis

Serve in large champagne flute or white-wine glass.

LEMONADE (CLARET)

2 tsps.   Powdered Sugar
Juice of 1 Lemon
2 oz.   Claret or Red Wine

Dissolve sugar and lemon in collins glass, then add ice and enough water to fill glass, leaving room to float wine. Decorate with slices of orange and lemon, and a cherry. Serve with straws.

> Age is something to brag about in your wine cellar and forget in a birthday book.

LEMONADE (MODERN)

1   Lemon
2 tsps.   Powdered Sugar
1½ oz.   Dry Sherry
1 oz.   Sloe Gin
Club Soda

Cut lemon into quarters and muddle well with sugar. Add sherry and sloe gin. Shake with ice and strain into collins glass. Fill glass with club soda.

LONDON SPECIAL

1 cube   Sugar
2 dashes Bitters
Chilled Champagne

Put a large twist of orange peel into champagne flute. Add sugar and bitters. Fill with champagne and stir.

PORT WINE COCKTAIL

2½ oz.   Port
½ tsp.   Brandy

Stir with ice and strain into cocktail glass.

PORT WINE SANGAREE

½ tsp.   Powdered Sugar
1 tsp.   Water
2 oz.   Port
Club Soda
1 tbsp.   Brandy

Dissolve sugar in water in highball glass. Add port and ice cubes. Fill with club soda to nearly top of glass and stir. Float brandy on top and sprinkle with nutmeg.

SIX GLASS PUZZLE

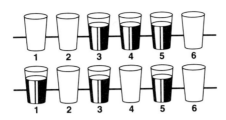

Place six glasses—3 filled and 3 empty—in a row as shown. Ask some-one to arrange the glasses so that they stand alternately one filled and one empty, etc. He must do this by moving or touching only one glass. METHOD: Lift glass 4 and pour its contents into glass 1, then put glass 4 back in its original place, producing the desired result, as shown.

Low-Alcohol Drinks

I f you're one of those folks who prefers a "light" cocktail with less alcohol, this section of recipes was tailor-made for you.

All the drinks on the following pages have one-third to one-half less alcohol than a standard drink—five ounces of wine, twelve ounces of beer, or a cocktail containing one and one-half ounces of spirit. Included here are the classic favorites such as the Bellini, Spritzer, and Mimosa, as well as a selection of other refreshing drinks.

Keep in mind, too, that many of the drinks in the previous sections of this book can easily be prepared as "light" cocktails simply by reducing the amount of spirit in the recipe. Of course, some drinks—such as a Martini or Manhattan—don't offer that flexibility. In general, however, tall drinks, particularly those made with clear spirits and juice mixers like a Screwdriver or Bloody Mary, can be adapted without noticeably affecting the taste. Don't hesitate to experiment and adapt recipes to suit your own taste or that of your guests.

When all such of us as have now reached the years of maturity first opened our eyes upon the stage of existence, we found intoxicating liquor recognized by everybody, used by everybody, repudiated by nobody.

It commonly entered into the first draught of the infant and the last of the dying man.

It is true that even then it was known and acknowledged that many were greatly injured by it; but none seemed to think the injury arose from the use of a bad thing, but from the abuse of a very good thing.

—*Abraham Lincoln, 1842*

ADONIS COCKTAIL

1 dash Orange Bitters
¾ oz. Sweet Vermouth
1½ oz. Dry Sherry

Stir with ice into cocktail glass.

ALOHA BUBBLY

2 oz. Pineapple Juice
½ tsp. Powdered Sugar
2 oz. Club Soda
2 oz. Dry White Wine
Club Soda

In tall, slender glass, put the pineapple juice, sugar, and 2 ounces club soda. Stir well. Fill glass with crushed ice and add the wine. Fill with club soda and stir again. Garnish with an orange or lemon peel spiral or whole fresh strawberry.

AMER PICON COCKTAIL

Juice of 1 Lime
1 tsp. Grenadine
1½ oz. Amer Picon

Shake with ice and strain into cocktail glass.

ANGEL FACE

1 oz. Gin
½ oz. Apricot-flavored Brandy
½ oz. Apple Brandy

Shake well with cracked ice and strain into cocktail glass.

BAMBOO COCKTAIL

1½ oz. Dry Sherry
¾ oz. Dry Vermouth
1 dash Orange Bitters

Stir with ice and strain into cocktail glass.

BELLINI

3 oz. Chilled Italian White Peach Juice (or Peach Nectar)
1 dash Lemon Juice
3 oz. Chilled Sparkling Wine (Dry)
1 dash Black Currant Juice or Grenadine

Pour white peach juice into champagne flute. Add dash of lemon juice (more if peach nectar is substituted) and dash of black currant juice or grenadine for color. Fill with chilled sparkling wine.

BITTERS HIGHBALL

¼ oz. Bitters
Ginger Ale or Club Soda

Fill highball glass with bitters, ice cubes, and ginger ale or club soda. Add a twist of lemon peel, if desired, and stir.

BITTERSWEET

1 oz. Sweet Vermouth
1 oz. Dry Vermouth
1 dash Bitters
1 dash Orange Bitters

Stir with cracked ice and strain into cocktail glass. Add a twist of orange peel.

BURGUNDY BUBBLER

| 1 oz. | Burgundy |
| 4 oz. | Ginger Ale |

Pour burgundy into large red-wine glass over ice. Fill with ginger ale. Add lemon, lime, and orange slices.

CAFÉ ROYALE

1 cube Sugar
Brandy
1 cup Hot Black Coffee

Put cube of sugar, well soaked with brandy, in teaspoon and hold so that it will rest on top of the cup of coffee and ignite. Hold until flame burns out. Drop contents in coffee.

COUNTRY CLUB COOLER

½ tsp.	Grenadine
2 oz.	Club Soda or Ginger Ale
2 oz.	Dry Vermouth

Into collins glass, put grenadine and club soda and stir. Add ice cubes and dry vermouth. Fill with ginger ale or club soda and stir again. Insert a spiral of orange or lemon peel (or both) and dangle end over rim of glass.

EAST INDIA COCKTAIL NO. 2

1½ oz.	Dry Vermouth
1½ oz.	Dry Sherry
1 dash	Orange Bitters

Stir with ice and strain into cocktail glass.

ECLIPSE COCKTAIL

Grenadine
1 oz.	Gin
2 oz.	Sloe Gin
½ tsp.	Lemon Juice

Put enough grenadine into cocktail glass to cover a ripe olive. Mix the remaining ingredients with ice and strain onto the grenadine so that they do not mix.

HOT SPRINGS COCKTAIL

1½ oz.	White Wine
1 tbsp.	Pineapple Juice
½ tsp.	Maraschino
1 dash	Orange Bitters

Shake with ice and strain into cocktail glass.

KIR

| 3 oz. | White Wine |
| 1 splash | Crème de Cassis |

Pour wine over ice in old-fashioned glass. Add crème de cassis, a twist of lemon, and stir.

L'Chaim
—a Hebrew toast

LAKE BREEZE

4 oz.   Cranberry Juice
2 oz.   Pineapple Juice
1 tsp.   Coconut Liqueur
Lemon-lime Soda

Shake with ice and strain into collins glass filled with ice cubes. Fill with soda.

MIMOSA

3 oz.   Chilled Champagne
3 oz.   Chilled Orange Juice

Pour into champagne flute or white-wine glass; stir.

PINEAPPLE COOLER

2 oz.   Pineapple Juice
½ tsp.   Powdered Sugar
2 oz.   Club Soda
2 oz.   White Wine
Club Soda

Put ingredients into collins glass. Stir. Add ice cubes. Fill with club soda and stir again. Insert a spiral of orange or lemon peel (or both) and dangle end over rim of glass.

PORT MILK PUNCH

1 tsp.   Powdered Sugar
2 oz.   Port
1 cup   Milk

Shake with ice and strain into collins glass. Sprinkle nutmeg on top.

PORT WINE NEGUS

½ cube   Sugar
2 oz.   Port

Pour into punch cup, fill with hot water, and stir. Sprinkle nutmeg on top.

QUEEN CHARLOTTE

2 oz.   Claret or Red Wine
1 oz.   Grenadine
Lemon-lime Soda

Pour into collins glass over ice cubes. Stir.

REFORM COCKTAIL

¾ oz.   Dry Vermouth
1½ oz.   Dry Sherry
1 dash   Orange Bitters

Stir with ice and strain into cocktail glass. Serve with a cherry.

SHANDY GAFF

5 oz.   Beer
5 oz.   Ginger Ale

Pour into collins glass and stir.

SHERRY COBBLER

1 tsp.   Powdered Sugar
2 oz.   Club Soda
2 oz.   Sweet Sherry

In red-wine glass, dissolve powdered sugar in club soda. Fill glass with ice and add sherry. Stir and decorate with fruits in season. Serve with straws.

SHERRY COCKTAIL

2½ oz.   Cream Sherry
1 dash   Bitters

Stir with ice and strain into cocktail glass. Add a twist of orange peel.

SPRITZER

3 oz.   Chilled White Wine
Club Soda

Pour wine into highball or white-wine glass over ice cubes. Fill with club soda and stir gently.

TOMBOY

½ cup   Chilled Tomato Juice
½ cup   Cold Beer

Pour tomato juice into highball glass. Add beer.

VERMOUTH COCKTAIL

1 oz.   Dry Vermouth
1 oz.   Sweet Vermouth
1 dash   Orange Bitters

Stir with ice and strain into cocktail glass. Serve with a cherry.

WINE COOLER

3 oz.   Red Wine
Lemon-lime Soda or Club Soda

Pour wine into red-wine glass over ice cubes. Fill with soda and stir.

XERES COCKTAIL

1 dash   Orange Bitters
2 oz.   Dry Sherry

Stir with ice and strain into cocktail glass.

THE MAGIC PENCIL

Hand someone a pencil and a piece of paper and ask him to write the number 1000 without lifting his pencil from the paper. METHOD: Fold the edge of the paper down and trace the figure, as shown.

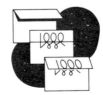

Crow's Nest, Batman Cocktail

These days, chances are that among your circle of friends and acquaintances there are those who do not consume alcohol at all. While it's certainly important that you respect their personal choice not to drink, there's no reason why nondrinkers cannot raise their glasses in a toast with a libation that's creatively prepared and attractively garnished.

Most everyone has heard of a Virgin Mary and Shirley Temple, and recipes for these old standards are included here. There are also nonalcoholic versions of other popular cocktails, such as the Unfuzzy Navel and Punchless Piña Colada. From the frosty Summertime Barbarian to the refreshingly tangy Yellowjacket, you'll find quaffs to offer nondrinkers that are delightfully different from ordinary soft drinks.

As mentioned in the previous chapter on low-alcohol drinks, feel free to be creative and experiment with omitting the alcohol in some of the standard cocktail recipes throughout this book, especially those made with a variety of fruit juices. And don't forget that presentation is just as important—attractive glassware, a pretty garnish, or a colorful straw adds appetite appeal to any drink.

BATMAN COCKTAIL

6 oz.   Orange Juice
½ tsp.   Grenadine
Club Soda

Pour into collins glass almost filled with ice cubes. Top with club soda, stir. Garnish with orange slice.

BEACH BLANKET BINGO

3 oz.   Cranberry Juice
3 oz.   Varietal Grape Juice
          (Chenin Blanc, etc.)
Club Soda

Pour ingredients over ice in highball glass. Top with club soda and garnish with lime wedge.

BUBBLETART

3 oz.   Cranberry Juice
1 oz.   Lime Juice
3 oz.   Mineral Water

Shake juices with ice and strain into highball glass. Fill with mineral water. Garnish with a lime wheel.

BUBBLY ORANGEADE

4 tsps.   Orange Juice
          Concentrate,
          thawed and
          undiluted
¼ cup   Club Soda

Stir together in collins glass and add ice. Garnish with an orange slice.

COFFEE ALMOND FLOAT

¼ cup   Instant Coffee
2 tbsps. Water
4 cups   Milk
2 tbsps. Brown Sugar
¼ tsp.   Almond Extract
Chocolate Ice Cream

Dissolve coffee in water in a pitcher. Add milk, brown sugar, and almond extract. Stir well and pour over ice cubes into parfait glasses. Top with a scoop of ice cream. Makes 4–6 servings.

COFFEE-COLA COOLER

2 tbsps. Instant Coffee
2 cups   Water
1 tbsp.   Maple Syrup
12 oz.   Chilled Cola

Dissolve coffee in water and stir in maple syrup. Slowly stir in cola. Serve over ice cubes in collins glasses. Garnish with lemon slices. Makes 3–4 servings.

CRANBERRY COOLER

2 oz.   Cranberry Juice
½ tbsp.   Lime Juice
Club Soda

Add juices to collins glass filled with ice. Top with club soda and stir. Garnish with twist of lime.

The only person who can handle a pint or a quart while driving is the milkman.

CREAMY CREAMSICLE

| 8 oz. | Orange Juice |
| 2 Scoops | Vanilla Ice Cream |

Combine ingredients in blender. Blend at low speed. Pour into highball glass and garnish with orange slice.

CROW'S NEST

4 oz.	Orange Juice
1 oz.	Cranberry Juice
$\frac{1}{2}$ tsp.	Grenadine

Shake with ice and strain into old-fashioned glass almost filled with ice cubes. Garnish with a lime slice.

FLAMINGO

4 oz.	Cranberry Juice
2 oz.	Pineapple Juice
$\frac{1}{2}$ oz.	Lemon Juice
2 oz.	Club Soda

Shake juices with ice and strain into highball glass. Top with club soda and stir. Garnish with lime wedge.

FRUIT SMOOTHIE

8 oz.	Chilled Orange Juice
1	Banana, peeled and sliced
$\frac{1}{2}$ cup	Ripe Strawberries, Blueberries, or Raspberries

Combine ingredients in blender. Blend at low speed. Pour into highball glass and garnish with assorted fruits.

FUZZY LEMON FIZZ

| 6 oz. | Peach Nectar |
| 4 oz. | Lemon-lime Soda |

Pour ingredients over ice in highball glass. Garnish with a lemon twist.

GRAPEBERRY

| 3 oz. | Cranberry Juice |
| 3 oz. | Grapefruit Juice |

Combine juices in large red-wine glass filled with ice. Add wedge of lime and short straw.

ICED MOCHA

2 cups	Milk
$\frac{1}{3}$ cup	Chocolate Syrup
1 tbsp.	Instant Coffee

Combine milk, chocolate syrup, and coffee, and mix well. Pour into collins glasses filled with crushed ice. Top with whipped cream and chocolate shavings. Makes 3–4 servings.

INNOCENT PASSION

4 oz.	Passion Fruit Juice
1 dash	Cranberry Juice
1 dash	Lemon Juice
Club Soda

Combine juices in highball glass filled with ice. Top with club soda, stir. Add a cherry and a long straw.

KIDSICLE

8 oz. Milk
½ scoop Vanilla Ice Cream
2 oz. Orange Juice
1 oz. Lemon-lime Soda
1 dash Grenadine

Combine milk, ice cream, and orange juice in blender and blend until smooth. Pour into parfait glass. Add soda and grenadine. Top with whipped cream and garnish with a cherry.

LAVA FLOW

4 oz. Light Cream
½ oz. Coconut Cream
3 oz. Pineapple Juice
½ Banana
½ cup Frozen Strawberries, thawed

Combine all ingredients except strawberries in blender with ice and blend until smooth. Put strawberries at the bottom of a parfait glass, then quickly pour in blended mixture for a starburst effect.

LEMON SQUASH

1 Lemon, peeled and quartered
2 tsps. Powdered Sugar
Club Soda

Muddle well in collins glass until juice is well extracted. Then fill glass with ice. Add club soda and stir. Decorate with fruits.

LEMONADE (CARBONATED)

2 tsps. Powdered Sugar
Juice of 1 Lemon
Club Soda

Dissolve sugar and lemon juice in collins glass, then add ice and enough club soda to fill glass and stir. Decorate with slices of orange and lemon, and a cherry. Serve with straws.

LEMONADE (FRUIT)

Juice of 1 Lemon
2 tsps. Powdered Sugar
1 oz. Raspberry Syrup
Water

Combine in collins glass. Add ice cubes and enough water to fill glass, and stir. Decorate with slices of orange and lemon, and a cherry. Serve with straws.

LEMONADE (PLAIN)

2 tsps. Powdered Sugar
Juice of 1 Lemon
Water

Stir sugar and lemon juice in collins glass. Fill glass with ice. Fill with water and stir well. Decorate with slices of orange and lemon, and a cherry.

Kong-Gang-Ui Wi-Ha-Y
—a Korean toast

LIME COLA

Juice of ½ Fresh Lime
Cola

Add juice to collins glass
filled with ice. Fill with cola.
Stir, add long twist of lime.

LIME COOLER

1 tbsp.   Lime Juice
Tonic Water

Add lime juice to collins
glass filled with ice. Top with
tonic water. Garnish with
lime wedge.

LIMEADE

Juice of 3 Limes
3 tsps.   Powdered Sugar
Water

Combine in collins glass,
then add ice and enough
water to fill glass. Stir, and
add a wedge of lime and a
cherry. Serve with straws.

LITTLE ENGINEER

4 oz.   Pineapple Juice
4 oz.   Orange Juice
½ oz.   Grenadine

Pour over ice in parfait glass.
Garnish with a paper flag.

ORANGE AND TONIC

6 oz.   Orange Juice
4 oz.   Tonic Water

Pour ingredients over ice
into highball glass. Garnish
with lime wedge.

ORANGEADE

Juice of 2 Oranges
1 tsp.   Powdered Sugar

Mix in collins glass. Add ice
cubes and enough water to
fill glass, and stir. Decorate
with slices of orange and
lemon, and two cherries.
Serve with straws.

PAC MAN

2 tsps.   Lemon Juice
1 tsp.   Grenadine
1 dash   Bitters
Ginger Ale

Add grenadine, lemon juice,
and bitters to collins glass
filled with ice. Top with
ginger ale. Notch an orange
slice and slide down side of
glass.

PASSION FRUIT SPRITZER

4 oz.   Passion Fruit Juice
Club Soda

Pour juice into champagne
flute and fill with club soda.
Garnish with a lime wedge.

PEACH MELBA

8 oz.   Peach Nectar
2 Scoops Vanilla Ice Cream
½   Whole Sliced
          Peach
3 oz.   Ripe Raspberries

Combine ingredients in
blender. Blend at low speed.
Pour in highball glass and
garnish with raspberries.

PUNCHLESS PIÑA COLADA

1 oz.   Cream of Coconut
1 oz.   Pineapple Juice
1 tsp.   Lime Juice

Combine ingredients in blender with 1 cup of crushed ice. Pour into collins glass. Garnish with slice of pineapple and cherry.

RUMLESS RICKEY

1 oz.   Lime Juice
1 dash   Grenadine
1 dash   Bitters
Club Soda

Add juice, grenadine, and bitters to old-fashioned glass with three to four large ice cubes. Top with club soda. Stir. Garnish with long twist of lime.

RUNNER'S MARK

4 oz.   V-8 Vegetable Juice
2 drops Tabasco Sauce
2 drops Lemon Juice
1 dash   Worcestershire
         Sauce

Combine ingredients in old-fashioned glass over ice. Stir, and garnish with celery stalk or scallion.

SHIRLEY TEMPLE

Ginger Ale
1 dash   Grenadine

Add grenadine to collins glass filled with ice; top with ginger ale. Decorate with orange slice and cherry.

STRAWBERRY WONDERLAND

1 oz.   Coconut Cream
2 oz.   Frozen Strawberries
3 oz.   Pineapple Juice
1 oz.   Sour Mix

Combine ingredients in blender with ice and blend until smooth. Pour into snifter. Top with whipped cream and garnish with a strawberry.

SUMMERTIME BARBARIAN

½ cup   Fresh Strawberries
½ cup   Fresh Pineapple
½ cup   Grapefruit Juice

Combine ingredients in blender with ice and blend until smooth. Pour into collins glasses. Garnish with kiwi fruit wheel. Makes 2 servings.

SUNSHINE SPLASH

3 oz.   Pineapple Juice
3 oz.   Orange Juice
1 oz.   Sour Mix
½ oz.   Grenadine
2 oz.   Lemon-lime Soda

Pour over ice into parfait glass and stir. Garnish with a pineapple slice.

TOMATO COOLER

8 oz. Tomato Juice
2 tbsps. Lemon or Lime
                Juice
Tonic Water

Combine tomato and lemon juices over ice in highball glass and top with tonic water. Garnish with a wedge of a lime, sprig of dill, and cucumber slice.

UNFUZZY NAVEL

3 oz. Peach Nectar
1 tbsp. Lemon Juice
3 oz. Orange Juice
1 dash Grenadine

Combine ingredients in shaker with ice. Strain into red-wine glass. Garnish with an orange slice.

VIRGIN MARY

4 oz. Tomato Juice
1 dash Lemon Juice
½ tsp. Worcestershire
                Sauce
2 drops Tabasco Sauce
Salt, Pepper to taste

Fill a large wine glass with ice. Add tomato juice, then remainder of ingredients. Stir and garnish with wedge of lime.

WAVEBENDER

1 oz. Orange Juice
½ oz. Lemon Juice
1 tsp. Grenadine
5 oz. Ginger Ale

Shake juices and grenadine with ice and strain into highball glass filled with ice cubes. Top with ginger ale and stir.

YELLOWJACKET

2 oz. Pineapple Juice
2 oz. Orange Juice
½ oz. Lemon Juice

Shake with ice and strain into old-fashioned glass filled with ice cubes. Garnish with a lemon slice.

The Egyptians had a rather quaint custom, which today, no doubt, would make some men quite nervous—if a gentleman offered a lady a sip of his beer, they were considered betrothed!

Party Planning Guide and Tips

A well-made libation can turn any time into party time, but a little advance planning can have you and yours toasting a special occasion or holiday in an especially memorable way. Any current happening like fall foliage, three-day weekends, or a pet's birthday; a shared interest like sports: a big win for a college team, the World Series, or the Olympics; and retro rage like a 60s gathering complete with bell-bottoms, body-painting, and psychedelic decals can spark great parties.

Are you a movie buff? What about a *Star Wars* blow-out, with participants dressed up like their favorite characters? Or a *Casablanca* cocktail hour where guests dress in 1940s black-and-white elegance with period piano music as a subtle background?

And don't forget the world of ethnic culture. Have your own Feast of St. Anthony with Italian wines to accompany pasta and divine pastries; celebrate Oktoberfest with German beer and hearty sausages, and toast a new year the Russian way with vodka and caviar. There are as many party ideas as there are cocktails. To get you started, how about a:

Coffee Klatsch

Everywhere you look there's another one: a coffee bar featuring exotic and high-quality coffees. So join the trend and host a weekend afternoon or evening get-together that will warm the spirit during the winter or cool it off on a sticky summer day. Served with an assortment of dipping cookies—Italian biscotti are more popular than ever—and cakes, hot coffee drinks like Black Gold, Mexican Coffee, Café Royale, and the venerable Irish Coffee (the purported invention of San Francisco's Buena Vista bar) will create a very special "coffee break." For those who prefer other hot drinks there's Amaretto Tea. And drinks made with coffee-flavored liqueurs or brandies will make cocktail hour even more special: Who could resist a Black Russian or a Cappuccino Cocktail? In warmer weather invite guests to your own outdoor cafe (just pull up some chairs around a backyard or terrace table covered with a flowered cloth) and offer Boston Iced Coffee or Frozen Cappuccinos. For those who prefer a nonalcoholic drink have a luscious Iced Mocha on hand.

Political Party

Whether you're toasting a winner or looking forward to trying again the next time, an election night party is sure to draw support from your own circle of constituents. Even if voting day is months away, why wait? Bring out the buttons and placards, the favorite foods of your candidate, and a batch of El Presidente Cocktails. For those who don't support your candidate, provide a Double Standard Scout, an Incider, or Journalist Cocktail—or even a shooter like the International Incident.

A Day at the Beach

It's two degrees above zero and the snow won't melt until spring. It's definitely time for sun and fun, so put the Beach Boys on the CD player and pitch a big umbrella in the middle of the living-room floor on top of colorful beach towels. Pull on your shorts, tank tops, and sunglasses, rub on some suntan lotion, and you're ready for Malibu. A perfect snack is a variety of Southwestern foods like fajitas, tortillas, and enchiladas. Fill big bowls with some of the new chips that feature vegetables as well as your favorite standbys, dip them in fiery salsa or smooth guacamole, and start pouring from a pitcher of Surfriders, Suntans, or Crocodile Coolers, or nonalcoholic Sunshine Splashes or Wavebenders. Pass a tray of various shooters, including the Blue Marlin, Sex on the Beach, and the aptly named Woo Woo. Don't forget Frozen Margaritas and Frozen Daiquiris—just because there's ice outside doesn't mean there shouldn't be ice inside. For convenience in summer or winter, remember ready-to-serve *Chi-Chi's Margaritas*. Just blend with ice then get ready to party. Surf's up!

Hawaiian Luau

While Trader Vic's of the San Francisco establishment of the same name lays claim to originating the Mai Tai, this popular drink has long been associated with the soft winds and perfect beaches of Hawaii. To set the mood, ask each guest to wear a flowered shirt and present each one with a paper lei upon arrival. For outdoor gatherings, light torches (buy them) and serve up pineapple, melons, bananas, and other tropical fruits on platters decorated with flowers. Barbecue chicken, fish, and pork and sit down at flower-covered tables to eat. Perfect drink choices include the Waikiki Beachcomber, the Blue Hawaiian, the Pineapple Fizz, or the low-alcohol Aloha Bubbly.

Caribbean Cruise

What better time to try your hand at a great Chi-Chi, a Tropical Special, a Papaya Sling, a Blue Lagoon, or even a Yellow Parrot? And don't forget the classic Cuba Libre. Plan a cruise ship style buffet featuring fish fritters, jerk or curried chicken or pork, black beans and yellow rice, fried plantain, and banana and coconut cream pies. Don't forget the reggae and calypso music.

After Sailing or Fishing Party

To celebrate your catch of the day—even if it's only some sun—relax with a Cape Codder, a Seabreeze, or an Angler's Cocktail. Grill fish and boil or steam lobsters, set out a pile of corn on the cob, toss a giant salad, and enjoy the sunset.

Cocktails on the 50th Floor

With soft lighting, Cole Porter playing on the stereo, and a video clip of Fred Astaire and Ginger Rogers dancing up a storm, your living room can be turned into a romantic penthouse perched stop a New York Art Deco skyscraper. Martinis, Manhattans, Champagne Cocktails, and the Rainbow Room's famed Planter's Punch are the order of the day.

Lone Star Fiesta

Maybe you've never lived anywhere but the city, but that's no reason not to enjoy a down-home, country-style party. Announce a dress code of jeans, boots, and Stetsons, and have Willie Nelson on tape. Before—or after—the line dancing, offer up an Alamo Splash, a South of the Border, a Tequila Sunrise or a Yellow Rattler. Serve up some chili and beans and cornbread.

Just Desserts

Guests with a sweet tooth will appreciate liquid confections like the Chocolate-Covered Strawberry, Raspberry Cheesecake, Peach Melba, Pineapple Upside Down Cake, Banana Foster, Death by Chocolate, and nonalcoholic Creamy Creamsicle. Often featuring ice cream, these drinks make perfect adult birthday party treats. Fresh fruit, cookies, petit fours, and candy-coated nuts make this an extra-delicious treat.

Winter Wonderland

The first snow of the season, an after-ski wind-down, trimming the Christmas tree; all savor the joys of winter. Hearty fare like goose, lamb, or beef, thick soups, potato casseroles, and warm pies make sitting on floor cushions even more comforting. Ladle out servings of Hot Rummed Cider or Winter Cider, Hot Burgundy Punch, or any kind of nog. For something different, prepare a Snowflake or Snow Bunny or a festive Scotch Holiday Sour and have those all-time favorite carols playing in the background.

Murder Mystery

On a dark and stormy night invite eight guests to play a board game that provides the clues. Draw the curtains and place candles throughout the house. Have each person dress the part, from the ingenue in peril to the tweedy English detective. Lower the lights, serve red wine, Bloody Marys, and, of course, shooters. Serve finger food like crustless sandwiches, a cheese board and crackers, and assorted nuts.

Hobo Heaven

Very casual dress is the theme, so cover tables with butcher paper, set place settings with paper towels, and serve food and beverages in galvanized tin buckets. Dine on hot dogs and beans, and po'boys, along with a Rusty Nail, a Hairy Sunrise, or a Midnight Cocktail. Appropriate music: "King of the Road."

Sadie Hawkins Day

For a girls' night out, why not stay in and have a slumber party? Bring your baby dolls and jammies, experiment with makeup, and order in pizzas. Have on hand a Beauty Spot Cocktail, a Diamond Fizz, or a Foxy Lady.

Of course, every day can be a holiday; it's not up to Congress to declare one. Here are some of our favorites:

New Year's Day: Brunch Punch, Brandy Milk Punch or a Mimosa will bring out the flavor of Eggs Florentine, an assortment of breads and muffins, and various preserves. Wear slippers: this is a day for quiet.

Presidents' Day: Do the honest thing and celebrate by offering late-afternoon cherry pie along with a Cherry Fizz or a Cherry Blossom.

Mardi Gras/Carnival: Oysters, crayfish, and fabulous desserts are the right fare to have with a Hurricane (a specialty of Pat O'Brien's in New Orleans), a New Orleans Buck, or a Basin Street Daiquiri.

Valentine's Day: A kiss is still a kiss, so wear your heart on your sleeve and offer up a Red-Hot Passion, an Amber Amour, a Kiss on the Lips, or a nonalcoholic Innocent Passion. Whatever you choose for dinner, make sure you have a decadent chocolate dessert. With after-dinner coffee or cappuccino, offer a classic romantic liqueur, Amaretto.

Saint Patrick's Day: Corned beef and cabbage and boiled potatoes are a must, as are an Emerald Isle Cocktail, an Irish Shillelagh, or an Irish Flag.

First Day of Spring: Buy the first daffodils or tulips to set the mood, comb the market for the freshest baby vegetables, poach a fillet of salmon and toss off winter doldrums with a Spring Feeling Cocktail, a Strawberry Sunrise, or a nonalcoholic Yellowjacket.

April 15 (Income Tax Day): A midnight supper of mashed potatoes, scrambled eggs, and soft rolls will help you make it through, as will an Income Tax Cocktail.

Cinco de Mayo (the fifth of May): Celebrate Mexico's holiday with mariachi music, chicken in mole sauce, a piñata, and a Margarita, a Chapala, or a Purple Pancho.

Independence Day: Barbecue your favorites, set up a dessert buffet with strawberry and vanilla ice cream topped with blueberries and assorted toppings, and serve an Americana, a 4th of July Tooter, or a Stars and Stripes.

Bastille Day: A Champs Elysées Cocktail is the beverage of choice to accompany French bread, pâté, and (why not?) Napoleons.

National Ice Cream Day (July 18): Frozen drinks like a Chocolate Almond Cream, a Chilly Irishman, or a Cloud 9 make this day extra special. Use as a super dessert after a meal of cold chicken and assorted salads.

National Bourbon Month (September): Kentucky Derby Day isn't the only time to savor this native American drink. Have a steak, a baked potato, a salad with the dressing of choice along with a Bull and Bear, a Thoroughbred Cooler, or a Southern Lady.

Halloween: Bob for apples, pass the candy corn, and have a Nightmare, a Frisky Witch, or a Zombie.

Thanksgiving: Turkey with all the trimmings has its particular drink: a Thanksgiving Special.

Repeal of Prohibition (December 5): If you really need an excuse to have a party, this is the day. Don Roaring Twenties attire and roll up the rug to dance the Charleston (or play the soundtrack from *The Sting*). Mix pitchers of gin cocktails kept cool in a baby bathtub filled with ice, and celebrate the end of the dry spell with your own speakeasy.

Christmas: Bake a ham, roast a goose, and serve up a Christmas Yule Eggnog.

New Year's Eve: Champagne Punch with your favorite elegant foods is a lovely way to ring in a new year of special days.

How Many

Whether you're hosting an intimate dinner party or throwing a bash for a crowd, the buying guide charts in this section can make it easy for you to determine how much liquor and wine you'll need.

FOR FOUR PEOPLE

Lunch
6 Cocktails/wine
6 Glasses wine with lunch
4 Liqueurs

Cocktails
8 Cocktails *or*
8 Glasses wine first 2 hours
6 Drinks an hour thereafter

Dinner
8 Cocktails/wine
8 Glasses wine with dinner
4 Liqueurs
4 Drinks an hour after
    dinner

Evening
16 Cocktails/wine

HOW MANY BOTTLES OF WINE FOR DINNER
Table Wines, Champagnes, Sparkling Wines
(average 2 servings, 5 oz. each, per person)

People	4	6	8	10	12	20
750ml.	2	2+	3+	4	5	8
1.5 Liter	1	1+	2	2	2+	4

Generally, bottle quantities recommended provide some small overages of wine from 10 oz. per guest formula. "+" indicates somewhat less formula and you may desire to have an additional bottle on hand.

Drinks to Plan

FOR SIX PEOPLE

Lunch
10 Cocktails/wine
10 Glasses wine with lunch
 6 Liqueurs

Cocktails
12 Cocktails *or*
12 Glasses wine first 2 hours
 9 Drinks an hour thereafter

Dinner
12 Cocktails/wine
12 Glasses wine with dinner
 6 Liqueurs
 6 Drinks an hour after
   dinner

Evening
24 Cocktails/wine

FOR TEN PEOPLE

Lunch
15 Cocktails/wine
15 Glasses wine with lunch
10 Liqueurs

Cocktails
20 Cocktails *or*
20 Glasses wine first 2 hours
15 Drinks an hour thereafter

Dinner
20 Cocktails/wine
20 Glasses wine with dinner
10 Liqueurs
10 Drinks an hour after
   dinner

Evening
40 Cocktails/wine

HOW MANY DRINKS PER BOTTLE

Cocktails, Mixed Drinks
(1.5 oz. liquor servings)

Bottles	1	2	4	6	8	10	12
750ml.	16	33	67	101	135	169	203
Liter	22	45	90	135	180	225	270
1.5 Liter	39	78	157	236	315	394	473

Table Wines, Champagnes, Sparkling Wines
(5 oz. wine servings)

Bottles	1	2	4	6	8	10	12
750ml.	5	10	20	30	40	50	60
Liter	6	13	27	40	54	67	81
1.5 Liter	10	20	40	60	81	101	121
3 Liter	20	40	80	121	161	202	242
4 Liter	27	54	108	162	216	270	324

C

The responsible advertiser for the following brands is Barton Brands, Ltd., Chicago, IL
Very Old Barton Bourbon Whiskey, 40% Alc/Vol (80 Proof), 43% Alc/Vol (86 Proof),
45% Alc/Vol (90 Proof), and 50% Alc/Vol (100 Proof)
Barton Vodka, 40% Alc/Vol (80 Proof)
Barton Rum, 40% Alc/Vol (80 Proof)
Barton Gin, 40% Alc/Vol (80 Proof)
Kentucky Gentleman Bourbon 40% Alc/Vol (80 Proof), 43% Alc/Vol (86 Proof),
45% Alc/Vol (90 Proof), and 50% Alc/Vol (100 Proof)
Amaretto di Amore Liqueur, 21% Alc/Vol (42 Proof) and 45% Alc/Vol (90 Proof)
Cafe di Amore Liqueur, 26.5% Alc/Vol (53 Proof)
Ten High Bourbon Whiskey, 40% Alc/Vol (80 Proof)
Inver House Blended Scotch Whiskey, 40% Alc/Vol (80 Proof)
House of Stuart Scotch Whisky, 40% Alc/Vol (80 Proof) and 43% Alc/Vol (86 Proof)
Lauder's Blended Scotch Whisky, 40% Alc/Vol (80 Proof)
Highland Mist Scotch Whisky, 40% Alc/Vol (80 Proof) and 43% Alc/Vol (86 Proof)
Northern Light Canadian Whisky, 40% Alc/Vol (80 Proof)
Speyburn Single Malt Scotch Whisky, 43% Alc/Vol (86 Proof)
Monte Alban Mezcal, 40% Alc/Vol (80 Proof)
Montezuma Tequila, 40% Alc/Vol (80 Proof)
El Toro Tequila, 40% Alc/Vol (80 Proof)
Sabroso Coffee Liqueur, 26.5/26.6% Alc/Vol (53.0/53.2 Proof)
Heather Cream Liqueur, 17% Alc/Vol (34 Proof)
Sambuca di Amore Liqueur, 42% Alc/Vol (84 Proof)
Fleischmann's Gin, 40% Alc/Vol (80 Proof), 100% Grain Neutral Spirits
Canadian LTD Blended Canadian Whisky, 40% Alc/Vol (80 Proof)
Chi-Chi's® Margarita Prepared Cocktail, 10% Alc/Vol (20 Proof)
Chi-Chi's® Mexican Mudslide Prepared Cocktail, 12.5% Alc/Vol (25 Proof)
Kentucky Tavern Kentucky Straight Bourbon Whiskey, 40% Alc/Vol (80 Proof)
Mr. Boston Five Star Brandy, 40% Alc/Vol (80 Proof)
Mr. Boston Cordials, Liqueur, 30% Alc/Vol (60 Proof), 21% Alc/Vol (42 Proof),
and 17% Alc/Vol (34 Proof)
Mr. Boston Flavored Brandy, 35% Alc/Vol (70 Proof)
Mr. Boston Egg Nog, Blended Whiskey, 15% Alc/Vol (30 Proof)
Mr. Boston Schnapps Liqueur, 24% Alc/Vol (48 Proof)
Jacques Bonet Brandy, 40% Alc/Vol (80 Proof)
99 Bananas Liqueur, 49.5% Alc/Vol (99 Proof)

The responsible advertiser for the following brands is Barton Beers, Ltd., Chicago, IL
Corona Extra
Corona Light
Modelo Especial
Negra Modelo
St. Pauli Girl Lager
St. Pauli Girl Dark
St. Pauli Girl N.A.
Double Diamond
Peroni

The responsible advertiser for the following brand is Monarch Import Company, Chicago, IL
Tsingtao

The responsible advertiser for the following brand is Consolidated Pacific Brands, Chicago, IL
Pacifico

The responsible advertiser for the following brands is Stevens Point Brewery Co., Stevens Point, WI
Point Special
Point Bock
Point Classic Amber
Point Pale Ale
Point Winter Spice
Point Maple Wheat

The responsible advertiser for the following brand is Inglenook Vineyards, Madera, CA
Inglenook Vineyards Chardonnay